KEVIN MULLALLY

Theological advisor: Dr Anthony Draper, All Hallows College, Dublin

GILL & MACMILLAN

Dedicated to the students and staff of Kylemore College, Ballyfermot

Gill & Macmillan Ltd
Hume Avenue
Park West
Dublin 12
with associated companies throughout the world
www.gillmacmillan.ie

ISBN–13: 978 0717 13472 4
ISBN–10: 0 7171 3472 5

Design, typesetting and print origination by Anú Design, Tara
Colour reproduction by Typeform Repro

*The paper used in this book is made from the wood pulp of managed forests.
For every tree felled, at least one tree is planted,
thereby renewing natural resources.*

Contents

Section 1

Community 2
Community at Work 22
Communities of Faith 29

Section 2

What is Religion all about? 94

Section 3

Christianity 117
- How the Bible came to be 119
- A Look at Judaism 126
- Christianity 130
- The Context 132
- Size of Palestine 135
- History of Palestine 141
- Jobs 151
- Money 154
- Political and Religious Groups 156
- The New Testament 161
- The Life of Jesus 170
- The Crucifixion 284
- The Resurrection 291

Acknowledgments

Special words of thanks to all those who supported and encouraged me over the time of writing these two books, especially my family; Mam, Dad, Niall and Conor, Cathy, Robbie, Fran, Tom, Sinead, Emma, Diarmuid, Siobhan, Amanda, Paul K., Therese, Paul T., Fiona, Joe, Piaras, Sean and Gottfried, and Fr Tony Draper.

Photo Credits

For permission to reproduce photos, the author and publisher gratefully acknowledge the following:

154R © akg-images/Erich Lessing; 13B, 96CR, 154L, 176 © Alamy Images; The Art Archive: 154C © Kanellopoulos Museum Athens/Dagli Orti; 141 © Museo Capitolino Rome/Dagli Orti; 6, 37 courtesy of the author; 13T © Jennie Woodcock/Bubbles; Bridgeman Art Library: 181R, 267 © Brooklyn Museum of Art, New York, USA; 284 © Prado, Madrid, Spain; 287 © Louvre, Paris, France, Giraudon; 34T © Camera Press Ireland; 25 courtesy of Conseil Général de la Société de Saint-Vincent de Paul; Corbis: 34B © Vittoriano Rastelli; 43 © Archivo Iconografico, S.A; 47 © Francis G. Mayer; 55 © Bettmann; 109TR © Chris Lisle; 181B © Dave G. Houser; 181TL © Elio Ciol; 181TC © Richard T. Nowitz; 285 © Otto van Veen; 86 © The Corrymeela Community, reproduced by kind permission. For more information visit www.corrymeela.org or email belfast@corrymeela.org; 85 © Empics; 122 © Getty; 14, 40, 96CL © Imagefile Ireland; 96B © Irish Image Collection; Lonely Planet Images: 109L © Diana Mayfield; 184 © Russell Mountford; 23, 61 © Mary Evans Picture Library; 35 © John McElroy; 96T © Science Photo Library/Pascal Goetgheluck; 109BR © Rex.

The author and publisher have made every effort to trace all copyright holders, but if any has been inadvertently overlooked we would be pleased to make the necessary arrangements as the first opportunity.

Section

Community

- Characteristics and Experiences
- Individual Needs v. Community Needs

Community at Work

- St Vincent de Paul (SVP)

Communities of Faith

- Roman Catholic Church
- The Methodist Church in Ireland
- The Quakers (Society of Friends)
- Challenges
- Ecumenism
- Interfaith Dialogue
- Sectarianism
- Religious Conflict

'Community'

TO KNOW

- Community.
- Exchange.
- Society.
- Parish.

If you think about it, this is a word that you often hear in everyday life. If you turn on the TV, you will hear about it; if you glance at the newspaper, you'll see articles written about it; and you'll hear people talking about it. But what exactly are they talking about?

Q

What do you think is meant by the word 'community'?
What picture or image comes into your mind when you hear the word 'community'?

Draw the word in your copy or write a few lines about your idea. You can discuss it with someone, if you like! Use this to help you to write your ideas.

I think community is ... because ...

COPY AND COLOUR

... so, to help us along we really need to examine 'community' a bit more ... Let's see!

The word **COMMUNITY** has been in use for centuries, and it comes from the Latin word *Communis*, meaning 'exchange' and 'shared by all'.

This, then, helps us to see that the word **COMMUNITY** is about people sharing something and exchanging something!

Q1. Name four places where you might hear the word 'community' used.
Q2. Why might people be using the word 'community'?
Q3. What word in Latin does it come from?
Q4. What does **Communis** mean?
Q5. What is community about?

Get a dictionary and look up the word 'community'. When you find a definition, put it in the box on the right ...

'Community' means:

Now do your own definition as well ...

I think 'community' means:

To help us understand it as best as we can, here are a few more good definitions:

- A group of people living in a certain place together.
- A group of people who share the same interests – jobs/religion/country/family.
- Society in general (town/village/city).

This picture helps us to see what these definitions mean.

'Community' is...

Same country.

Same job –
Nursing Community, for example.

People Living in a Certain Place Together.

Christian Community –
same Religion.

It's important to remember that every day we are part of different communities. As we have seen, communities are groups of people with the same interests, activities, ideas or beliefs.

Q **Can you think of some of the communities that you are part of? (Make a list in your copy.)**

Now compare your list with this list here.

- Family community.
- Your road/area/neighbourhood.
- Your city.
- Your country.
- Your class/school.
- Your parish.
- Your Church/religious community.

Pick three of these communities and in your copy draw a picture for each one.

'What is a **PARISH**?' you might ask. It is:

TO KNOW →

A community of people of religious/Christian (Catholic/Protestant) belief who meet and worship in and around a church/chapel.

'My Church Community'!

COPY AND COLOUR

Being part of the **'Parish Community'** means that you are part of your **'Church Community'**.

As a baptised Catholic, you have a role to play in your Catholic community.

Who's in my Church Community?

- me and my family;

- other baptised Catholics;
- people of different faiths who live in the area;
- people of no faith;
- priests/nuns/Brothers.

NB

As a baptised member of my Church Community, I am called upon to:

- follow the message of Jesus contained in the Gospels;
- help promote and create the Kingdom of God in the world around me;
- attend and participate in liturgical celebrations and Mass in my church;
- follow the leadership of the Church given to us by the Pope, bishops, councils, etc;
- help those who are less well-off in my community;
- respect and reach out to people of other faiths and of no faith.

LET'S ASK OURSELVES:

Q1. Give two definitions of 'community'.

Q2. Where does the word **COMMUNITY** come from?

Q3. Name some of the communities that you might belong to.

Q4. What is a **PARISH**?

Q5. Can you think why communities are a good thing?

Q6. In your opinion, how can communities work at their best?

As we look in more detail at people's experience of being in communities, we see that there are certain characteristics that communities have. These characteristics seem to help **COMMUNITIES** to work better.

1 Co-operation! 2 Sharing!

3 Roles! 4 Communication!

If a community has these characteristics, it should be working well.

1. **CO-OPERATION:** people work together for the same aims of the community. No one person tries to be better than another. It's about having an understanding that working together is better than ignoring others and being selfish.

2. **SHARING:** everybody has what they need. If one person needs something, they get it from others who share with them. In a good working community, people are not selfish; they understand that sharing is for the good of everybody in the community.

3. **ROLES:** in the community, people use their gifts and talents in different ways for the good of all the people. This means that they have a ROLE. Some people are good at leading, others at entertaining, others at caring and so on.

4. **COMMUNICATION:** happens when people are honest about their views and needs. Good communication is about people talking to each other about their likes and dislikes, needs and wants, problems and difficulties and so on.

We will look at leadership later!

Community breakdown starts when all this doesn't happen!

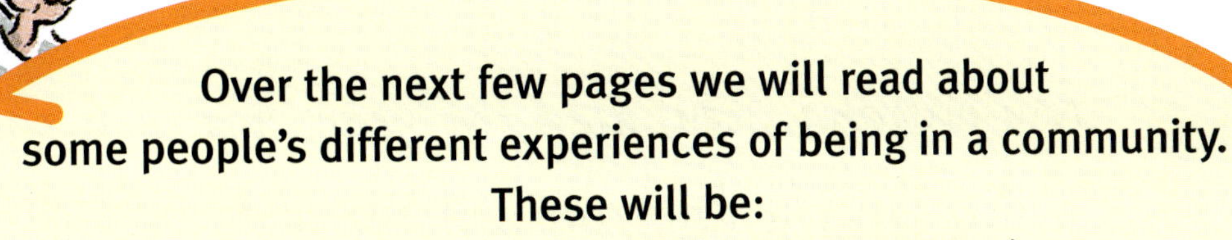

Let's look at these experiences!

Hiya!

My name is May and I'm a mother of four. We live on the north side of Dublin in a normal housing estate. My four children are aged from 4 up to 17, all with their own needs, responsibilities and personalities.

My husband, Joey, died two years ago in a car crash, so now I'm the boss, running the show, and it's not an easy show at that!

Thinking of my family as a little community is strange, but it is a community trying to operate as best as it can. My role in this family community is the boss. I look after the house, pay the bills (I've a part-time job) and look after the kids. I suppose being a mum is a tough job, but I love it and love my kids. That probably is the most important thing – that I'm here for the kids. That's more important than the four walls of the house.

Communication is a funny thing in our family. Sometimes it happens and happens very well; other times it doesn't and there are fights – the result of bad communication, I suppose!

We co-operate most times, but some days any one of us can be feeling selfish and want things our own way and sometimes things don't get done. Jenny is the youngest and demands the most attention. Joe is the eldest – I want him to do well in his Leaving Cert Applied; he also looks after the others. Patty (aged 10) does a bit of housework at the weekends; and Cleo does the garden. These are the basic roles and they all abide by my rules. There you have it – my family community!

Interview people in your own family and see how they feel about the **Family Community**.

Try these questions about May and her family community!

Q1. Where does May live?

Q2. What happened to her husband?

Q3. What is May's role in the family community?

Q4. What are the important things she does in the community?

Q5. What happens when there is no communication in this family?

Q6. What are the different roles in the community?

Q7. What makes this family a good community?

Q8. What might make it a bad community?

From reading May's family story, fill in these blanks:

May is a mother of f_____ children. She lives on the n_____ s_____ of Dublin. Her children are aged from f_____ to s______. They each have their own n______, r______________ and p______________. Her husband J_______ died two years ago in a c_____ c_____. May sees her family as a c_______. She pays all the b_______ and looks after the k______. C______ happens and sometimes it doesn't. When it doesn't, there are a_______. All the family members have different r_______. May's family is a c_______.

COPY AND COLOUR

Parish Community!

Róisín works in her local parish. This is her experience of working in her community:

Hello. I've been working in my parish for the past six years. I love every minute of it. My four children have all flown the nest, so I love keeping busy helping in the parish community. I believe that one of the most important things that I do is working as part of the team that visits local people in their houses.

This is properly called a VISITATION TEAM. We work as a team, co-operate and rely on each other as we do our job. We basically make sure that everybody is kept in touch with parish life; we give them all the news and they, in turn, tell us what's important. We also try to be witnesses to Jesus' message in the Gospels in our lives.

Sometimes, people don't like me calling because they want nothing to do with the parish. This is disappointing. But overall the people are lovely and usually very nice. I believe that it's important to keep in touch with the local parish community.

Next we talk to a student who is part of his

School Community!

COPY AND COLOUR

My name is Dave and I am 17. At the moment, I am a fifth-year student in my local secondary school. In some ways, it's funny to think of my school as a community, but it is one. Firstly, I'm part of my class community called 'Shannon' (named after rivers). As a student in the school, I have a lot of responsibilities. The basic ones go without saying: Co-operating with teachers, the VP, and the Principal – giving respect to them and to school mates; making sure to give everything 100 per cent; doing my homework; being in and on time; and also being honest. I'm also involved in the first-year soccer league. I referee and do up the leagues. I believe that I am a role model to the juniors. I have to work well with them and all the people in the school community. I'm quite important, now that you look at it.

Some questions for you to work on!

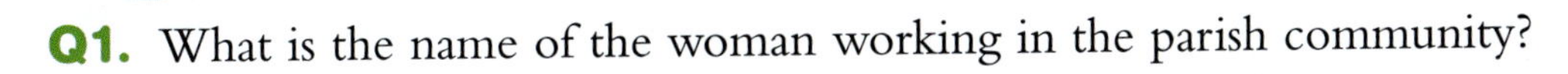

Q1. What is the name of the woman working in the parish community?

Q2. What is one of the most important things she does?

Q3. What is the **VISITATION TEAM**?

Q4. What is their job?

Q5. Why might somebody not like her calling to their house?

Q6. How do they work as a team?

JOURNAL IDEA

Find someone who works in your parish. Ask them what they do.

TRY THIS

Everybody is part of a parish. Try to complete this **FACT FILE** (you may need to go and ask people at home):

- Name of the parish: ______________________
- Name of one priest: ______________________
- Name of your local church: ______________________
- Number of people living in your parish: ______________________
- What roles are there? ______________________
- How old is the parish? ______________________
- What ceremonies take place in the parish church? ______________________

You could also do a fact file for the parish your school is located in.

To do

Q1. How old is Dave?

Q2. What year is he in?

Q3. What's the name of his class?

Q4. What are his responsibilities?

Q5. Why is he a 'role model'?

Q6. What communities is he part of?

Q7. Why is school a community?

Ask a senior student if they have any role in the school community.

Characteristics of a Good Community are:

Another important aspect of being part of a community is to **BALANCE** the needs of the community with your own needs – the **NEEDS** of the individual.

Community Needs!

In your copy:

Make a list of what you think individual needs might be.

Share them with the class.

A community, or the community we are in, should be a good place to be in. We should feel happy. If we don't, something is wrong and we should ask ourselves why we're not happy in the community!

The people we read about in the previous pages would have known why it was worthwhile to remain in the community. They also realised that they had to take care of themselves and their individual needs, as well as the community's needs. They had a **BALANCED** idea of themselves and their community.

The famous psychologist, ABRAHAM MASLOW, came up with the idea that, as individual humans, we all need specific things to be able to do our very best.

These are:

1. **Basic Needs** – food and water.

2. **Safety Needs** – security, safety, protection.

3. **Love Needs** – to feel cared for, to give and receive love.

4. **Confidence Needs** – to feel worthwhile and respected; to have self-esteem and self-confidence.

5. **To be the best person you can** – develop to your full potential.

These are the basic needs that we all have.

So, for a **COMMUNITY** to work well, the needs of each of the individuals should be looked after. When this happens, the community should work to its best ability. A balance has been made between you – **THE INDIVIDUAL** – and others – **THE COMMUNITY AS A WHOLE**.

Draw a Pyramid Poster showing the 5 needs identified by Maslow

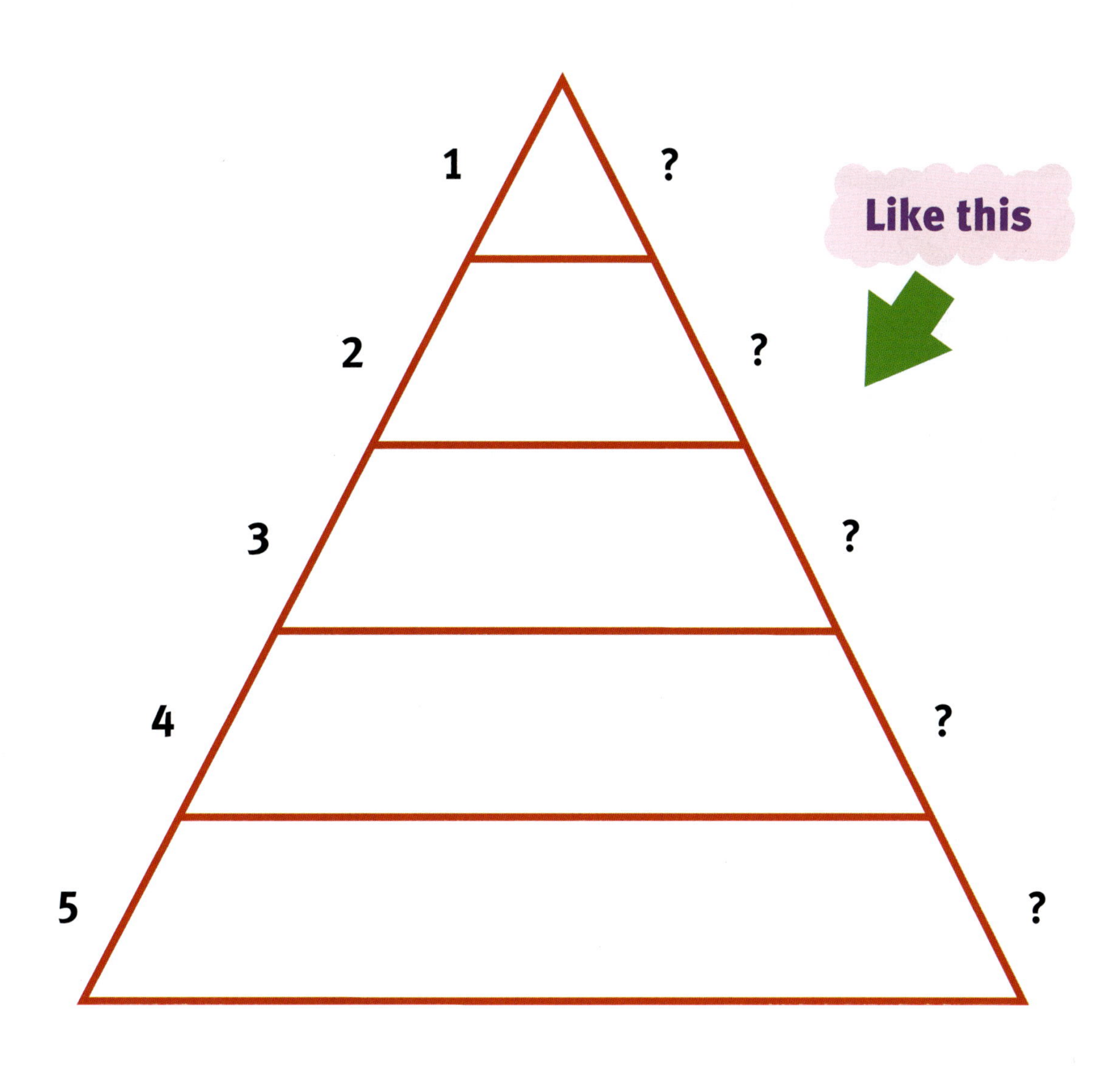

Basically it means that each of us has a need or a want to be part of something. We are, and need to be, part of the **FAMILY COMMUNITY**; we choose to be part of a team, a group, a bunch of friends. We are part of the **SCHOOL COMMUNITY**, part of our **NEIGHBOURHOOD COMMUNITY**. None of us likes to feel alone. Being part of a community is good for us and our development as mature adults.

In the Church we know that we are not alone – we are a Catholic family of believers in Jesus and his Church. We are called to help each other, be with each other, love each other, be witnesses to Jesus and to develop as people spiritually and in our relationship with God the Father, imitating Jesus his Son, and using our gifts given by the Spirit.

Community Wordsearch

N J D G K M S B Q B Q C N S U
C O O P E R A T I O N O O H G
E I O B H D E R B Q I M I A J
E T N J A G I R E T H M G R W
H G B D A L E I A A F U I E O
E E N L I A A C F A Y N L D L
D U L A K V I N M Y F I E K S
L I M D H N I I C S Y T R H A
V O O F U C L D E E C Y E Q M
J W O M C Y X L U N E E D S T
N U M H A T O E H A I R A P O
V O L V C R A Y Q Y L V G M W
C J E T O S I N U M M O C M N
S H A R I N G V W H N I W F C
W V V B V M K V G O K M Q H Q

AREA
BALANCE
COMMUNICATION
COMMUNIS
COMMUNITY
CO-OPERATION
EXCHANGE
FAMILY
INDIVIDUAL
MASLOW
NEEDS
RELIGION
ROLES
SCHOOL
SHARED
SHARING
TOWN
VILLAGE

TO KNOW

- International.
- Organisation.

COPY AND COLOUR

As well as being in the communities mentioned earlier – family, school, neighbourhood, Catholic and so on – some people choose to be in other communities.

There are people who choose to be in organisations and communities that work on a **local** / **national** / **international** level. One such community organisation is →

- The Society of St Vincent de Paul is an organisation that many people are familiar with because it has groups in every community and parish. Let's see what it does as a community organisation.
- While we are looking at the St Vincent de Paul community at work, we need to keep a few important points at the back of our minds. These are:

A Service
– the work the members do.

B Commitment
– how they will do their best at all times.

C Inspiration
– why they do the work and for whom.

D Vision
– how the work helps people and the future generations.

E Leadership
– how the community organisation is run.

Vincent de Paul

'Inspiration of the Society'

(1581–1660)

- Vincent de Paul was born in 1581 in the village of Pouy (near Dax, France) at the foot of the Pyrenees. The de Paul family was poor, but managed to get by.

- In 1595 Vincent's father, seeing how talented his son was, sent him to a boarding school run by the Franciscan order – a Catholic order of priests and Brothers.

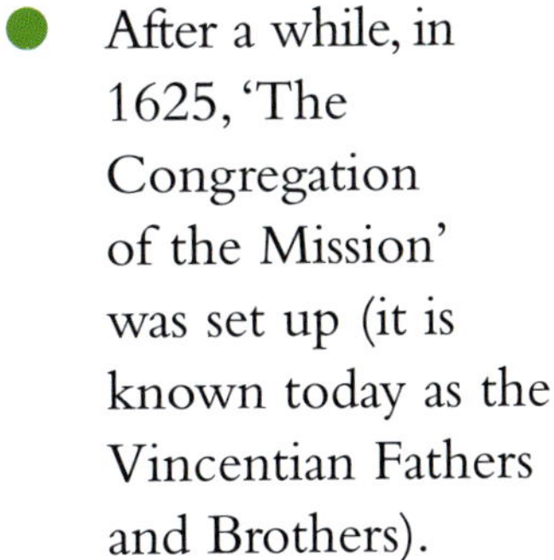

'To go all over the Earth to inflame people's hearts to do what the Son of God did.'
(Vincent de Paul)

- In those days, certain prisoners from the jail were made to row on the big merchant ships or battleships. Vincent felt a calling from God to go and speak to them, to tell them the love Jesus had for them.
- Vincent travelled from village to village, preaching to these prisoners condemned to the oars, and giving a Mission.

- A number of years later, having graduated from university and the seminary, Vincent was ordained a priest. He was nineteen years old.

- After a while, in 1625, 'The Congregation of the Mission' was set up (it is known today as the Vincentian Fathers and Brothers).
- Vincent's mission was 'to go all over the Earth to inflame people's hearts to do what the **Son of God** did' – show God's love for all people. Missionaries came from all over Europe to join Vincent and to help spread Jesus' Good News.
- Vincent died in 1660 and was declared a saint in 1737.

St Vincent de Paul was born in _______, in the village of _______ at the foot of the _______ Mountains. The family was _______ but managed to get by. In _______ he was sent to _______ school. It was run by the _______ order. After graduating, he became a _______. He was _______ years old. At that time prisoners were made to _______. Vincent travelled from _______ to village _______ to these prisoners, and giving a Mission. After a while, in 1625, the '_______ _______ _______ _______' was set up. Its mission was 'to go all over the Earth to _______ people's _______ to do what the Son of God did'.

In your copy, using **eight boxes** draw a cartoon strip telling the story of St Vincent de Paul.

Try these True / False sentences:

- Vincent was a Catholic. **T / F**
- Vincent was born in 1680. **T / F**
- His village was at the foot of Mount Everest. **T / F**
- The family had loads of money. **T / F**
- He was sent to boarding school. **T / F**
- He became a butcher. **T / F**
- He helped the poor and needy. **T / F**

LET'S HAVE A LOOK

- The Society of St Vincent de Paul is a local, national and international voluntary Catholic organisation.
- Anyone is free to join the organisation.
- The inspiration for the work of the organisation is St Vincent, Jesus, the Gospels and Church teaching.

TO KNOW → **Conference: local people coming together as an organised group.**

The founder

of the organisation was a man called

Frederic Ozanam

(1813–1853)

He was born in Milan, Italy, in 1813. He was a very intelligent man and studied Law in Paris. While there, he saw how some people lived in great poverty. Because of this, he wanted to do something to help; his Christian beliefs demanded that he help in some way.

VINCENT
SVP
DE PAUL

'Love of God, Love of Neighbour'

Frederic, together with the Sisters of Charity and some friends, began their Mission to follow Jesus' command: **'Show love to your neighbour'**. This gradually led to the first Conference of the Society being formed in 1833. At this Conference, it was decided that St Vincent de Paul should be the patron saint of the Society (because of his love for the poor). Frederic died in 1853, aged forty. In 1997, Pope John Paul II beatified him (gave him the title **'blessed'**).

- Nationwide, the Society has a membership of 9,000, organised in more than 1,000 Conferences.
- The Society of St Vincent de Paul is spread across the thirty-two counties of Ireland, constantly working for God's Kingdom.

Give these a go!

Q1. What is the inspiration for the work of the organisation?

Q2. Who is the founder of SVP?

Q3. What made him want to help the poor?

Q4. What nuns did he contact?

Q5. What did he do then?

Q6. How many members has the SVP in Ireland?

Q7. What happened in 1997?

The Work of the Society of St Vincent de Paul

Just as with St Vincent and Blessed Frederic, the purpose of the Society's work is to help the needy in our communities through

Assistance to people in need ...

Contact is made with the people in need, enabling people to help themselves.

Acceptance of people as they are ...

People are not judged or looked down upon. They are accepted as people of God.

Advice when asked for ...

Is given on different matters, but only when asked for. Members do not tell people what they should do.

Dignity of the person maintained ...

Nothing should make people feel that they're not needed or loved.

Respect of the person, always ...

These are human beings, loved by God and gifted with the Holy Spirit.

Prayer ...

Asking God to help the organisation in its work and **praying** for all in need.

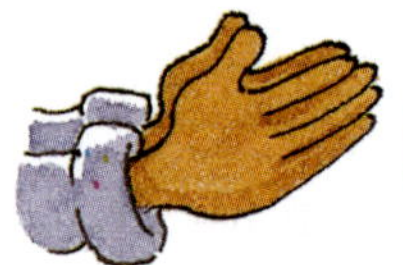

Social Justice is always fought for ...

The Society of St Vincent de Paul continually stands up for the rights of the poor and needy in our society.

... All this is achieved through a wide range of activities and projects.

- **financial support;**
- **advice and counselling;**
- **personal development;**
- **spiritual development and love of God;**
- **youth clubs** ● **education grants;**
- **job preparation** ● **drugs projects;**
- **halfway houses** ● **homeless hostels;**
- **lobbying the Government**

... to name but a few.

Organisation of

- SVP operates 1,100 Conferences across the country, pinpointing people's needs.
- SVP has a National Council. This co-ordinates thirteen Regional Councils who support smaller Area Councils and Conferences.

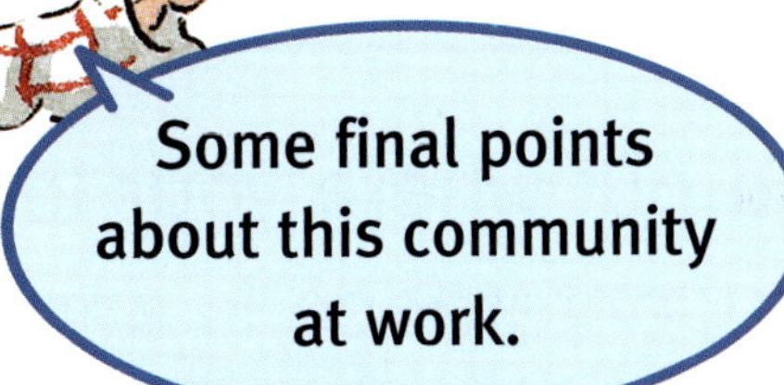

- SVP helps all people in financial / practical /emotional and spiritual need.
- SVP lives and promotes Catholic social teaching, as well as manifesting Gospel values and Jesus' love for all.

Ensure that poverty and social exclusion are eliminated.

In your copy answer these questions as best you can:

- What is the service of SVP?
- What is the Society's inspiration?
- How is SVP organised (leadership)?

How does SVP promote the **5** things below?

Respect • Advice • Acceptance • Dignity • Spirituality

1. Name six activities and projects that SVP offers.
2. How many Conferences are there across the country?
3. Who supports the work of SVP?
4. Who does SVP help?

Find out where your local SVP Conference is and get information on what it does in your local area.

Communities of Faith!

TO KNOW

Denomination = a religious group, usually part of a bigger religion or community of faith.
Lay = a person not ordained to priesthood or priestly ministry.

COPY AND COLOUR

Remember A community of faith is a group of people who share the same religious belief, have holy men and women, holy books and worship guidelines and who follow the rules laid down by a particular religion or faith. They also try to make the society they live in a better place by giving good example to others, and reaching out to those in need.

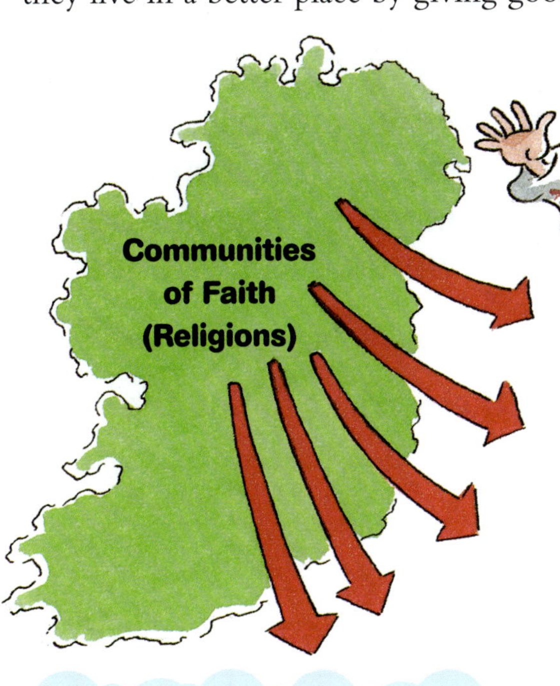

There are many communities of faith all around the world, but let's look at some of the many communities of faith in Ireland.

- Catholic (Catholicism);
- Church of Ireland (Anglicanism);
- Presbyterian (Presbyterianism);
- Methodist (Methodism);
- Baptist;
- Lutheran (Lutheranism);
- Salvation Army;
- Quakers (Society of Friends);
- Islamic (Islam);
- Jewish (Judaism);
- Buddhist (Buddhism);
- Greek Orthodox.

NB: other communities of faith can be groups of Brothers and nuns or religious people.

Unmuddle each of these communities of faith:

Put the right word here

MLSAI ______________________

RTEHULAN ______________________

SDMHITOET ______________________

CLITAOHC ______________________

RSKUQAE ______________________

SWJEIH ______________________

Find them in this puzzle wheel. Highlight them:

RABCARSTCAATHOLICMJUDAISMKSTQUAKERSMADGHMETHODISTLOSKMUVMBAPTISTCOPUVKELRESCATHOLICUTK

Q Explain each of the following: **'lay' / 'denomination'.** In your copy, put both words into sentences.

Unscramble these bricks to find the words:

COM	OF	ITI	TH	FAI	MUN	ES

HOL	IC	T I	CAT	M	SLA	TIS	BAP

Focus on ...

As you can see, there are many communities of faith in Ireland, so let's …

Christian Faith Communities

Over the years, from the time of Jesus, splits in Christianity occurred for various reasons, resulting in all these Churches.

Keep in mind the communities'
- founder;
- denomination;
- vision;
- belief;
- commitment;
- mission.

Anglican

Christian Orthodox

Roman Catholic

Presbyterian

Methodist

Quaker (Society of Friends)

The Faith Community of **Christianity** (religion) is based around and on the life, death and resurrection of **Jesus of Nazareth, the Christ**. Jesus worked and lived in Palestine (Israel) 2,000 years ago. (You will read more about this in a later section.)

As part of our exploration of communities of faith we will look at the

Roman Catholic Church

TO KNOW

Roman: from and based around Rome, Italy.
Catholic: meaning 'Universal'.
Church: believers in Jesus Christ / building for Christian worship.

Christians believe that Jesus is present in his Church through his Spirit. The Church can be called the **'Body of Christ'**.

- The Roman Catholic Church is part of Christianity, as are the Protestant Churches and the Orthodox Churches.
- **Let's have a look at …**

... Beginnings

The Catholic Church traces its origins back to the 'Twelve Apostles' (Chosen by Jesus to help spread his word). They were witnesses to Jesus' life, death and post-resurrection experiences. Of the twelve Apostles, Jesus chose **Peter** to be a leader in the Church.

We will read about the other Apostles later.

In the **BIBLE**, the Sacred Scripture of the Catholic Church, we read in the **Gospel of Matthew**, in the New Testament, that Jesus said to Peter, 'You are Peter and on this rock I will build my community (Church) … I will give you the keys of the Kingdom of Heaven.'

- After the death and resurrection of Jesus, Peter, along with James, became the leader of a Christian community in Jerusalem.
- Later on, he became the **Bishop of Rome**, in Italy. Rome became the centre of the Catholic Church.

TO KNOW

About half of all Christians are Catholic – 750 million people.

The Catholic Church teaches that it is the continuation of the Church founded by Jesus and the authority given to Peter and the Apostles.

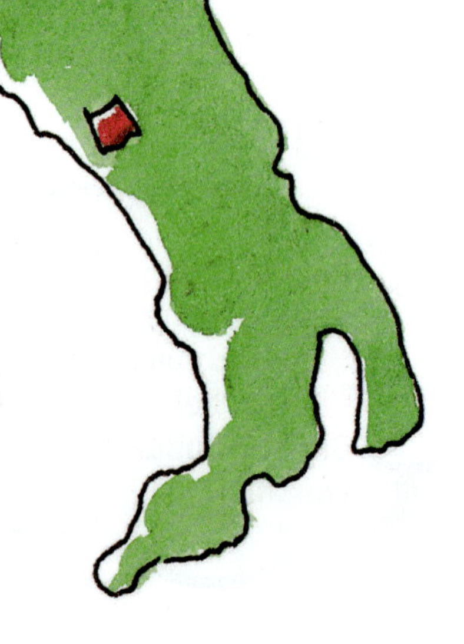

Q1. Name three Christian faith communities.

Q2. Which person is **Christianity** based around?

Q3. Where did he live?

Q4. What does **CATHOLIC** mean?

Q5. The Church can be called something else – what is it?

Unmuddle these

TOLHCAIC
MRANO
RPTEE
SPOTLEAS
IBELB
VRELDEAE

Fill in these blanks

The ______ Church traces its ______ back to the twelve ______. They were ______ to Jesus' ______, ______ and post-resurrection experiences. Of the ___ apostles, Jesus chose ______ to be a leader in the Church. The ______ is the Sacred ______ of the Catholic Church. In the Gospel of ______, Jesus said to Peter: 'You are ______ and on this ______ I will build my ______ … I will give you the ______ of the Kingdom of ______.' Peter became the leader of the ______ community in ______ . Later, he travelled to ______ and became the bishop there. Rome became the centre of the Catholic ______.

Mix and Match

Match the word to its definition:

Catholic	Christian Faith Community
Church	Universal
Anglican	Number of Catholics
Peter	Centre of Catholic Church
Rome	Believers in Jesus Christ
750 million people	Head of Jesus' Church

More Qs

A. Who was the first Bishop of Rome?

B. In your opinion, why is the Church called Catholic?

C. What did Jesus mean by: 'I will give you the keys of the Kingdom of Heaven'?

D. How many Christians are Catholic?

E. What does **Body of Christ** mean?

••• From the Apostles, St Peter's authority has been handed down to other religious men over the centuries •••

TO KNOW

Apostle = one of the twelve original followers of Christ.
Succession = leadership passing from one person to the next.

This is properly called

- St Peter and the Apostles were chosen by Jesus to have authority over the Church.

The Pope

(In Latin = *papa*)

- The authority is handed down from one generation to the next.

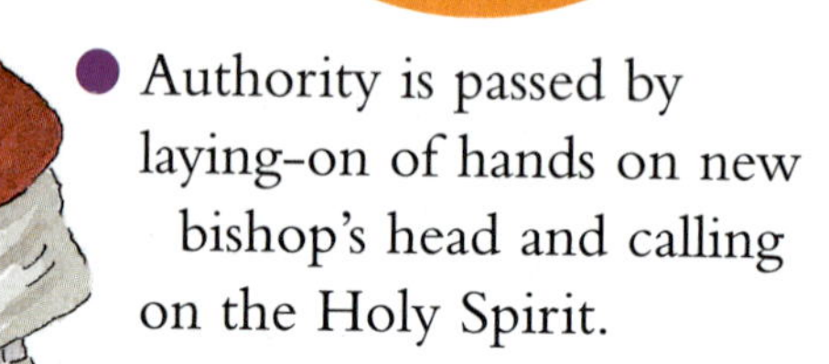

- Authority is passed by laying-on of hands on new bishop's head and calling on the Holy Spirit.

- The Pope is the leader of the Catholic Church.
- The Pope is the successor of St Peter in Rome.
- He has authority over all Roman Catholics the world over.
- He is called **The Vicar of Christ**, meaning the representative of Christ on Earth.
- Also called **The Supreme Pontiff**.
- The Pope lives in **The Vatican**.
- Since the First Vatican Council (1870) the Pope can make an **infallible statement** (meaning that it can't be wrong) about matters of faith. (This happens very rarely.)
- He is elected through the cardinals and the inspiration of the Holy Spirit.

‘Cardinals’

Who are they?

TO KNOW

Hierarchy = the different levels of authority in the Catholic Church.

- The title ‘Cardinal’ is given to a priest or bishop who becomes a special dignitary of the Catholic Church. They are chosen by the Pope.
- Cardinals can take part in voting for a new Pope. They are also usually on Vatican Councils and Commissions and have authority over dioceses and Catholic Church areas.
- At present in Ireland there are two cardinals – **Cardinal Desmond Connell** and **Cardinal Cathal Daly**.

In Ireland, there are twenty-seven dioceses. There are also four archdioceses. An archbishop has authority over these areas. The archdioceses of Ireland are:

Armagh
Cashel
Dublin
Tuam

4 Provinces
Ulster / Munster / Leinster / Connacht

‘Bishops’

Bishops are consecrated to that role by the laying-on of hands. They have authority over a ‘diocese’.

{NB: a diocese is an area made up of Catholic parishes.}

It is the bishops’ role to interpret, teach and spread Catholic teaching to the diocese. It is also their role to help create the Kingdom of God with other bishops, priests and the people of God.

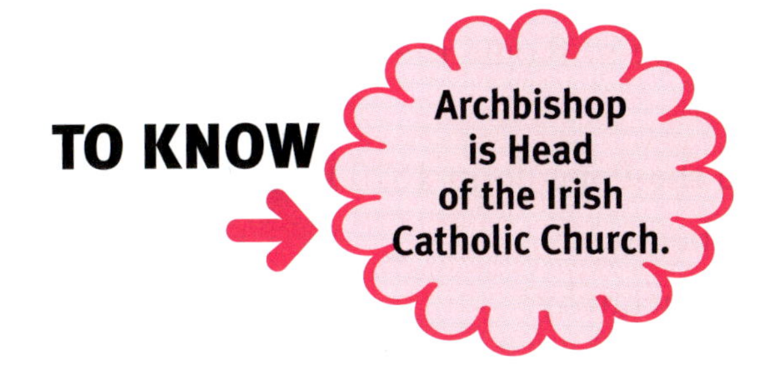

When you find them, list them in your copy and use each one in a sentence.

Quick Research

- Find out who the Irish cardinals are.
- Where do they live?
- Find the names of four Irish bishops.
- Where do they live?

Answer these

Q1. What does **Apostolic Succession** mean?

Q2. Explain **Apostolic**.

Q3. Jesus gave Church authority to whom?

Q4. Who is this authority handed down to?

Q5. What is the English for '*Papa*'?

Q6. Give two other titles for the Pope.

Q7. What is the Pope's job?

Q8. Where does he live?

Word tiles – figure these out!

LIC	ON	STO	SU	SSI	APO	CCE

IST	OF	AR	CHR	VIC

Try these

A. Why is the Pope in Rome the successor to St Peter?

B. What could the Pope do in 1870 that he couldn't do before?

C. What is the Hierarchy?

D. What does a cardinal do?

E. How are bishops consecrated?

F. What is the bishops' job?

G. What is an archdiocese?

As we mentioned before, a diocese is made up of a number of parishes, all overseen by a bishop. To help the bishop with the running of the parishes are

'Priests'

- Priests are men who are ordained by the bishop of the diocese to work in parishes.

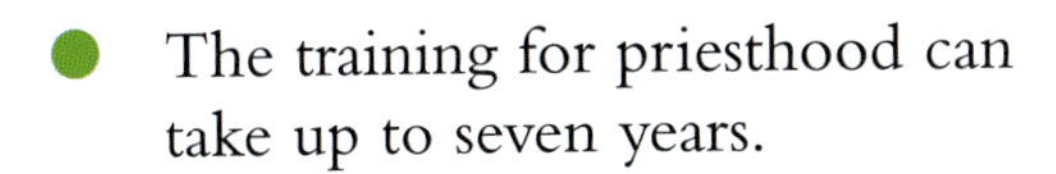

- The training for priesthood can take up to seven years.

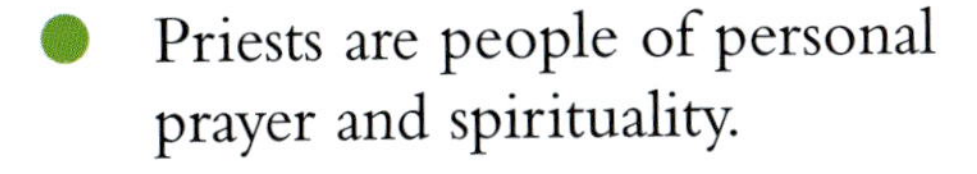

- Priests are people of personal prayer and spirituality.
- Priests are appointed to a parish for a number of years.
  This is what they do!

- preside over liturgical celebrations;
- administer the Sacraments;
- proclaim the Word of God and explain Christ's and Church teaching;
- bear witness to Christ and to Gospel values in the community;
- make themselves always available to all believers for discussion, advice, etc.

TO KNOW

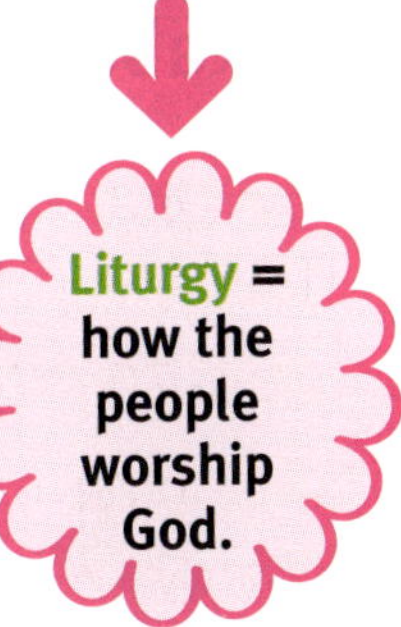

NB: people who feel a calling to be a priest, nun or Brother have a **Vocation** to that way of life for God.

Of course, not all people who are members of the Catholic Church are **cardinals, bishops or priests**. Most of the people in the Catholic Church Community of Faith are called

like you and me!

'Lay' means 'different from the clergy', or 'not ordained'.

Catholic laypeople, because of their baptism, are called to help spread the message of Jesus Christ. This they can do by ...

Collaborating with the priest in the parish.

Participating in the Mass, Sacraments and liturgical celebrations.

Being witnesses to Christ's message.

Working to help the needy at home, in the parish and abroad!

Using gifts and talents for the good of others in the parish and community.

By doing these things laypeople can help to make the community better for all and can help to create God's Kingdom.

'Lay Christians are entrusted by God by virtue of their baptism and confirmation the right and duty to work so that the divine message of salvation may be known by all people throughout the earth'. (Cat. 900)

Priests and Laypeople work together!

Draw and name four things a layperson does to spread Jesus' message.

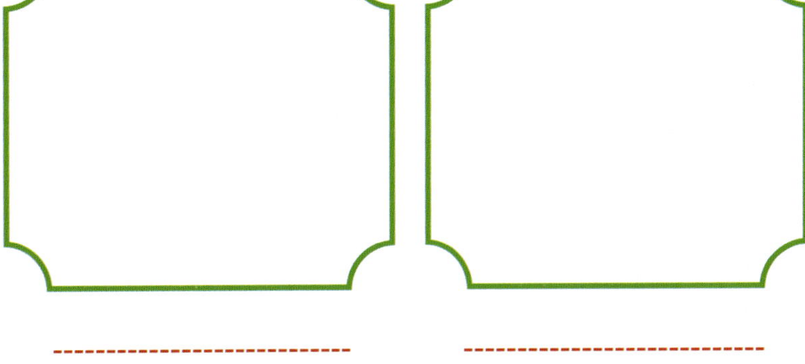

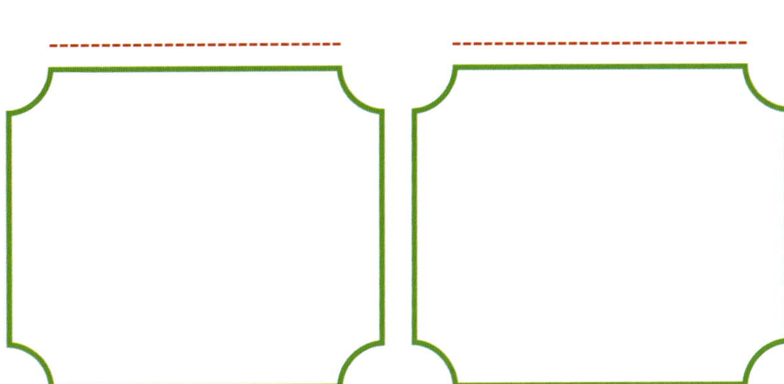

1. What does **lay** mean?
2. Explain why you are a layperson.
3. What is our role as baptised laypeople?
4. List three things you can do to help spread the message of Jesus.
5. What is a diocese?
6. Who helps the bishop to run the diocese?
7. List four things that a priest does.
8. What does **liturgy** mean?

Find out how laypeople help in your parish church.

- Who are they?
- What do they do?

A. Name your parish.
B. What diocese is your parish in?
C. Who is the bishop of your diocese?
D. Explain **Ordination**.
E. Name some **liturgies**.
F. How can a layperson help at **liturgies**?
G. What does it mean to be **spiritual**?
H. A **vocation** is …?
I. Where do priests go to study?

As we know, all communities of faith have very important beliefs. These beliefs are different across some faith communities. Let's look at

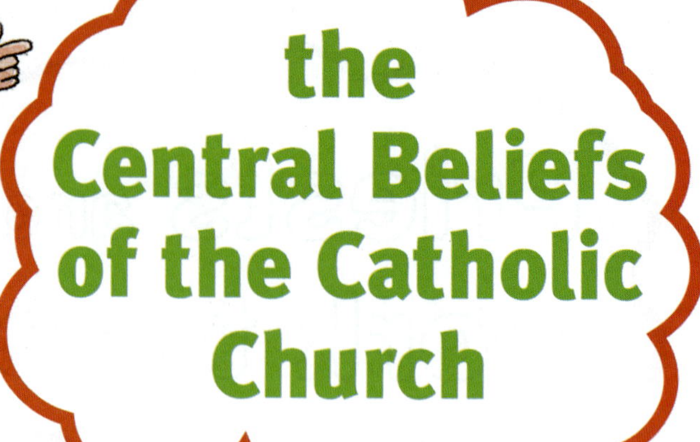

Over the centuries God revealed, or made himself known to us through the Prophets and finally through his son, Jesus Christ. All the revelations are contained in the Bible and the tradition of the Church.

'God has revealed himself fully by sending his own son Jesus Christ in whom he has established his covenant for ever.'
(Cat. Art. 1. 3. 73)

Revelation, then, is transmitted through **HOLY SCRIPTURES** and **TRADITION**.

TO KNOW

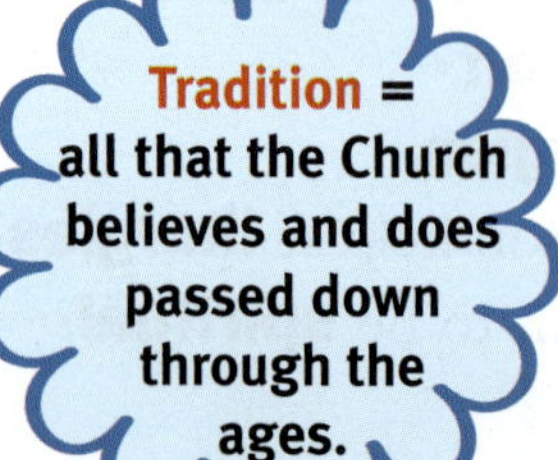

'God becomes man'

- Jesus, the only son of God, took on human nature, without losing his **Divine nature**. He became **INCARNATE!**
- The Incarnation is all about the union of human and Divine natures in Jesus Christ.
- Jesus was born of the Virgin Mary, 'Mother of God'.

Jesus' Death

AND

- God loved us and sent his only son to rescue us from our sins (1 John 4:10).
- Through Jesus' death God reconciled the world to himself (2 Cor. 5:19).
- Jesus freely gave himself up to save us. He pointed to this at the Last Supper – **'This is my body ... this is my blood given up for you'** (Lk 22:19).
- Christ came 'to give his life as a ransom for many' (Mt 20:28). 'He loved his own to the end' (John 13:1).

- The Resurrection is Jesus rising from the dead, the entry of Christ's humanity into the glory of God.
- By God's power, Christ was saved from death and decay.
- Christ is the 'first born from the dead' (Col. 1:18) and we all share in his resurrection.

- Jesus enters Heaven and lives with God the Father forever.
- He goes before us all to God's Kingdom.

The Holy Spirit

- Given to Jesus at his baptism.
- Given to the Apostles at Pentecost.
- Given to us at **Baptism** and **Confirmation**.
- God has sent the Spirit of his Son into our hearts.
- The Holy Spirit builds, strengthens and makes holy the Church.

Figure out the **2** central beliefs from these tiles

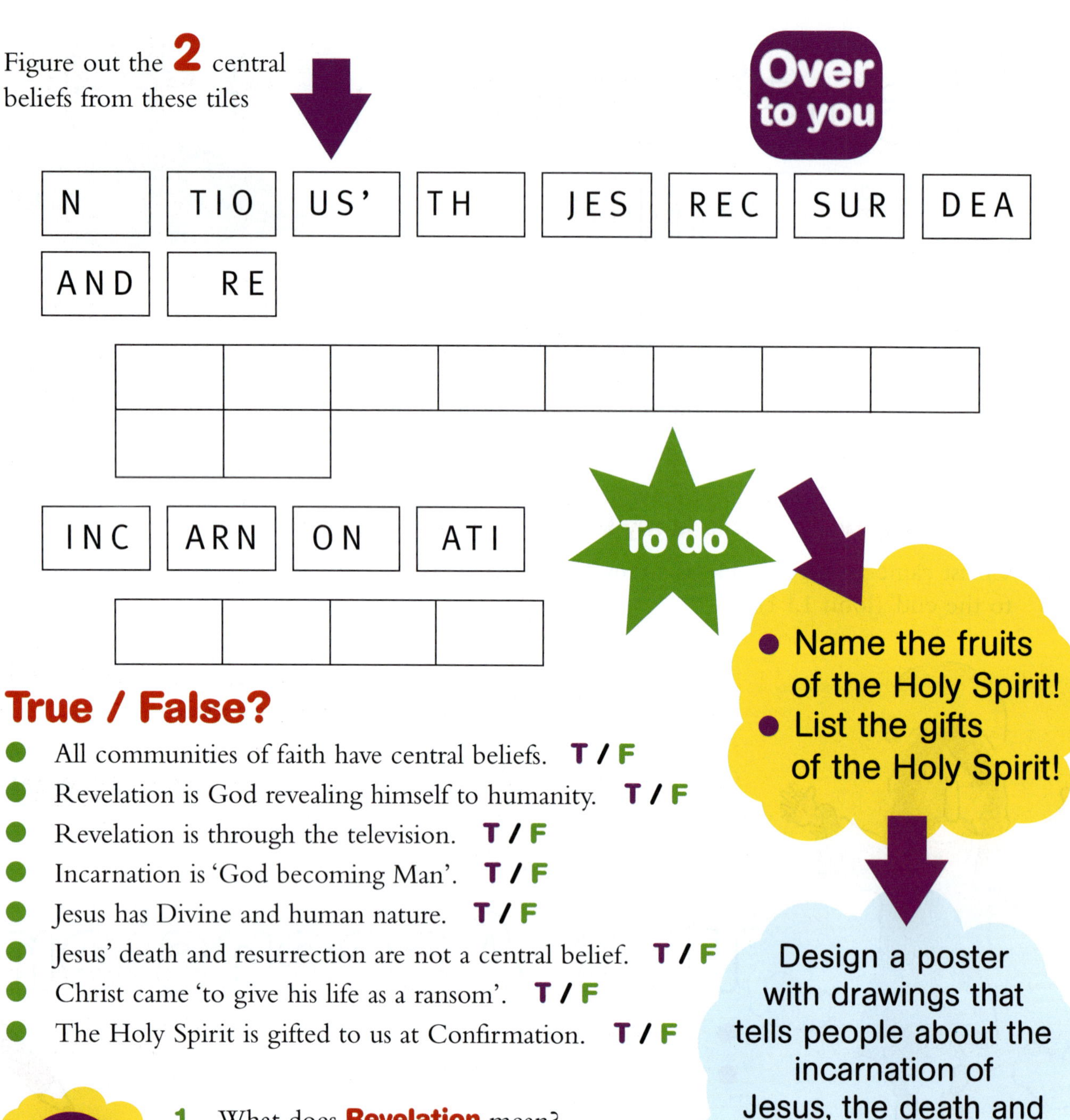

- Name the fruits of the Holy Spirit!
- List the gifts of the Holy Spirit!

Design a poster with drawings that tells people about the incarnation of Jesus, the death and resurrection of Jesus and Jesus' ascension into Heaven!

True / False?

- All communities of faith have central beliefs. **T / F**
- Revelation is God revealing himself to humanity. **T / F**
- Revelation is through the television. **T / F**
- Incarnation is 'God becoming Man'. **T / F**
- Jesus has Divine and human nature. **T / F**
- Jesus' death and resurrection are not a central belief. **T / F**
- Christ came 'to give his life as a ransom'. **T / F**
- The Holy Spirit is gifted to us at Confirmation. **T / F**

Q

1. What does **Revelation** mean?
2. How does **Revelation** happen?
3. What does **Tradition** mean?
4. Name the phrase for Jesus becoming human.
5. What two natures did Jesus have?
6. Who was Jesus' mother?
7. What is the Resurrection?
8. Why is it so important?
9. Why did Jesus die?
10. What happened at the Ascension?
11. What is the message of the Resurrection?
12. How important is the Holy Spirit?
13. What was the climax of Revelation?
14. 'The Word became Flesh' means …?

The Trinity

- **God the Father**, **God the Son** and **God the Holy Spirit** existing together forever.
- As Catholics, we worship God in the Trinity and the Trinity in unity. The Father is one, the Son is one, and the Holy Spirit is one, and yet the three – Father, Son and Spirit – are one. The Father loves the Son, Jesus, who in turn loves the Father and together the love between them is the Spirit.
- The Holy Spirit as the third person of the Trinity is God, one and equal with the Father and the Son, of the same substance and the same nature, he is the spirit of the Father and the Son, with the Father and the Son he is worshipped and glorified'. (Cat. 245)
- They are inseparable in what they are, and inseparable in what they do.

The Eucharist

- It is heart and summit of the Church's life.
- The bread and wine change to Christ's body and blood during the Mass **(as Jesus did at the Last Supper)**.
- The Eucharist is the memorial of Christ's work of saving us brought about by his life, death and resurrection, made present by the actions of the priest and people at Mass.
- Christ, through the priest, offers the eucharistic sacrifice.
- Christ is present in the species of bread and wine.
- The blessing of the Holy Spirit is called on and the priest pronounces the words of **Consecration**:
  'This is my body which will be given up for you … This is the cup of my blood …' (words spoken by Jesus at the Last Supper).
- By this Consecration the **Transubstantiation** of the bread and wine into Christ's body and blood occurs.

Transubstantiation = to change the substance of something to another substance.

TO KNOW

Eucharist = from Greek *Eucharistein* + *Eulogein* meaning 'Thanksgiving to God'.

Christ's Presence!

Jesus is present in his Church in many ways.

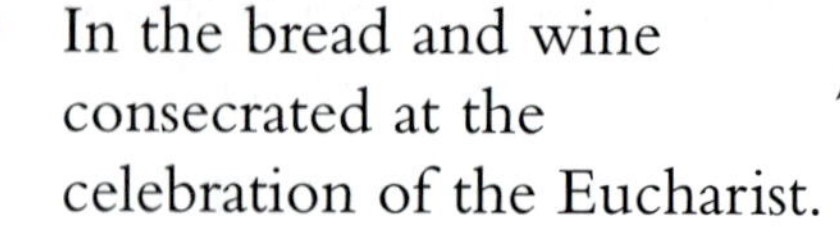

- In the bread and wine consecrated at the celebration of the Eucharist.

- In the 'Word' **(Scripture)**, by nature of 'Revelation'.

- In the gathered community. He is the Head of the **Body of Christ**!

- In the person of the **priest** presiding over the liturgical celebrations.

- In the **Sacraments** of the Church:

Baptism

Eucharist

Confirmation

Reconciliation

Holy Orders

Marriage

Last Rites

Through all these, Christ is present in the world.

We will study these further in a later section.

Fill in the blanks:

The Trinity is the ______ of ______ the Father, ______ the ______ and God the ______.

As Catholics, we worship God in the ______ and the Trinity in ______ . The Father is ______ , the ______ is one, and the Holy Spirit is one, and yet the three are ______ .

They are ______ in what they ______ and what they ______ .

Q

1. What is the heart and summit of the Church's life?
2. What happens to the bread and wine during the Mass?
3. What is the 'Eucharist'? What does the word mean?
4. How is 'Christ' present?
5. How is the Eucharist 'Memorial'?

Finish these sentences

- The Eucharist is the heart …
- The bread and wine change …
- The Trinity is the unity of …
- The words of Consecration are …
- Christ is present in the Sacraments. These are …
- He is also present in …
- In the community, Christ is the head of …
- Holy Orders concern becoming a …
- Penance is …

Name and draw three ways in which Christ is present to us!

To do

Write the words of 'Consecration' in a bubble in your copy!
Retell the story of your Confirmation day.

Unmuddle these words and use each one in a sentence:

- RITNIYT
- TEUHRSCAI
- DEBRA + NWIE
- EMMRILOA
- RPESNCEE
- CPRISTRUE
- CTYMMIOUN
- SRMTSENACA
- TRGALLIUIC

TO FIND OUT

- When do baptisms happen in your parish church?
- How are they celebrated?

The Kingdom of God!

- In the Church, the **Kingdom of God** (Reign of God) is present. A kingdom of peace, love and justice!
- In and through the Church it will be fulfilled at the end of time.
- The Kingdom has come in the person of Christ.
- Christ calls all people to himself by his words and deeds, through the Apostles and their successors.
- Everyone is called to enter this Kingdom. It belongs to the poor and lowly, those who have accepted it with humble hearts.
- The Lord's Prayer ('Our Father') calls on God's Kingdom to come.

The Virgin Mary

Mary has a very special place in Catholic belief, teaching and worship. She is the mother of Jesus, the Mother of God.

- Mary conceived Jesus by the power of the Holy Spirit.
- She was betrothed to Joseph.
- She gave birth to Jesus in Bethlehem, 'the Virgin Birth'.
- She was with Jesus when he was on his cross.
- By her prayers she helped the beginnings of the Church.
- 'She is the Mother of the Members of Christ' (Cat. 963).
- She is a model of holiness for all Catholics.
- She is 'full of grace'.
- She is blessed among all women.
- She is with God forever in Heaven.

The Church believes that Our Lady has appeared in a number of places around the world. **Lourdes, Knock and Fatima** are three places where apparitions have occurred.

Mother of God

- She was born without sin, the **Immaculate Conception**.
- She was assumed into Heaven, body and soul – **the Assumption of Our Lady**.
- Decay did not come to her holy body.
- Pope Paul VI proclaimed her **Mother of the Church**.
- Pope Piux XII proclaimed her **Universal Queen**.
- Announced as **Immaculate Conception** in 1854.
- Dogma of **Assumption** announced by Pius XII in 1950.

Complete this fact file about Mary:

Betrothed to ____________

Gave birth in ____________

Born without sin ____________

Full of ____________

Entered Heaven ____________

Pope Paul VI called her ____________

____

In 1854 ____________

Appeared in ____________

Blessed among ____________

1. How will the Kingdom of God be fulfilled?
2. How does Christ call people?
3. Who does the Kingdom belong to?
4. What prayer calls for God's Kingdom to come?
5. List some titles for the Virgin Mary.

Fill in these blanks:

In the ________ , the Kingdom of ________ exists. In and through the Church it will be ________ at the ________ of ________. The ________ has come in the person of ________. Christ calls all ________ to himself, by his ________ and ________, through the ________ and their ________. Everyone is ________ to ________ the Kingdom. It belongs to the ________ and ________, those who have accepted it with ____________.

Find out as much as you can about one of the places around the world where Our Lady has appeared. Write it up and add photos and drawings.

The beliefs or **CREEDS** of the Catholic Church are contained here.

The Apostles' Creed

TO KNOW

Creed = Latin for I believe, ***'Credo'***.

I believe in God, the Father Almighty, creator of Heaven and Earth.

I believe in Jesus Christ, his only Son, Our Lord. He was conceived by the power of the Holy Spirit and born of the Virgin Mary. He suffered under Pontius Pilate, was crucified, died and was buried.

He descended to the dead. On the third day he rose again. He ascended into Heaven and is seated at the right hand of the Father. He will come again to judge the living and the dead.

I believe in the Holy Spirit, the Holy Catholic Church, the Communion of Saints, the forgiveness of sins, the resurrection of the body and life everlasting. Amen.

NB: the Apostles' Creed is called this because it is a faithful summary of the Apostles' faith.

From the Council of Nice A.D. 325; Constantinople A.D. 381.

The Niceno-Constantinople Creed

We believe in One God, the Father, the Almighty, maker of Heaven and Earth, of all that is seen and unseen.

We believe in One Lord, Jesus Christ, the only Son of God, eternally begotten of the Father, God from God, light from light, true God from true God, begotten not made, of one being with the Father. Through him all things were made.

For us men and for our salvation, he came down from heaven, by the power of the Holy Spirit he became incarnate of the Virgin Mary, and became man. For our sake he was crucified unto Pontius Pilate, he suffered death and was buried. On the third day he rose again in accordance with the Scriptures, he ascended into heaven and is seated at the right hand of the Father. He will come again in glory to judge the living and the dead and his Kingdom will have no end.

We believe in the Holy Spirit, the Lord, the giver of life, who proceeds from the Father and the Son, with the Father and the Son he is worshipped and glorified. He has spoken through the prophets. We believe in one holy, Catholic and apostolic Church. We acknowledge one baptism for the forgiveness of sins. We look to the resurrection of the dead and the life of the world to come. Amen.

Everything that the Catholic Church holds dear – its beliefs, teachings, vision, mission, future message, etc – is contained in the 'Catechism of the Catholic Church'.
Get hold of a copy and have a look; it's good to know your faith even deeper!

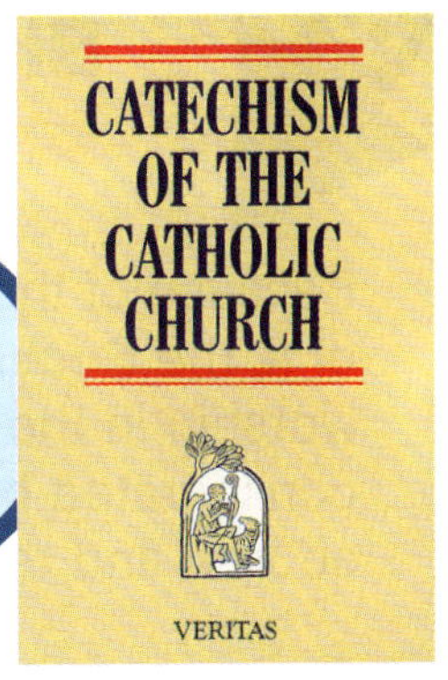

Central to the worship of Catholics is the **Mass**. This celebration is given different names.

'The Holy Sacrifice of the Mass'

'The Breaking of Bread'

'Celebration of the Eucharist'

TO KNOW

Mass = from Latin '*Missa Est*' meaning 'Go, the Mass is ended'.

It is important because

- it is the action of the Church that makes present the sacrifice of Christ on the cross;
- it remembers and celebrates Christ's Last Supper on Holy Thursday;
- in it, we follow his command to 'eat his body and drink his blood';
- it is Christ present in communion;
- it is the memorial, celebration, re-enactment of Christ's death and resurrection. It is made up of

WELCOME

Gathering and Welcome

Liturgy of the Word

Liturgy of the Eucharist

Communion Rite

Dismissal and Blessing

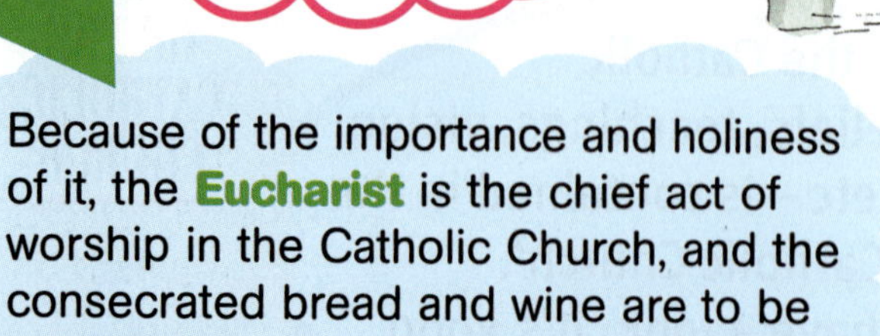

Because of the importance and holiness of it, the **Eucharist** is the chief act of worship in the Catholic Church, and the consecrated bread and wine are to be adored and revered by all the faithful.

'The Church obliges the faithful to take part in the Divine Liturgy on Sunday and feast days and, prepared by the Sacrament of Reconciliation, to receive the Eucharist at least once a year, if possible during the Easter season. But the Church strongly encourages the faithful to receive Holy Communion on Sundays and feast days, or more often still, even daily.' (Cat. 1389)

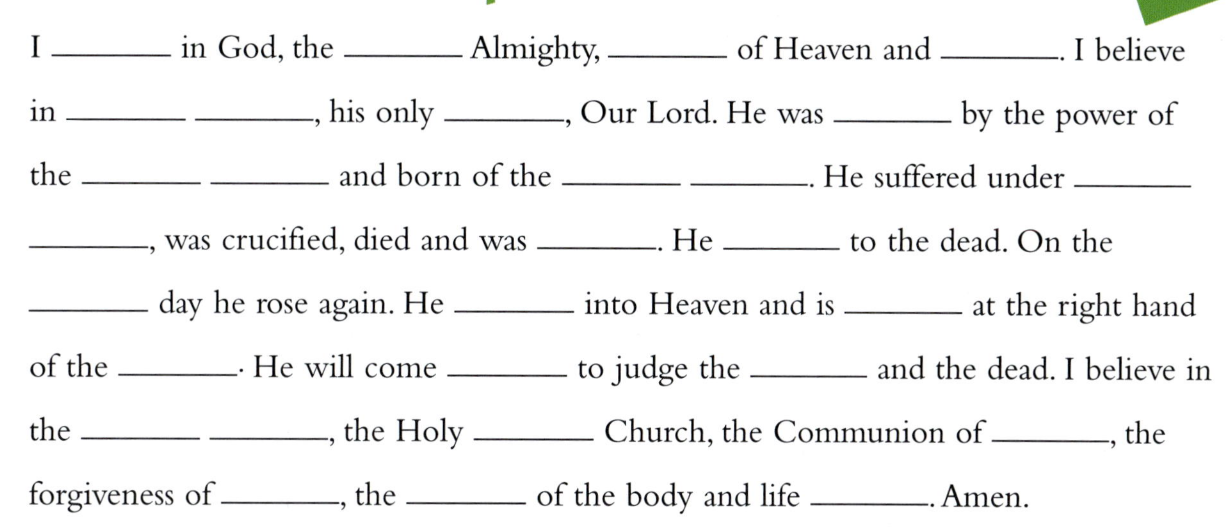

Fill in these blanks: Apostles' Creed

I _______ in God, the _______ Almighty, _______ of Heaven and _______. I believe in _______ _______, his only _______, Our Lord. He was _______ by the power of the _______ _______ and born of the _______ _______. He suffered under _______ _______, was crucified, died and was _______. He _______ to the dead. On the _______ day he rose again. He _______ into Heaven and is _______ at the right hand of the _______. He will come _______ to judge the _______ and the dead. I believe in the _______ _______, the Holy _______ Church, the Communion of _______, the forgiveness of _______, the _______ of the body and life _______. Amen.

1. Why is the Apostles' Creed called that?
2. What does it say about God the Father?
3. What happened to Jesus on the third day?
4. List the reasons why the Mass is important.

To do

Compare the two creeds and make a list of the differences that are mentioned.

Name the five parts of the Mass and draw a picture for each part:

Catholic Church Wordsearch

I	D	X	O	N	P	L	I	E	G	Q	B	B	H	R
Y	L	I	M	A	F	L	C	G	P	R	T	T	S	O
C	F	M	S	N	D	Y	U	N	E	Z	A	T	I	L
C	O	M	M	U	N	I	C	A	T	I	O	N	R	E
S	Y	O	L	B	L	O	K	H	A	W	I	B	A	S
U	I	S	P	O	A	D	F	C	N	Q	N	W	P	D
N	G	N	O	E	O	L	V	X	W	H	D	T	V	B
C	E	H	U	W	R	I	A	E	K	Z	I	M	R	P
V	C	E	N	M	L	A	Z	N	H	M	V	S	M	M
S	M	A	D	L	M	W	T	L	C	A	I	H	C	U
S	Q	C	A	S	N	I	O	I	W	E	D	A	D	E
X	S	G	F	D	N	R	C	L	O	A	U	R	T	S
R	E	L	I	G	I	O	N	F	S	N	A	I	P	Y
Y	T	I	N	U	M	M	O	C	P	A	L	N	J	W
S	H	A	R	E	D	A	E	R	A	A	M	G	C	A

AREA
BALANCE
BREAKDOWN
COMMUNICATION
COMMUNITY
CO-OPERATION
EXCHANGE
FAMILY
INDIVIDUAL
MASLOW
NEEDS
PARISH
RELIGION
ROLES
SCHOOL
SHARED
SHARING
TOWN
VILLAGE

Points to Remember

- The Roman Catholic Church is a Christian Faith Community!
- It began with Jesus choosing the Apostles and Peter as leader.
- Its spiritual capital is the Vatican in Rome.
- The Pope is the Head of the Church, a successor to St Peter.
- The Hierarchy of the Church is made up of the Pope, cardinals, bishops and priests.
- The Bible is the revealed Word of God.
- Members of the Church who are not ordained to priesthood are called the laity; they work with the priest to bring about God's Kingdom.
- Core beliefs are:

  Incarnation – God became man;

  Jesus' death and resurrection;

  The Holy Spirit;

  The Trinity;

  The Eucharist /the Mass;

  The presence of Christ;

  The Kingdom of God;

  The resurrection of all believers;

  The Virgin Mary.
- Its primary worship is the celebration of the Eucharist – Mass.
- Its beliefs are contained in creeds.
- The 'Catechism of the Catholic Church' contains articles of faith, belief, vision, worship and spirituality.

Time to Think and Pray

Light a candle, play some soft music, burn incense, focus on Scripture or a cross … open your heart to God.

'Do not be afraid;
I am with you;
I have called you
each by name …
follow me, I will
be your guide …
I love you;
you are mine.'

Be With Me

- Be with me, Lord, in the hard times. **R /** Be with me, Lord.
- Be with me, Lord, when I struggle. **R /** Be with me, Lord.
- Be with me, Lord, when I'm scared. **R /** Be with me, Lord.
- Be with me, Lord, when I laugh. **R /** Be with me, Lord.
- Be with me, Lord, when I cry. **R /** Be with me, Lord.
- Be with me, Lord, when I pray. **R /** Be with me, Lord.

Scripture Reading

'The washing of the feet'
(John 13:1–20)

Play 'The Servant Song'.

Checklist: organise a class celebration of the Eucharist …

- Priest
- Readings
- Theme
- Altar
- Gifts
- Bread and Wine
- Prayers of the Faithful
- Music
- Readers
- Reflections
- … other …

Reflect …

I am one of Christ's family; let me show it to the world. I am a baptised Christian; let me be it. I will spread Christ's message; let me do it. I will help others in need … I will do it, I am a servant as Jesus was. I am a mirror for Jesus; show his reflection.

OK, let's look at another community of faith – the Methodist Community.

Remember, keep in the back of your mind:

NB:
name comes from ... 'Living according to the method laid down in the Bible'.

the founder;
the denomination;
its vision;
its belief;
its commitment;
its mission!

the Methodist Church ... in Ireland

'Friends of all, enemies of none!'

The President of the Methodist Church in Ireland today is Revd W. Winston Graham, and he is based in Belfast.

Brief history: Methodism was originally part of the Church of England and one of its most important members was a man called John Wesley (1703–1791).

John was a great preacher and put a lot of emphasis on living good Christian lives. Many of the people in Methodism felt that they didn't belong to the Church of England, but John Wesley and Methodism gave people a new sense of purpose and hope. These feelings of purpose and hope were based on the Bible, and worship and love of God.

Wesley himself said …

'To Spread Scriptural Holiness Throughout the Land …'

As a part of its vision, the Methodist Church has the 'Four All'

'4 All'

This was very attractive to people who didn't feel part of the Church of England.

After John Wesley died (1791), Methodism split from the Church of England, and then again into smaller groups (Churches). From these small groups, **Methodism** spread around the world.

The Methodist Church arrived in Ireland in the 1740s. Many of its earliest members were English. As it did in England, it split from the Church of Ireland and became a separate Christian denomination here.

It is estimated that there are *c.* 5,000 members in Ireland today.

(North America has the largest Methodist population. Worldwide, the Methodist Church has 70 million followers.)

Some work for you to do

- Draw the symbol for the Methodist Church 

Q1. Who is the President of the Methodist community of faith in Ireland?

Q2. Who is one of the most important members of Methodism?

Q3. Who was John Wesley?

Q4. What did Methodism give to those people who were unhappy with the Church of England?

Q5. Where does the name Methodism come from?

Q6. What happened after Wesley died?

Q7. When did Methodism arrive in Ireland?

List the '4 all' below:

____

____

____

____

____

Choose the correct answer:

- Methodist Church President:
  - Martin Luther
  - Pope Benedict XVI
  - Revd W. Winston Graham
- Founder of Methodism
  - John Wesley
  - Guru Nanak
  - Mohammed
- Wesley died in:
  - 1870
  - 1640
  - 1791
- Methodist Church arrived in Ireland
  - 1866
  - 1791
  - 1740
- Methodism was part of:
  - Judaism
  - Orthodox Church
  - Church of England
- Methodist vision:
  - To wear black
  - To read books
  - To spread Scripture

Overall, in **Methodism** there is an emphasis on:

- The Holy Spirit.
- Belief in the Doctrines of Christianity.

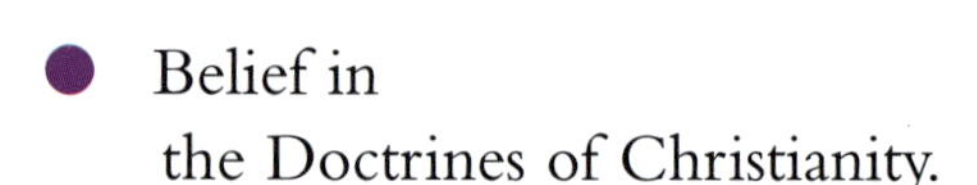

- Close relationship with God.

- Concern for the needy, poor and less fortunate in our society.

- Simple and equal worship (ministers and laypeople work together).

... OK, let's look back at our checklist from earlier and give some answers.

Methodist Checklist

Founder: John Wesley (1703–1791) **Denomination:** Christian
Vision: 'Friends of all, enemies of none' **Belief/s:** 4 All
Commitment: relationship with God, working for the needy
Mission: to spread Scriptural holiness.

Finally, structure:

- Local Methodist churches form a **Society** or congregation.
- Many Societies form a **Circuit**, with one or more ordained minister.
- A group of Circuits forms a **District**, overseen by a Chairperson. They meet to discuss important issues.
- The final authority is the **Conference**. It looks after matters of belief, worship, discipline and order. (The first Conference in Ireland was called by Wesley in 1752, in Limerick.)

Worship:

- Sunday services, morning and evening.
- Readings from Old and New Testaments/prayers, hymns and preaching.
- Monthly celebration of the Last Supper. (Holy Communion – for Methodists, Holy Communion is not the real presence.)
- Baptism.
- Ordination of women as well as men (in Ireland, since 1978).

Methodist Community of Faith Fact File:

COMPLETE THIS

- Founder: ____________
- Mission: ____________
- Vision: ____________
- Belief: ____________
- Commitment: ____________
- Denomination: ____________
- Sacred Text: ____________
- Emphasis on: ____________

In your own words, explain how the Methodist Church is organised (its structure).

RESEARCH
JOURNAL IDEA

Find out where your nearest Methodist church is and get some information about:

- ministers;
- worship times;
- celebrations;
- address;
- local history.

Try these questions

Q1. What was the vision of John Wesley?

Q2. Why did Methodism grow?

Q3. How many followers, worldwide, does it have?

Q4. What does 'All Can Be Saved' mean?

Q5. In your view, what are people saved from?

Q6. What is one of the Methodist Church's main concerns?

Q7. How do people worship in the Methodist Church?

Q8. Why were people attracted to the Methodist Church?

COPY AND COLOUR

'Friends of ALL, Enemies of NONE'

Methodist Wordsearch

M	L	L	A	A	C	R	W
Y	I	W	M	H	O	S	E
Q	V	S	U	U	D	K	S
G	Z	R	S	N	P	K	L
B	C	I	E	I	L	L	E
H	P	I	E	A	O	O	Y
Q	R	T	C	A	T	N	L
F	E	N	G	L	A	N	D

ALL
CHURCH
ENGLAND
FRIENDS
MISSION
WESLEY

Methodist Teaser

Unmuddle these words

All the letters in the circles make a word or phrase. Find it.

TEOSITMDH — 1, 15, 7

WESEYL — 8

AECDHRPE — 6

VIOSIN — 14, 5, 13

FORU LASL — 11, 12

PERDAS SEICTRURP — 10, 9, 2

WOHSIRP — 4

PAREYR — 16

DGO SCPTCEA — 3

1 2 3 4 5 6 7 8 9   10 11 1 1 12 13 14 15 16

The next Community of Faith we will take a look at is

COPY AND COLOUR

THE Quakers!

TO KNOW

Properly called 'The Religious Society of Friends'.

(Society of Friends)

The founder of the Quaker Movement was a man called George Fox (1624–1691). At the age of nineteen, George Fox left his home in England. He wanted to find answers to the big questions in life, e.g. death, love, God, etc. On his travels, he met with many religious and spiritual leaders, but none of these – not even Christian leaders – managed to answer his questions.

In essentials: **UNITY**
In non-essentials: **LIBERTY**
In all things: **CHARITY**

When he was twenty-three, he heard a voice. It said to him: **'There is one, even Christ Jesus, who can speak to your condition'!**

Quaker Philosophy

With this, George Fox became a travelling preacher, saying that worship of God did not need buildings or ministers. He also promoted the idea of **The Inward Light**

This **Inward Light** (or Inner Voice) is a part of God's spirit implanted in every person's soul.

COPY AND COLOUR

George Fox also called this ...

'The Seed of Christ'

Because of this, George Fox says, everyone has the ability to understand the Word of God and give opinion on religious and spiritual matters.

And so, in time, the Quaker movement began to get into trouble with the English authorities and the Church of England. One big problem was that they didn't pay tax to the Church, or take an oath of loyalty to the King.

Because of all this, George Fox was imprisoned on many occasions. On one appearance in court, he replied to the judge by saying, 'Quake at the voice of the Lord!'

'Quake at the voice of the Lord!'

COPY AND COLOUR

The judge responded by calling Fox a 'Quaker', and the name stuck. Basically, Fox criticised the Church because it had too much emphasis on 'outward things', like property, land and money, rather than on 'inner meanings', e.g. spirit, soul, love, etc.

The beliefs of the Quakers can be summed up this way:

Belief in God, Jesus Christ, Holy Spirit • Belief in the Bible •
Direct communication with God (no need to ordain) •
God's will understood through the community •
Everyone has 'Light of Christ' • Simplicity, honesty, integrity •
Equality of men and women •
Peace, no war, reconciliation • Love and goodness •
Life is Sacramental • Experience God throughout life •
All people are connected to God.

Q

Let's do some work

1. What is the proper name of the 'Quaker' Community of Faith?
2. Who was the founder of the Quaker movement?
3. Why did he leave home?
4. Who did he meet on his travels?
5. What happened to him when he was twenty-three?
6. What did he do after he heard the voice?
7. While preaching, what did he speak about?
8. What's another name for the 'Seed of Christ'?

Fill in these blanks:

The founder of the ______ is ______. He was born in ______. When he was ______, he left his ______ in ______. He wanted to find ______ to life's ______. On his travels, he met many religious ______. None of them had ______. When he was ______, he heard a ______. It said '______ ______'. From that moment, he became a ______. He preached about the ______ ______ or ______ of Christ. This meant that everyone has the ______ to understand the ______ of God and give ______ on religious matters!

In your own words, explain how Quakers got their name.

Below, list eight Quaker beliefs

1. ______
2. ______
3. ______
4. ______
5. ______
6. ______
7. ______
8. ______

Organisation of the Quakers

Local groups and congregations around the country join together and hold regular meetings. These are called

Preparative Meetings.

These preparative meetings are grouped together.

They are **Regional Monthly Meetings.**

These are grouped into

Quarterly Meetings

(one every three months).

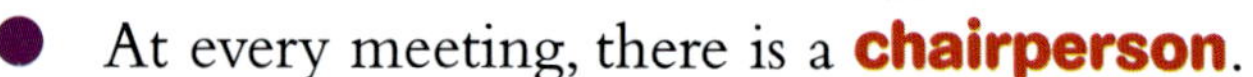

- At every meeting, there is a **chairperson**.
- One of the chairperson's tasks is to figure out 'the feeling of the meeting' (figuring out what the group is saying and what decisions need to be made).
- At the meetings, everybody has the right to speak – the meetings are very 'democratic'.
- The work of these meetings includes:
  - allowing new members;
  - recording of births /marriages /deaths;
  - discussion of premises and grounds.

The Quakers have spread all over the world. In Ireland, there are about 1,600 members **(900 in Ulster / 500 in Leinster / 200 in Munster)**. Local congregations have their own 'elders' and 'overseers'. Worldwide, there are a quarter of a million Quakers. The Religious Society of Friends is a Christian denomination.

As we had for other Communities of Faith, here's a quick checklist for the Quakers.

Founder: George Fox **Denomination:** Christian
Vision: God's spirit in all / peace / love
Belief(s): equality, God, Jesus Christ, Holy Spirit, Direct communication, Light of Christ
Vision: all gain perfection by spiritual development
Mission: reconciliation, peace, simplicity, spreading Scripture.

OVER TO YOU

True / False

- There are local Quaker groups around the country. **T / F**
- Their meetings are called 'assemblies'. **T / F**
- 'Regional Meetings' are held once every ten years. **T / F**
- Monthly meeting are grouped into 'Quarterly Meetings'. **T / F**
- At every meeting there is a chairperson. **T / F**
- The chairperson sings songs. **T / F**
- He/she is a dictator. **T / F**
- The work at the meetings includes making biscuits for the needy. **T / F**

Let's try our art skills! Design a poster about the **Quaker movement**. Put on it information on the following:

- who founded the church;
- in what year and why;
- its vision;
- some beliefs;
- its sacred text;
- its mission.

'Quakers' Wordsearch

Q U A K E K V K P Z X C A K V Y Z H F I E
X I W K Z P A F A P Z S Y N D G Y P N E Q
Z C Y U L U Y D Y X V Y E I P T O W L T U
I N N E R M E A N I N G S E I U A N G D A
Z L R O V A M M Y A R O G R D R W Y B Z L
E Y W F B G K P H V V Y G L D O Z T Y I I
Q U A R T E R L Y V R E S L G L F I L K T
H L I C B I F W I D T B I I A Z O C C S Y
R J J D H W Y M N N K G D T N J O I H B H
Y N G Z W R E X I Y H R N G I F R L I R U
T A K J A E I W L T A E F X M O S P Q J I
L I M N T E I S P W M W S M L C F M N B G
G B R I Y X F B T A S R D E N Y P I G O F
T C N I B J S U R I B D G M K R D S D Q B
B G P E P I O C O O A I N Y H O F X X Q Z
S F S M C S A R Y P S N B E V K O L S U C
K V V Y Q S Y X P V L Y D L I N X W X D E
F C M A E H B L K D Y F P V E R V X U N Q
B M Y C C X Z P O Y T H S P M K F D O E I
G P A G F W R W K H S R E K A U Q H L T L
Y E E V I T A R A P E R P J S S T N X N G
P B Y V L X B O E K N W B M Q T L L W Z L
X V L G D Y V D E N O M I N A T I O N J U
V S E Q I R D P B U H W D D S J N L O Q M
W D B O V X A W O T S I R H C F O D E E S

BIBLE
EQUALITY
GOD
INNER MEANINGS
MEETINGS
PREPARATIVE
QUARTERLY

CHRISTIAN
FOX
HOLY SPIRIT
INTEGRITY
OUTWARD
QUAKE
SEED OF CHRIST

DENOMINATION
FRIENDS
HONESTY
INWARD LIGHT
PEACE SACRAMENTAL
QUAKERS
SIMPLICITY

*(Not an exhaustive list.)

While looking at **Communities of Faith**, we can't ignore the fact that in today's world they face many challenges. Have a look at these headlines:

CHALLENGES to Communities of Faith and world religions!

Mass Attendance Falls!

Individualism on increase!

Science makes another discovery!

People have more money!

Anti-Church feeling increases!

Religion is not needed!

People don't believe in God anymore!

All wars are religious!

If we examine these headlines in a little depth, we can say that the challenges facing Communities of Faith and religion are immense in today's world, and we can list them as follows:

- **Secularism** – a view that society does not need religion.
- **Indifference** – people don't care one way or the other.
- **Materialism** – people have so many material things that they believe they have no need for religion.
- **Egotism** – people believe they are right, and that they have no need for Church or God.
- **Atheism** – a belief that there is no God.
- **Falling numbers** – the practice of faith by people is falling.
- **Scandals** – sex abuse scandals that disgrace the Churches.

The Communities of Faith realise these challenges and, where possible, they are answering these challenges.

Q

1. What is it that Communities of Faith can't ignore?
2. Name two of the headlines that tell us about challenges.
3. List four of the challenges mentioned and explain them.
4. Can you add any more challenges to the list?
5. Are the Churches trying to deal with the challenges?
6. Why, do you think, might young people be turning away from religion?

QUICK SURVEY

Go to your classmates and ask them why young people may not be part of a Community of Faith.

WRITE ANSWER HERE

____

____

____

____

____

____

Keep an eye

Over the next few days, keep an eye on the news and newspapers to see any further challenges to the Churches!

Crossword for you to do

Across

4. News that grabs our attention.
6. What the Churches face.

Down

1. Belief that there is no God.
2. Having too much.
3. Society doesn't need religion.
5. People don't care.

As you can see, there are many Communities of Faith around today. A lot of these are denominations of Christianity. They all follow the person of Jesus Christ and God's Word in the Bible, yet have different beliefs about certain things.

With this in mind, it's time to look at a concept called:

What is that? Here's a definition:

Ecumenism is the bringing together of different denominations of Christianity in order to increase respect and understanding between them. Also, working towards unity on basic issues of belief and worship.

The push for this unity between Christian denominations is called **the Ecumenical Movement.**

'Ecumenical' comes from the Greek for **'inhabited world'**.

Make a poster with this picture and the definition.

'Unity Among Christians'

COPY AND COLOUR

Ecumenism became important during the 1900s. The Christian Churches met in 1910 at the **World Missionary Conference** and from that moment determined dialogue commenced between the different Churches. The Pope called the Second Vatican Council in 1962 and at this he set up **the Secretariat for promoting Christian unity**, a further skip forward for ecumenism.

Ecumenical activities:

- Dialogue and discussion has been ongoing between all the Christian denominations (Orthodox / Protestant / Catholic).
- Much work has been done in the areas of co-operation / disaster relief / peace / development studies.
- There are, however, obstacles that remain. These include the ordination of women, papal authority, beliefs about the Virgin Mary, and contraception.

However, Ecumenists believe that much progress can be made through continuing to stress the points on which the Churches agree.

Ecumenical Teasers

NT	EC	UME	NIC	EME	MOV	THE	AL

Unscramble and find the circled word!

ICMESMUNE

UNYIT

THCINSARI

REGTETOH

PONTEASTRT

TICCAOHL

MEVEMNTO

NUICOCSL

MOSSIIYARN

LUEDOAGI

PYRERA

IFBELE

SAHIRNG

Let's work

Fill in the information

1. What does 'Ecumenism' mean?
2. What is the movement called?
3. What Churches are involved?
4. What did the Pope create?

List some of the Ecumenical events that have happened:

1. ____
2. ____
3. ____
4. ____
5. ____
6. ____
7. ____
8. ____
9. ____

Name some of the obstacles:

1. ____
2. ____
3. ____

How can the Churches overcome these obstacles?

Ecumenism in Ireland!

The **Irish Council of Churches (ICC)** leads the way in promoting Ecumenism in Ireland today.

It is made up of most of the Christian denomination Churches:

- Church of Ireland
- Methodist
- Presbyterian
- Society of Friends, and others ...

The Roman Catholic Church is invited to be an observer, but is not officially on the Council.

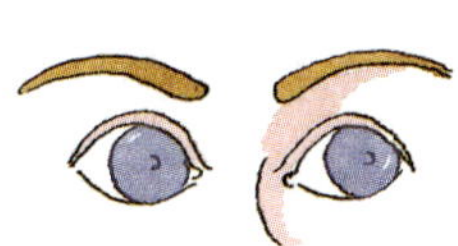

1998 saw the Council's **75th Anniversary!**

Its President is Revd Robert Herron from the Presbyterian Church.

The ICC has had a number of inter-Church meetings.

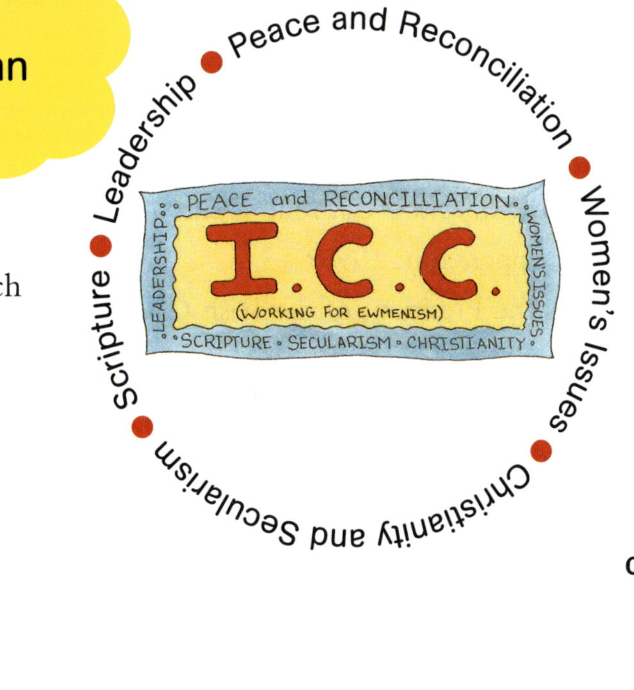

These inter-Church meetings with the Catholic Church have also been positive and have promoted issues important to Irish Christians in today's society.

Irish Ecumenism Wordsearch

Q I L A D K V E C L B R C H S
G T Q J F S J M Z D G Z I C O
N O I T A I L I C N O C E R C
N T Q C I L O H T A C T S U I
H A G M R L U I N E N Z D H E
J Z I K E R I R R A E R N C T
Y I G R C T E C T I F G E R Y
P V L H E C H S N T S S I E O
Z O E A N T E O P U R H R T F
Y S R O E T Y K D K O P F N P
S G C B O W N B S I A C S I E
H E R R O N Y S S S S R Z Y A
G O P M Y I K K V E U T Z B C
B T E H S E C U L A R I S M E
W N C C I S W W M T C P L F P

CATHOLIC
CHURCHES
CONCERN
COUNCIL
FRIENDS
HERRON
ICC
INTER-CHURCH
IRISH
METHODIST
PRESBYTERIAN
PROTESTANT
RECONCILIATION
SECULARISM
SOCIETY OF PEACE
WOMEN

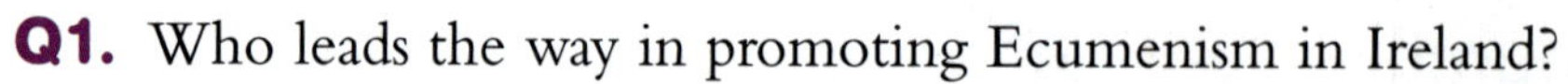

Q1. Who leads the way in promoting Ecumenism in Ireland?

Q2. Who is involved in Ecumenism in Ireland?

Q3. What role does the Catholic Church have?

Q4. What happened in 1998?

Q5. Who is the President of the Irish Council of Churches?

Q6. What are the main areas of concern?

Q7. What are the inter-Church meetings?

Q8. Do you think that Ecumenism is important? Give reasons.

TO KNOW

Interfaith = between different religions.
Dialogue = talking to someone.
Secular = a belief that society needs no religion.

As we saw, Ecumenism is about talking, working and agreeing among Christians. Our next subject is talking, working and agreeing among different religions around the world. It is called:

Let's see how it happened!
At the 1910 'World Missionary Conference' (WMC), as well as Ecumenism, relations with other religions (especially in Asia and Africa) were discussed. At another WMC in Jerusalem, in 1928, Christians were called 'to join hands with all believers to confront the growing impact of a secular culture'!

Definition: a discussion or exchange of ideas and opinions between Christian and non-Christian religions.

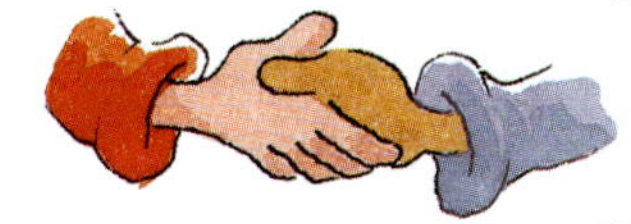

After the Second World War, greater emphasis was placed on Interfaith Dialogue in a broken world. The World Council of Churches (WCC) met in 1961.

Out of this conference emerged the first document and discussions on **Christian Relations with Peoples of Other Faiths!**

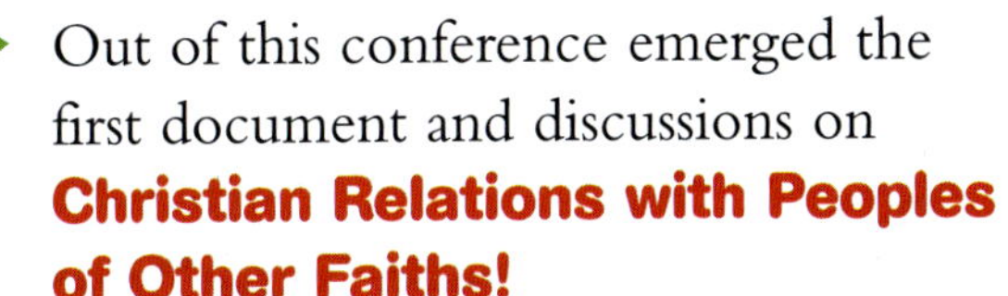

Later, in 1967, in Sri Lanka, a meeting of the WCC proved to be a landmark for 'Interfaith Dialogue' **(the Vatican Secretariat for non-Christians was present).**

1970 saw the next important development: The WCC in Lebanon met with Hindu, Buddhist, Muslim and Christian delegations.

Not only did they consult about Dialogue, they actively took part in it!

COPY AND COLOUR

... In 1971, the WCC created the sub-unit on

'Dialogue with People of Living Faith' and Ideologies

(now called Office on Inter-Religious Relations)

This **SUB-UNIT** has organised ongoing dialogue with:

Jews

Muslims

Buddhists

Hindus

Interfaith Dialogue came to be seen as an encounter between people who live by different faith traditions, in an atmosphere of mutual trust and acceptance.

Today, the Catholic Church sees **Interfaith Dialogue** as an integral part of its legitimate activities.

Interfaith Dialogue calls on the Churches to seek new self-understanding and vision in their relations with other faith traditions. It calls on Churches to delve deep into their resources to deal with the reality of a changing 'pluralistic' society and world, and new approaches to mission and witness.

COPY AND COLOUR

‘There can be no peace among the nations without peace among the religions.’

(Hans Küng, Theologian)

Fill in the blanks:

At the 1910 W__________ M __________ C__________ , as well as E __________ , relations with other religions were discussed. In J ______, in 1928, all Christians were called to join H__________ with all B __________ , to confront a S __________ culture. After W______ W______ II, greater emphasis was put on I__________ D__________. In 1961, the W__________ C__________ of C__________ worked on developing interfaith dialogue. Out of this conference emerged C________ R________ with peoples of other faiths. In 1970, the WCC met with H __________, B __________ and M __________ delegations. They spoke about I ____________________ Dialogue.

1. What was discussed at the 1910 World Missionary Conference?
2. What were Christians asked to do at the 1928 Conference?
3. What was the big development from the 1961 meeting?
4. What happened in 1970?
5. Define 'Interfaith Dialogue'.

Finish these sentences:

- In 1971, the WCC created ...
- Today the 'Dialogue' sub-unit is called ...
- It organises dialogue with ...
- The Catholic Church sees interfaith dialogue as ...
- Interfaith Dialogue came to be seen as an ...

Give two reasons why Interfaith Dialogue is important.

RESEARCH
JOURNAL IDEA

How does Interfaith Dialogue happen in your area or close to you? Who is it between? What do they do?

Sectarianism

Religious Conflict

Of course, we must remember that we live in a world where people do not always get on. For one reason or another, we disagree, we fight, we create violence and injustice. Even though, as we have seen, there is a great deal of work going on to help religions work and live together, there are still instances of violence between people of different religions. There are still places where people of different faiths and denominations don't get on and cause pain and suffering to each other, for their own reasons and purposes. With this in mind, we need to look at these two areas.

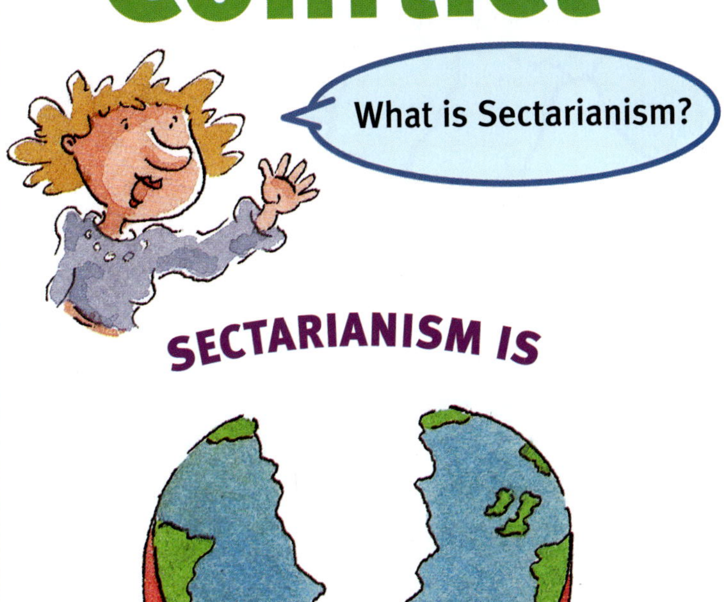

ACTIONS
ATTITUDES
STRUCTURES
BELIEFS that exist in a community or society, involving religion and politics in a negative way.

Q Name a place where sectarianism happens.

It is people and organisations wanting to express their identity and culture and differences, but usually ending up doing this in a destructive way, resulting in insulting others, dominating them, creating boundaries, intimidating and belittling those who are also trying to express their identity and differences.

Sectarianism can become a very serious problem in certain parts of the world. We don't have to go very far to see examples of sectarianism in our own country.

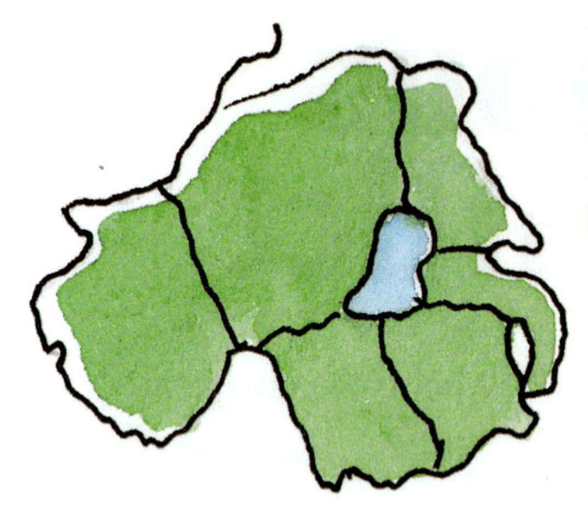

Sectarianism in Northern Ireland

Sectarianism is an issue for all the people on the island of Ireland, and to stamp it out is a challenge for us all!

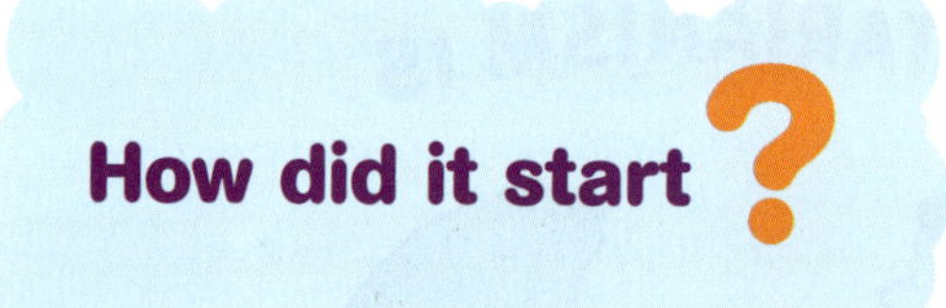

The history of sectarianism in Ireland is very long and complex, but we will try to put down the basic and most important historical details.

- Seventeenth century: arrival of English and Scottish settlers.
- They brought with them Protestant beliefs and Church.
- Celtic Catholicism threatened, beginnings of tensions.
- Two separate identities emerge: Native Catholic Irish / Protestant English and Scottish Settlers.
- Majority settled in northeast Ireland.
- 1641: Catholic uprising against Protestant settlers, with many killed on both sides.
- English soldier and captain, **Oliver Cromwell**, responded in 1649 by killing and attacking Catholics involved in the uprising.
- Eighteenth century: tension between farmers over land and tax; rise of the Orange Order in Ulster.

- Nineteenth century: **Industrial Revolution** and competition and rivalry between Catholics and Protestants for jobs.
- Nineteenth century: beginnings of the movement for **Home Rule** seemed to be identified with the Catholic Church (though not exclusively).
- At the same time, **Ulster Unionism** was growing. Linking with the Orange Order.

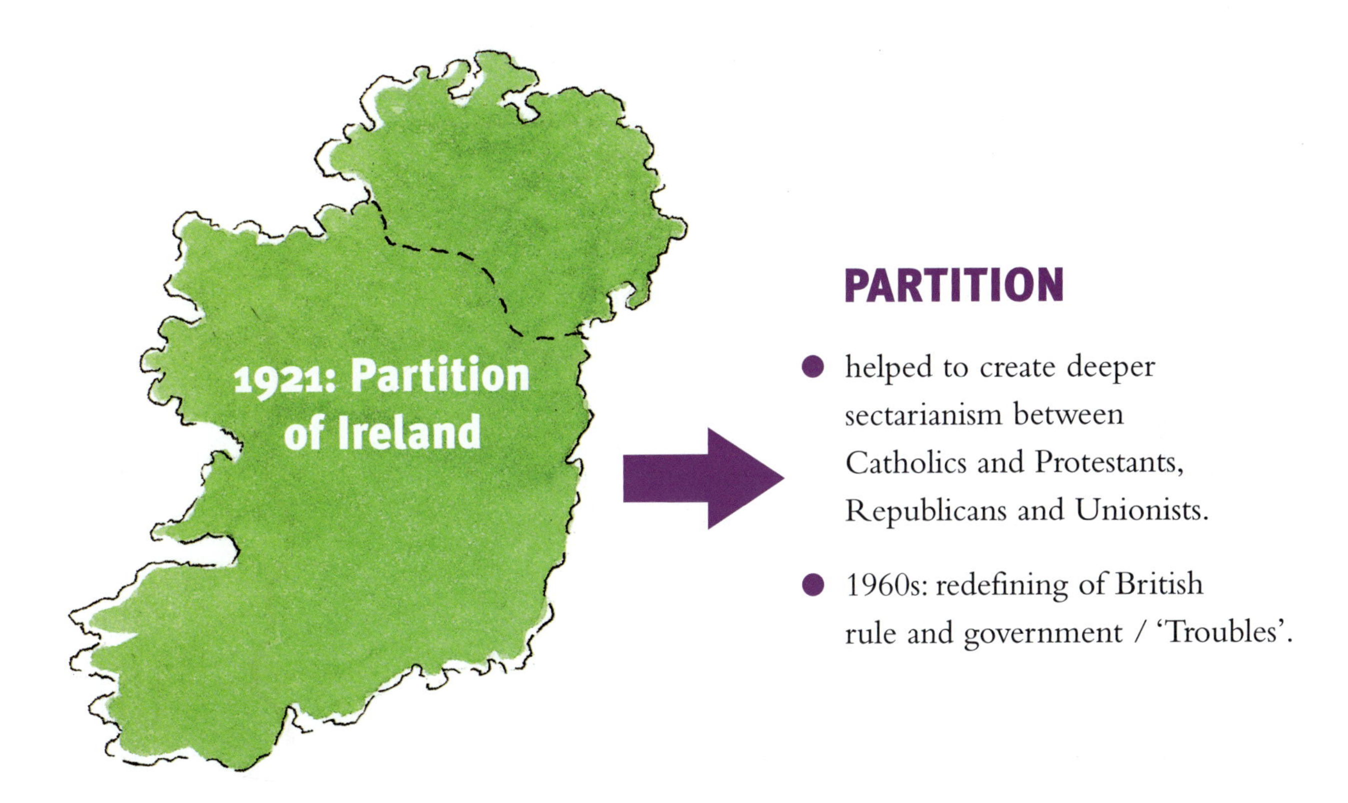

PARTITION

- helped to create deeper sectarianism between Catholics and Protestants, Republicans and Unionists.
- 1960s: redefining of British rule and government / 'Troubles'.

All of this has led to the current situation in Northern Ireland:

Questions to Answer!

Q1. What does 'sectarian' mean?

Q2. How does sectarianism happen?

Q3. What are the negative things that sectarianism causes?

Q4. As well as religion, what else is usually involved?

COPY AND COLOUR

THINK

In your own words, explain how sectarianism began in Ireland.

1. Who arrived in the seventeenth century?
2. What did the settlers bring with them?
3. Who felt threatened and why?
4. Where did the English and Scottish mostly settle?
5. What happened in 1641?
6. What was the English response?
7. What happened in the nineteenth century?
8. In 1921 what happened to Ireland?

RESEARCH
JOURNAL IDEA

- Keep a close eye on TV and papers. Make a note of sectarian issues that come up.

- Why were the Native Catholic Irish so threatened?
- What do you think caused the uprising in 1641?
- Why, do you think, did the Orange Order begin?
- Ulster Unionism began to grow in the nineteenth century. Why?
- How, do you think, did the Catholics of Northern Ireland feel after Partition?

Q: How?

Sectarianism is very much a problem for the communities of Northern Ireland and the people of Ireland.

Revd Robin Eames (Church of Ireland leader) said:

'**Sectarianism** is the number one cancer. It is in the air that people breathe, it is in the attitude that makes people say and do things.'

But there is hope and there are many people who are working to cross the boundaries that sectarianism has created. Let's see ...

- Schools, colleges and students have organisations against sectarianism.
- Unions and workers have rallied against sectarianism.

- Socialist groups campaign against sectarianism.
- EU Programme for Reconciliation.
- Trinity College 'learning together education for reconciliation'.
- Churches call for an end and actively work to bring about an end to sectarianism.

- Local, national and international politicians work for an end to sectarianism.
- Anglo-Irish Agreement.
- Good Friday Agreement, etc.

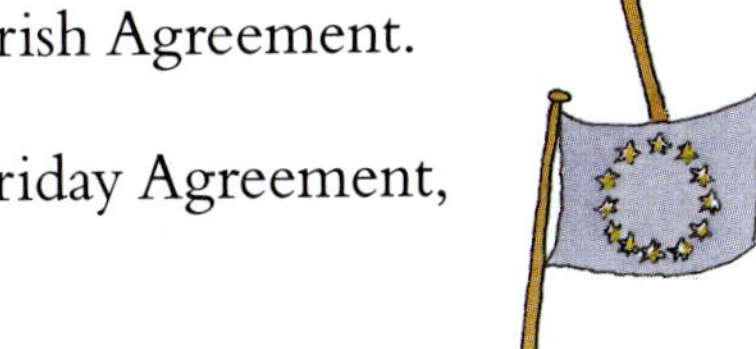

One organisation that is working hard to bridge the gap of sectarianism is Corrymeela.

TO KNOW

Reconciliation = to forgive each other and become friends again.

Corrymeela

Corrymeela is a group of people of all ages and Christian traditions who, individually and together, are committed to the healing of social, religious and political divisions that exist in Northern Ireland and the wider world.

- Be a sign that Catholics and Protestants can share and work together for reconciliation.

- Provide opportunities for dialogue, meeting, communication and learning about each other and the promise of respect, trust and co-operation.

- Support victims of violence and injustice. Allow healing of wounds and promote social and individual change.

- Address issues of faith and morality and develop new expressions of Christian Community.

Projects and Activities

• Residential (Catholic / Protestant) school • Residentials for all • Training and learning • Adult and youth Church projects • Support for new reconciliation plans • Support for victims.

Conflict and Tolerance Wordsearch

I	C	R	E	Y	E	B	H	A	G	C	F	F	R	U
R	Z	U	O	P	E	C	T	L	L	J	U	X	E	O
E	T	B	L	L	O	T	N	E	V	O	J	G	L	Q
L	G	O	I	T	I	H	B	E	F	U	S	K	I	K
A	R	E	L	T	U	X	M	M	R	M	W	M	G	K
N	F	W	U	E	M	R	K	Y	Y	E	K	R	I	Y
D	V	D	F	M	R	W	E	R	T	C	F	P	O	H
K	E	G	R	E	F	A	R	R	I	X	A	F	N	G
T	A	E	R	H	T	V	N	O	T	S	Y	R	I	L
N	O	I	T	A	I	L	I	C	N	O	C	E	R	D
S	E	C	T	A	R	I	A	N	E	S	S	H	Y	K
E	C	N	E	L	O	I	V	J	D	K	N	Z	V	Q
M	L	U	A	U	Q	D	J	W	I	A	D	B	V	H
J	U	P	I	N	U	G	O	O	D	W	O	R	K	P
R	Q	D	P	W	R	L	T	I	Z	V	X	F	M	X

ATTITUDE
CULTURE
HOPE
RECONCILIATION
THREAT

BELIEF
DIFFERENCE
IDENTITY
RELIGION
TOLERANCE

CORRYMEELA
GOODWORK
IRELAND
SECTARIAN
VIOLENCE

1. What work is being done to cross the boundaries that sectarianism has caused?
2. Design a poster against sectarianism (be sure to mention all the good that is going on, especially Corrymeela).
3. Create a small tourist brochure inviting people to come to Corrymeela and include: pictures, aims, objectives, work that is done.

Of course, sectarianism doesn't happen only in Ireland. Religious conflict and sectarianism happen in places all over the world.

COPY AND COLOUR

Here are some of the areas of religious conflict. There are more too.

Religious CONFLICT

'A conflict and clash between people of different faiths and religions. Usually for different reasons but can be because of domination, threat and survival. Conflict is likely if one religious group gains power in a divided country.

We can see religious conflict not only in Northern Ireland but also in places like:
Palestine – conflict between Jews, Muslims and Christians;
South Asia – conflict between Hindus and Muslims;
Pakistan – conflict between Muslims, Hindus and Christians.

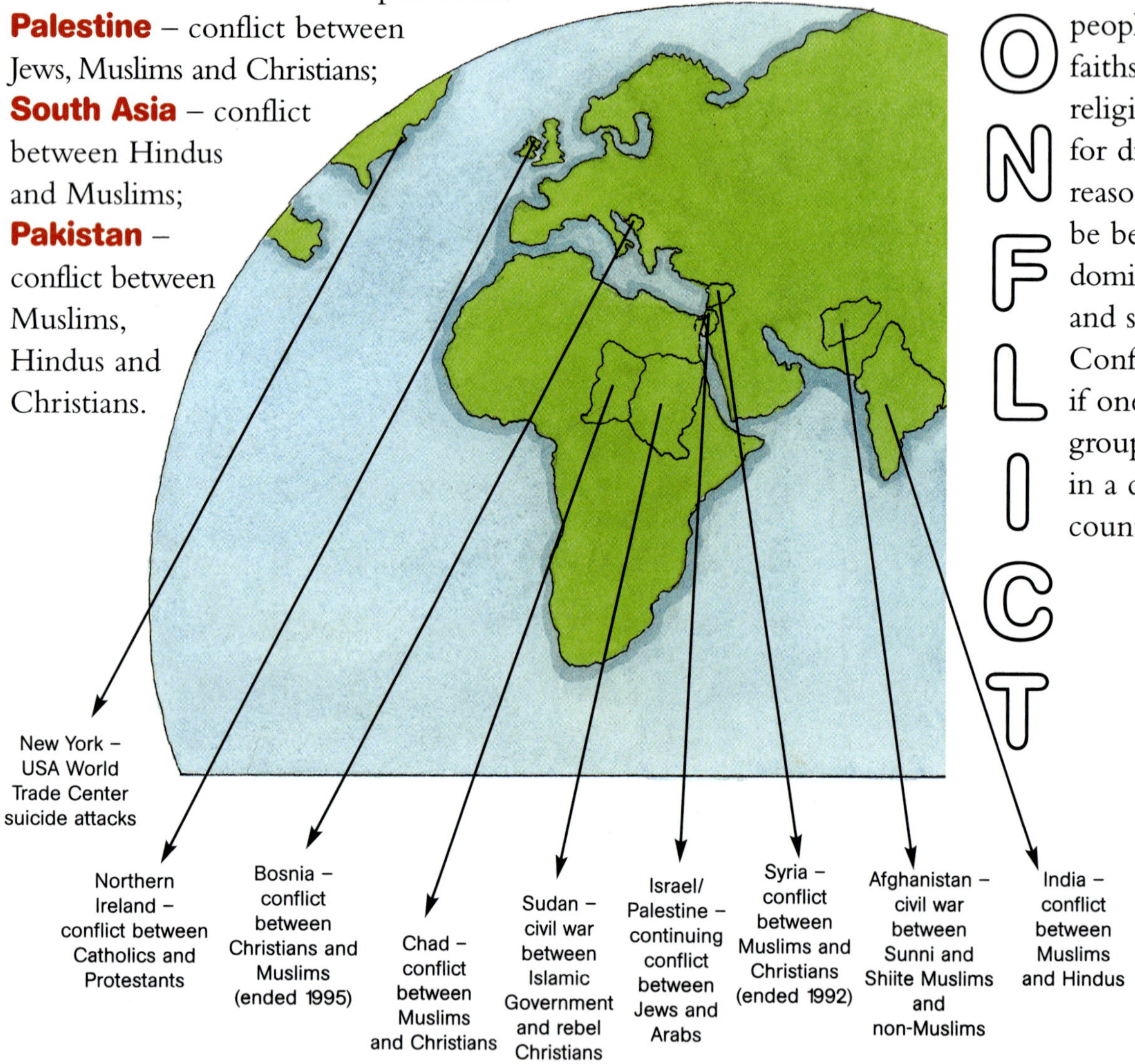

New York – USA World Trade Center suicide attacks

Northern Ireland – conflict between Catholics and Protestants

Bosnia – conflict between Christians and Muslims (ended 1995)

Chad – conflict between Muslims and Christians

Sudan – civil war between Islamic Government and rebel Christians

Israel/ Palestine – continuing conflict between Jews and Arabs

Syria – conflict between Muslims and Christians (ended 1992)

Afghanistan – civil war between Sunni and Shiite Muslims and non-Muslims

India – conflict between Muslims and Hindus

Every day we hear and read about religious conflicts. These conflicts in many cases involve groups of people who are seen as **'fundamentalists'**.

Q

What is a fundamentalist?
People who are fundamentalist usually believe their religious view and belief to be the only right one and will accept no other, and accept no change under any condition.

All the world religions are calling for an end to

Religious Conflict

and urging their followers to follow their **'Golden Rule'**.

We are called to be tolerant of people of different beliefs.

Most world religions have a Golden Rule. This rule basically tells followers not to do harm to their neighbour, and to treat their neighbour as they themselves wish to be treated.

'Religious tolerance consists of valuing the right of a person to hold beliefs that you believe to be wrong.' (Anon)

COPY AND COLOUR

In this box, write your definition of religious conflict.

In this box, write down the one you read on p.88.

In your copy, make a list of all the places mentioned where conflict occurs.

Design and make a poster calling for peace between religions around the world.

1. What does 'fundamentalist' mean?
2. What are all the religions calling for?
3. What do religions ask their believers to follow?
4. Basically, what is the Golden Rule?
5. How can people be tolerant?

Write a letter to religious leaders asking them to do more to stop religious conflict.

Time to Think and Pray

Let us pray ...

- We pray for all Christians, that they will one day join together as a United Church.
- We pray that violence and hurt will end between all Christian people – that God's spirit of love will dominate all hearts.
- We pray that followers of religions around the world will listen to and obey their Golden Rule – 'Love your Neighbour'.

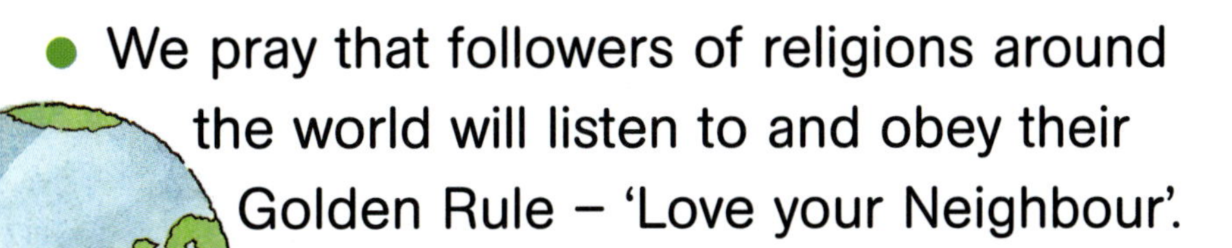

We offer all our prayers to God ...

I ask that I will always have the strength to stand up against those who bully and intimidate.
May I always show Christ's love to all people, no matter who they are, every day of my life.
Amen.

Light a candle ... think about:

- Have I ever hurt another person?
- Have I ever hurt a person because they were different from me?
- Am I afraid of 'difference', or do I seek it?
- How open-minded am I? ... How accepting? ... How tolerant?

Help me to be open-minded, accepting and tolerant and forgive me when I am not!

Section 2

What is religion all about?

- What is religion?
- Primal religions
- Many gods or one God?
- What do different religions have in common?
- Families of religion
- Universal religions
- Founders and prophets
- Symbols of religion
- Points to remember
- Journal ideas
- Time to Think and Pray

What is Religion all about?

This is a very good question. Many people have asked this over the years and have made a good attempt at answering it. It's a question that's not that easy to answer, but we'll try. Over the next few pages, we'll discuss what religion is all about!

To begin, think about the following:

- What do I think religion is?
- Where did religion come from?
- Why do we have religion?
- What is a religion?
- Do we need religion (do you think)?

TO KNOW

Polytheism = belief in many gods.
Monotheism = belief in one God.

Answer these questions again when you've finished reading this section.

- Religion, in some form or another, seems to have been around always.
- Not only that but it seems to have been in existence across the world (worldwide – from the Inuit eskimos to the Aborigines in Australia).

Archaeologists and historians can tell us that religion has been around for centuries.

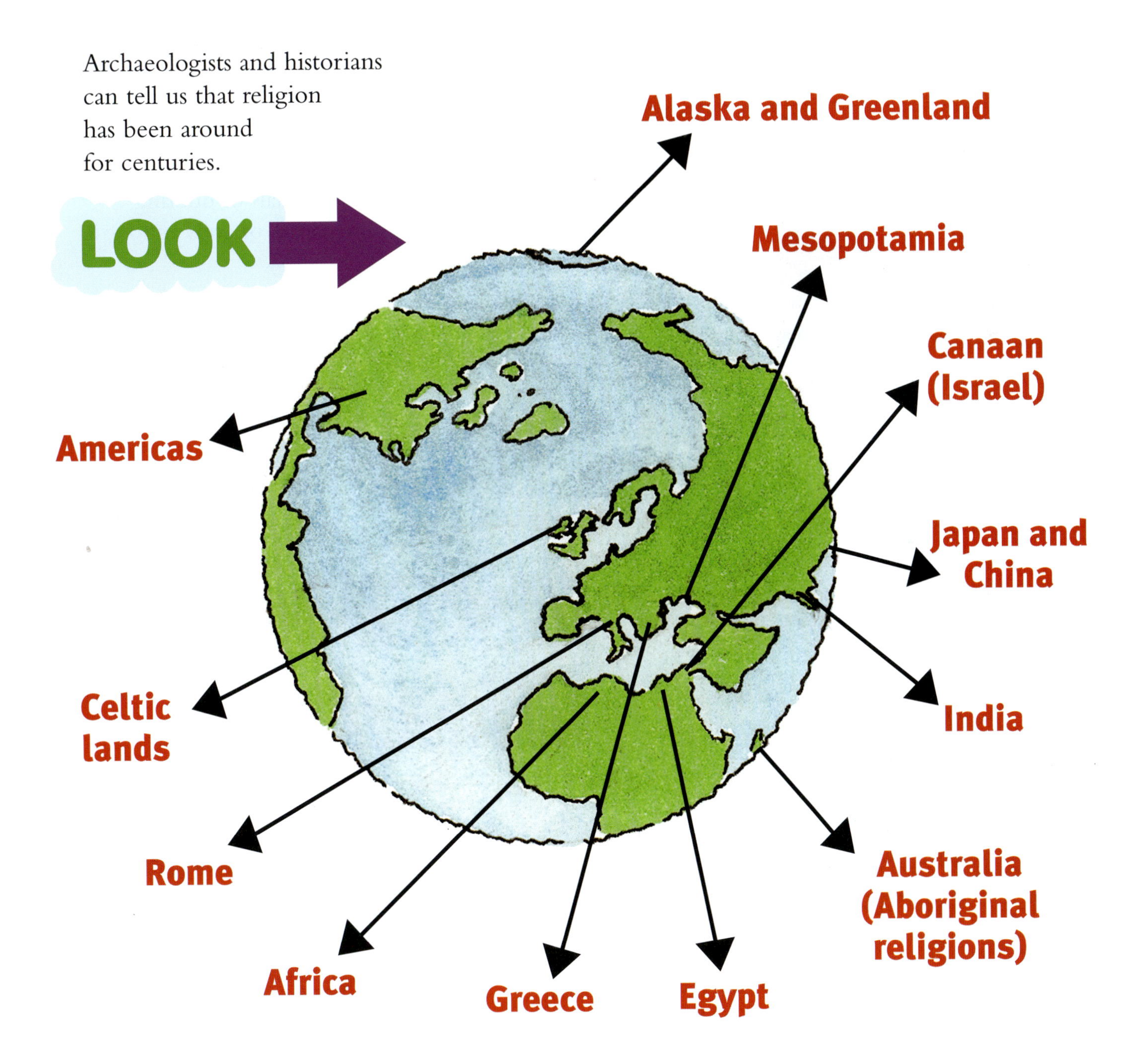

- For example, all of these places had some form of religion centuries ago.

Historians and archaeologists can also make a good estimation as to when religion began:

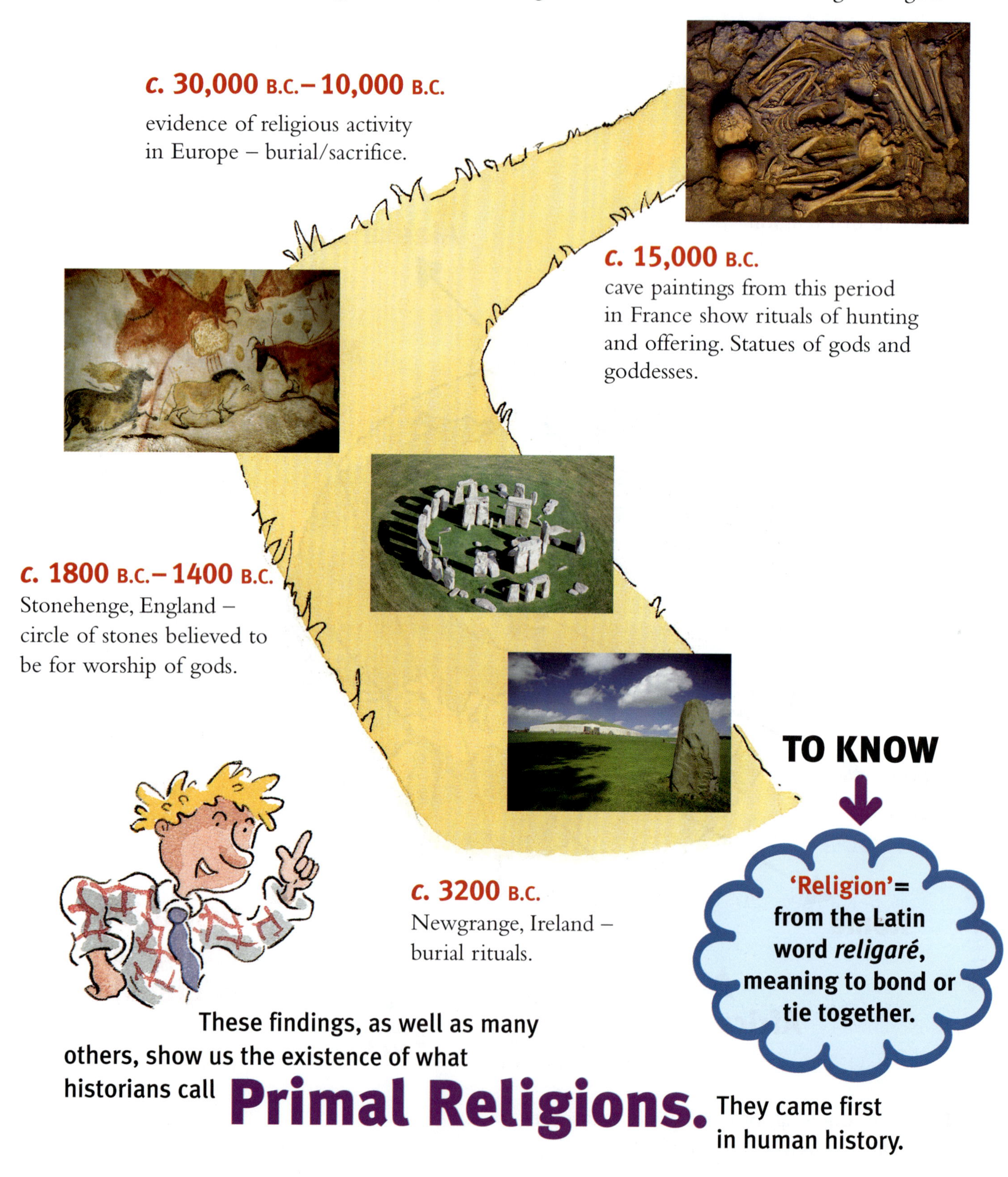

c. 30,000 B.C.– 10,000 B.C.
evidence of religious activity in Europe – burial/sacrifice.

c. 15,000 B.C.
cave paintings from this period in France show rituals of hunting and offering. Statues of gods and goddesses.

c. 1800 B.C.– 1400 B.C.
Stonehenge, England – circle of stones believed to be for worship of gods.

c. 3200 B.C.
Newgrange, Ireland – burial rituals.

TO KNOW

'Religion'= from the Latin word *religaré*, meaning to bond or tie together.

These findings, as well as many others, show us the existence of what historians call Primal Religions. They came first in human history.

Q Why did people all around the world develop 'Religion'?

Centuries ago, when our ancestors were around, they had no science, no TV, no computers – nothing to give them answers.

They wondered about a lot of things – the sun, rain, thunder and lightning, death and the world around them.

They began to understand that the world around them was powerful, and believed that things like the sun and the moon, the sea and the weather were gods and needed to be worshipped so that they would treat them well.

The people put together words, pictures and rituals of worship to the world around them, and hoped that the gods would be good to them in this life, and after death.

So began religion and religious worship and ritual.

TO THINK AND DO

Q1. How long has religion been around for?

Q2. Historians can name areas of early religious activity. Name some.

Q3. What does the word 'Polytheism' mean?

Q4. What does the word 'Monotheism' mean?

Q5. What is the earliest date that historians can give us for when religious activity began?

Q6. What was Newgrange used for?

Q7. What is the name given to early religions?

Q8. What does 'primal' mean?

Q9. Our early ancestors began to ask questions about what?

Q10. What did they begin to do for the gods and why?

CLOZE TEST

Centuries ago our a______ had no s______, no t______, no c______, nothing to give them answers. They w______ about things – the s______, the r______, t______ and l______, d______ and the world around them. Gradually they saw the s______ and s______ the w______ as g______ and began to w______ them. They created rites and r______ to w______ the gods. They wanted to have g______ lives and live in p______ with the gods.

Further thinking

A Give two reasons why religion began.

B Why was religious rite and ritual so important?

C How did our ancestors deal with death?

D How would they have seen the world around them?

E Today, how do we deal with big questions of life and existence?

F How did religion help early people to live good lives?

Many gods or One God?

As the centuries passed, our ancestors began to think that it wasn't the sun, moon, or weather that were gods. Rather, they decided that there were gods controlling those things – supernatural beings in charge of everything …

For example …

The **Egyptians** had their gods …

Ra

Sobek

and the **Greeks** had theirs …

Zeus

Poseidon

This belief in many gods is called → **'Polytheism'!**

The followers of the different religions worshipped their gods and, as with their ancestors, hoped that the gods would be good to them.

As time moved on, some of our ancestors began to believe in only

One God!

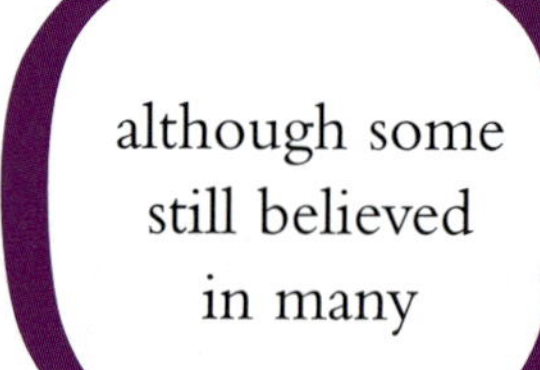

(although some still believed in many)

- This one God was the creator of everything and looked after the people who worshipped him.
- People prayed, worshipped and had religious rituals for their God.

This belief in one God is called → **'Monotheism'!**

… from this sprang religions whose followers believe in one God:

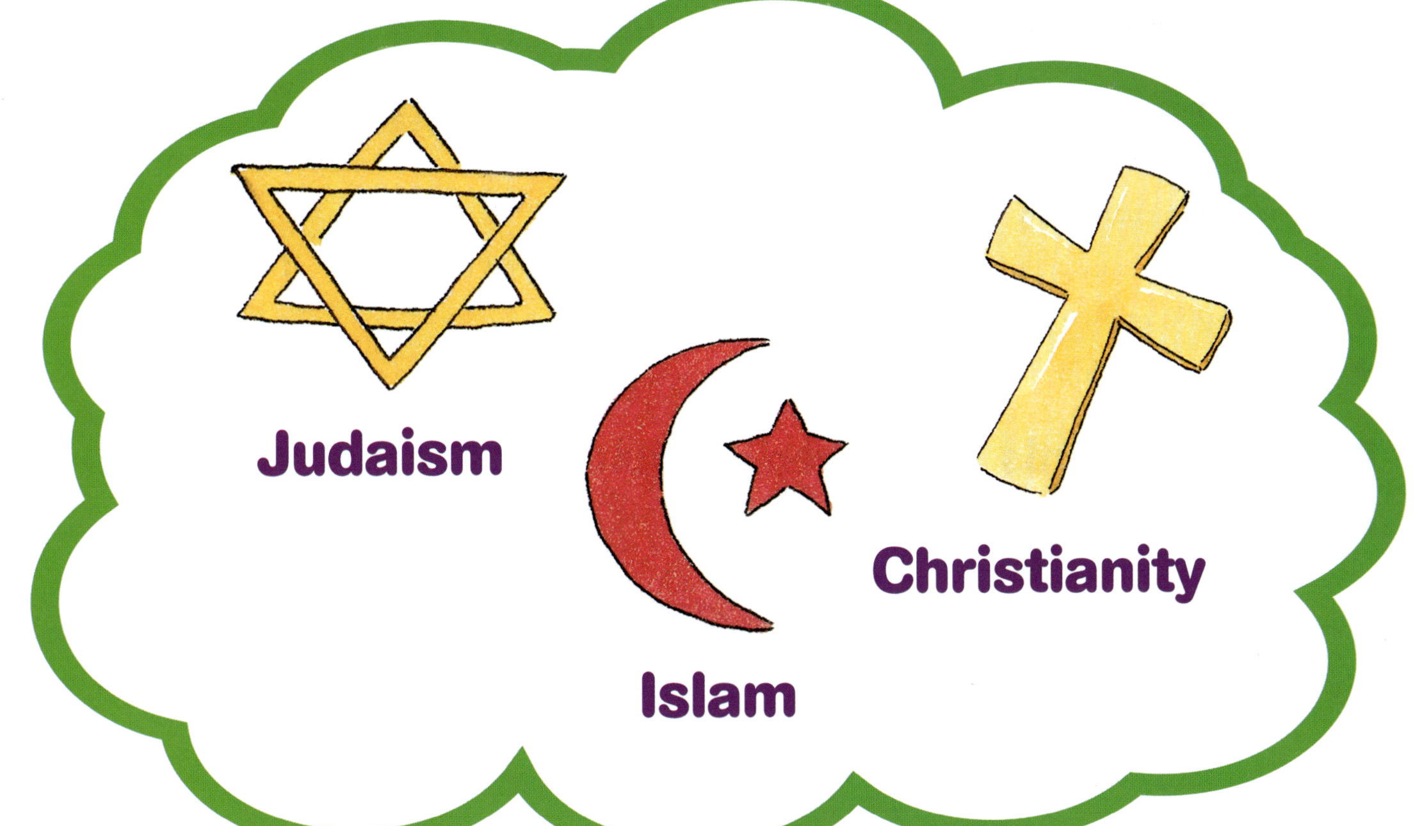

… and from **'Polytheism'** sprang religions whose followers believe in many gods:

... over to you ...

Figure out whether these sentences are **TRUE** or **FALSE**:

- The Egyptians had only one god. **T / F**
- The Greeks had gods named 'Zeus' and 'Poseidon'. **T / F**
- Believing in many gods is called 'Multigodism'. **T / F**
- Followers of many religions believe that their one God created everything. **T / F**
- Believing in one God is called 'Monotheism'. **T / F**
- Judaism is a religion that has a belief of Monotheism. **T / F**

Pick out the words you recognise.

When you find some, write them here:

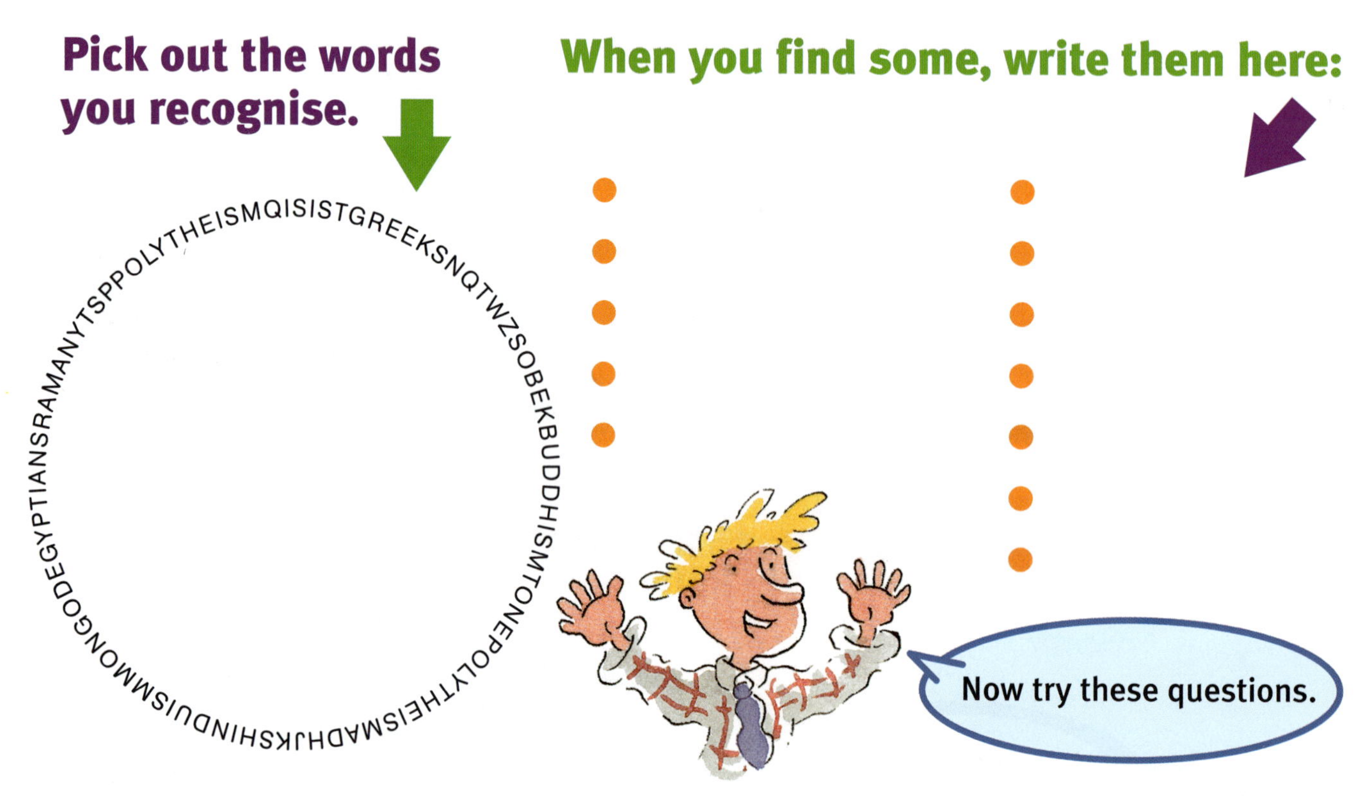

Q1. Name some Egyptian gods.

Q2. Name two Greek gods.

Q3. Why did the Greeks and Egyptians have many gods?

Q4. Explain the word 'Polytheism'.

Q5. Explain 'Monotheism'.

Q6. Name two religions that follow Monotheism and name two that follow Polytheism.

A. What was the purpose of having many gods?

B. Why was having one God different?

C. What did this one God do?

D. What do Christianity, Judaism and Islam have in common?

E. Is it easier to believe in one God? Why?

What do Different Religions Have in Common?

What makes a religion, a religion?

In general, religions have a number of things in common. **These are:**

1. Faith! People who believe in God or gods have faith. This faith helps them to worship, pray, believe, live good lives and communicate with their God or gods.

2. Cult! Everything that is done when people worship their God/gods – rituals, songs, prayers, buildings.

3. Creed! What the believers believe about their God/gods and religion – their statement of belief.

4. Code! The way people live their lives according to guidelines given by their religion.

5. Community! The community of people of the same religion who worship together.

6. Writings! The holy writings, books (Scriptures) of the religions.

How many religions can you name?

Let's look at Families of Religions

Families of Religions!

When we look at the religions of the world, we can put them into two groups!

1. **'Primal Religions'**
2. **'Universal Religions'**

Primal means original, primitive.

These were the religions around centuries ago …
and they include religions of

These religions have several things in common.

1. They are **LOCAL** – they belong to a tribe or culture and to no one else around them.

2. They depend on **ORAL TRADITION** – the passing-on of the religion through storytelling and not having anything written down.

Let's have a look at

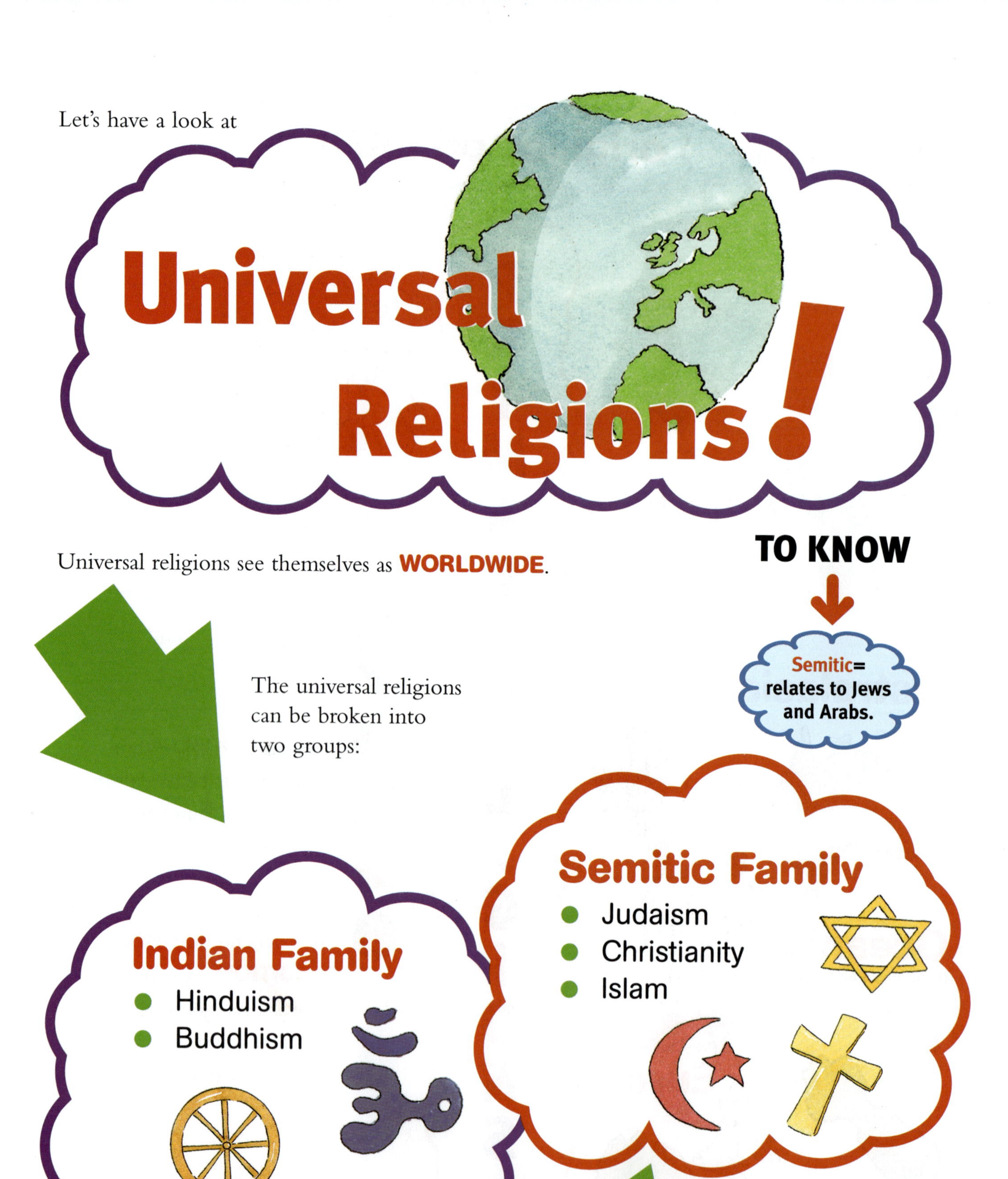

All share the same history and geography.

All About Religion Wordsearch

G P J V Z W I G D S J E S I Z L E S J T
L B Z X U O L Q N K U J T S J J E R E R
P U Z Y C K B A C N P X O L T R Q H A U
P O C R E L I G I O N F N A U F P W P M
Y F L U K T A V T O Z C E M J O R M O L
H B Q Y P H E H I A U D H A R G Q H P X
I Z R Y T R T P M B O Y E P N N A S L D
N E G E S H K N E G T N N C M M F N S Y
D E G A L C E S S I N L G Y M A I O I K
U O L N A I B I N R D B E E I X S I P X
I X I J A Z G A S U I M D T Q G B T X A
S L P W M R I A F M A T H M T D W S W N
M E J P T T G N R J D N U I S D E E R C
M S R U S O S W D E I B C A S I I U B K
G W L I N G U U E A D R Z J L N A Q U L
D P R I M A L T S N P I H S R O W D R Y
P H S E I R U T N E C R H E P X G K U R
C O V H T M V F K N J B Y D S O M W G J
X F A R G W K M O N O T H E I S M Z H D
P O D B R G X Q P P K S Y A C E E W I G

CENTURIES
CHRISTIANITY
CREED
EGYPTIANS
FAITH
GOD
GURU

HINDUISM
ISLAM
JESUS
JUDAISM
MONOTHEISM
MOHAMMED
NEWGRANGE

POLYTHEISM
PRIMAL
PROPHET
QUESTIONS
RELIGARE
RELIGION
RITUAL

SEMITIC
STONEHENGE
UNIVERSAL
WORSHIP

These universal religions have some characteristics in common – like the ones we mentioned earlier. Let's have a 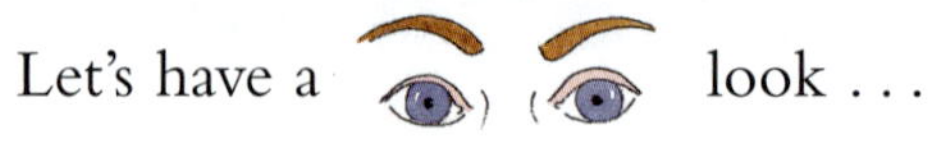 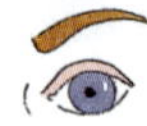 look . . .

	CULT	CREED	CODE	COMMUNITY	WRITINGS
BUDDHISM	Meditate on Buddha's image daily. Walk three times around Buddha's shrine in the temple. Worship what it represents. Meditation. Belief in Karma. No precise gods/no worship of them.	Ultimate goal is to reach Nirvana. Noble truths: • Duktha (Life is Suffering) • Samudaya (Causes of Suffering) • Magga (Path of Wisdom) • Nirvana (State of Perfection)	Noble eight-fold path: • Right Understanding, Thought, Speech, Action, Livelihood, Effort, Mindfulness • Concentration • Self-control through meditation	Community of Buddhist monks and nuns and laypeople worship as individuals at shrines and temples and as community.	Three Baskets (Tri-Pitaka) and Buddha's sayings, rules for monks and nuns and for knowledge of life. Pali Version and two Mahayana versions.
CHRISTIANITY	Prayer, especially 'Our Father', and, for Catholics, the Rosary. Celebration of Sacraments: Baptism, Eucharist, Confirmation, etc. Liturgical seasons and festivals, especially Easter and Christmas.	Statements of belief, such as Nicene Creed, Apostles' Creed, which, depending on the denomination, tell the nature of God, his mother, the Trinity and succession to the Apostles.	Christian codes are • The Ten Commandments • The Beatitudes And the command • 'Love your neighbour.'	Christianity includes Catholicism, Protestantism and the Orthodox Churches. Usually based around a diocese with a parish. Celebrations of Mass and other services and Sacraments.	The Bible made up of the Old Testament and the New Testament, which includes Acts of the Apostles, Letters of St Paul and the Revelation of St John.
HINDUISM	Worship God (Brahma, Vishnu Shiva) at shrines. Prayer at dawn, noon and the evening. Meditate using the 'Om'. Give offerings in large temples. Yoga.	Believe in the Veda Scriptures • Karma • Reincarnation • Transcendence to be sought after • Sacredness of life • All religions belong to God	The Laws of Manu (1500B.C.) • Five daily duties • Universe was created, as well as many gods.	Worship individually or in small groups. As a community, worship only at festival times. Priest in temple offers gifts to gods. Have shrines and temples. Puja ceremony.	*Bhagavad Gita* = poem about Prince Arjuna talking to Lord Krishna. Part of bigger epic, *Mahabharata*. Also a book called *Upanishad/Veda*.
ISLAM	Prayer five times a day. Do the Ra'ka facing Mecca. Pray anywhere, also gather to pray in the mosque. Pilgrimage to Mecca very important. Festival of Ramadan. Worship Allah.	Have statement: 'There is One God and Mohammed is his Prophet.' Also have belief in angels, prophets, predestination and Judgment Day.	Five pillars of Islam, which are Muslim obligations: • Creed • Fasting • Prayer • Pilgrimage • Poor dues and doing good to neighbour	Worshipping community prays in the mosque at prayer times. Leadership and guidance from the Imam and Mullah.	Qur'an (Koran) – sayings of the Angel Jibra'il to Mohammed in the seventh century. Written by God before time.
JUDAISM	Celebrate the Sabbath (Friday evening–Saturday evening). Go to the synagogue to pray. Read from the Hebrew Scriptures, the Old Testament. Many celebrations, including Bar Mitzvah, and festivals such as Passover.	Thirteen Principles of Faith stating many aspects of belief in God and the prophets and the coming of the Messiah.	Ten Commandments and 612 Commandments in the five books of Moses and the Mishna	Very family-oriented, especially during Passover. Worship in the synagogue for Sabbath and festivals. Rabbi is leader and leader of ceremonies.	Hebrew Bible (Old Testament). Three parts – the Torah, the Prophets and the Writing. Contains laws, guidance, history and story of relations with God.

Of course, these religions didn't just spring up out of the blue. Someone or something started them ...

'Founders and Prophets'

B.C.E. = Before Christian Era.

Hinduism (2000 B.C.E.)

Had thousands of Gurus, reflecting many teachings. A Guru (teacher) is someone enlightened through knowledge and life. No named founder – probably enlightened wise men *c.* 2000 B.C.E.

Judaism (1850 B.C.E.)

Began with the choosing of Abraham, by God, for a new covenant (agreement). Covenant continued and reaffirmed by Moses.

Buddhism (500 B.C.E.)

The Buddha was an Indian prince, Siddharta Gotama. He became the enlightened one (Buddha) when he understood the cause of suffering in life and the way to end it.

Christianity (4 B.C.E.)

Founded by Jesus Christ. Born in Palestine (A.D. 4). Crucified in A.D. 29. Believed to be the Son of God. Born to humanity to save them and to rise from the dead.

Islam (A.D. 622)

Began with the prophet Mohammed and his visions. Many prophets important to Islam. Islam means submission to God.

Finally, these religions have symbols. The symbols represent what the religion is all about and allow us to recognise them at a glance. Let's look at them and explain each of them in turn.

Judaism

(worldwide following: 20 million members)

The Star of David is the symbol of the Jewish religion. David was a great King of Israel.

Christianity

(1.5 billion members)

The Cross is the symbol of Christianity, representing the way Jesus Christ died.

Islam

(1 billion members)

The star and crescent moon are used because Islam follows a lunar calendar when setting dates for its festivals.

Hinduism

(800 million members)

This is the 'Om', the sacred word used in Hindu meditation.

Buddhism

(300 million members)

The eight-spoked wheel represents the 'eight-fold way' of Buddha.

Across

1. Holy book of Islam.
5. Belief in one God.
8. Latin for tying together.
11. Built the pyramids.
12. Founded by Mohammed.
13. What our ancestors asked.
14. Something our ancestors didn't have.

Down

2. Ancient Irish burial ground.
3. The opposite to primal religions.
4. Belief in many gods.
6. A teacher in Hinduism.
7. Another word for praise to the gods.
9. Founded by Jesus Christ.
10. The basic belief of a religion.

Some more work for you to do ...

Complete this exercise:
In the space below, write the six characteristics that religions have in common.

- ______________________
- ______________________
- ______________________
- ______________________
- ______________________
- ______________________

Write a sentence or two explaining each one.

____
____
____
____
____
____
____
____
____
____

Some questions for you:

Q1. Name the **CODE** for Judaism.

Q2. In relation to **CULT**, what does Islam do?

Q3. What is the Sacred Book of Christianity?

Q4. Who has the **LAWS OF MANU** as their code?

Q5. Who walks around a shrine in a temple three times as part of their cult?

Q Draw the symbols for Judaism and Christianity and explain them.

Judaism

Christianity

Explain the **BUDDHIST** symbol: ______________________________

Explain the symbol of **ISLAM**: ______________________________

A Approximately how many followers does Judaism have?

B How did Judaism begin?

C How important is the symbol for a religion? Explain.

D What does the word 'Semitic' mean?

Points to Remember!

Keep in mind:

- Religion has always been around.
- Evidence exists of religious ritual throughout history.
- People were trying to make sense of the world around them.
- Religion: 'A Bond Between Humans and God'.
- Religions today are universal.
- Universal religions are: Judaism, Christianity, Islam, Hinduism, Buddhism, etc.
- Belief in one God is Monotheism; belief in many gods is Polytheism.
- Religions have cult / creed / code / community / scripture.
- Religions usually have a founder and prophets.

Don't forget that you will have to write a journal about a specific topic towards the end of your studies. Have a practice and think about some of these.

Research Journal Ideas!

- The big questions of life and how religions try to answer them.
- Early evidence of religious activity in a particular / your area.
- The change from worshipping many gods to worshipping one God.
- How does one particular religion worship its God / gods?
- Investigate cult / creed / writings, etc. of a particular religion.
- The religions in your area – similarities and differences.

Time to Think and Pray!

Thinking back over the first questions asked ...
What do I think religion is? Where did it come from?
Why do we have it? What is religion?

Find an answer in your mind. Think about these ...
How am I here? Why am I here? What is the purpose of my life? Why do people die? Why do bad things happen?

Religions try to answer these questions. Think about the answers to these questions.

we pray ...

that we will always be open to the belief in a God ...

that we will let God work in our lives ...

that we will always respect people of different religions from our own ...

that we will work to make the lives of others happy ...

that we will take time out to pray ...

that we will do our best to offer worship to our God ...

that we will be good ambassadors of our religion and of God.

Amen.

Section 3

Christianity

- **How the Bible came to be**
  - Putting the New Testament Together
  - Check a Reference
- **A Look at Judaism**
- **Christianity**
- **The Context**
- **Size of Palestine**
- **History of Palestine**
- **Jobs**
- **Money**
- **Political and Religious Groups**
- **The New Testament**
  - The Gospels

The Life of Jesus

When Was Jesus Born?
Jesus Growing Up
The Baptism of Jesus and His Public Life Begins
Jesus is Tempted
Jesus' Disciples
Proclaiming the Kingdom of God
The Beatitudes
The 'Our Father'
Jesus, the Preacher
Jesus, the Miracle-Doer
Last Days of Jesus – 'Conflict'
Jesus Goes to Jerusalem
Holy Week
Trouble in the Temple
The Plan
The Last Supper
Final Hours of Jesus
Before the Religious and Political Leaders
Journey to the Cross

The Crucifixion

The Death of Jesus
Jesus' Burial

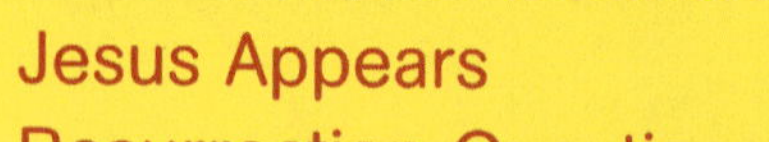

The Resurrection

Jesus Appears
Resurrection Questions

How the Bible came to be!

How did we get the Bible that way?

Let's have a  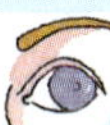 look!

The Bible is a collection of books.

When you take up a Bible, you might think that you are taking up **ONE** book. But you're not ...

The Old Testament

BOOKS OF THE LAW

Usually seen as one

BOOKS OF HISTORY

BOOKS OF WISDOM

THE PROPHETS

The New Testament

TO KNOW →

The Bible was originally written on scrolls, which were an early form of paper.

As you can see from our bookshelf, the Bible is made up of **72 Books** in all.

Some of the books are long. Others are quite short. Some are very ancient, and others not quite so old.

The books contain history, poetry, philosophy, hymns and songs, letters and sermons.

The Bible is divided into two sections:

1. **The Old Testament** (Hebrew/Jewish Holy Scriptures)
2. **The New Testament** (The Christian Holy Scriptures)

The Old Testament
(Hebrew Scriptures)

- Contains history and law of the Jewish people and their religion and is their Holy Writings.
- Is made up of the first **45** books detailed earlier.
- Was originally written in Hebrew and Aramaic (ancient languages of the Jews).

The earliest manuscripts of the Old Testament that have been found so far are called the **'Dead Sea Scrolls'**.

They are about 2,000 years old. They were found in caves beside the Dead Sea in Israel.

As well as the **Dead Sea Scrolls**, archaeologists and historians also have ancient documents from the ninth and tenth centuries. These are copies of the first five books of the Old Testament, properly called **The Pentateuch**.

Many of the documents that have been found were written centuries ago by Jewish scribes, and have somehow been preserved.

Another version of the Old Testament important to historians is **'The Septuagint'**. This is the Old Testament translated into Greek. Many Greek-speaking Jews and Christians used this version of the Old Testament.

TO KNOW → **All these pieces of historical evidence help us to say how the Old Testament came together!**

Q1. What is the Bible made up of?
Q2. How many books are there in the Bible?
Q3. Name the two parts of the Bible.
Q4. How many books are in the Old Testament?
Q5. Name the first five books of the Old Testament.
Q6. Name the Books of Wisdom.
Q7. How many books are in the New Testament?
Q8. Name the first four New Testament books.
Q9. What is the Holy Book of the Jews?
Q10. Name the Holy Book of the Christians.

OOLDLTVOTESTAMENTUXA66BEUBIBLESOPTOHOLYSCRIPTURESLAWMENMJEWISHSHSCRIBEBOOKSXTUMN

Find the words that we have used. When you find them, write them in your copy and use each one in a proper sentence.

Fill in the blanks:

The Bible has _______ books in it. It is made up of the Old _______ and the _______ Testament. The Old Testament has _______ books in it. The New Testament has _______. The Old Testament has books about _______, _______, _______ and the Prophets. The first four books of the New Testament are _______, _______, _______, _______. The earliest copies of the Old Testament that have been found are the _______ _______ Scrolls.

Match correctly

Septuagint	First five books of the Old Testament.
Dead Sea Scrolls	Man who wrote out the Old Testament.
Pentateuch	The Old Testament.
Scribe	The Greek translation of the Old Testament.
Hebrew Scriptures	Earliest historical manuscripts of the Old Testament.

RESEARCH
JOURNAL IDEA

Find out as much as you can about the **Dead Sea Scrolls**. Write up your findings in your journal. Dates / Names / Country / How they were found / Importance.

Putting the New Testament Together

Matthew

Luke

Paul's Letters

Titus

Jude

Mark

John

Peter 2

Peter 1

James

John 1/2/3

When piecing together the **New Testament**, Scripture scholars had many historical manuscripts to work from. From around the fourth century they had the **Codex Sinaiticus** and the **Codex Vaticanus**, containing the books of the New Testament. They also had the New Testament written in Greek, Latin, Egyptian and Syriac. From these and others a standard Greek New Testament was put together in the fifth century and revised in **A.D. 1516** by a scholar called Erasmus. The **King James New Testament** version appeared in the seventeenth century, and since the eighteenth and nineteenth centuries scholars have been able to see which New Testament books are accurate. This means that they have been able to make up the final **Catholic New Testament** edition.

TO KNOW

The New Testament contains all the stories about Jesus' life, death and resurrection. It also covers the spread of Christianity and the Church. It is the Holy Book of Christianity.

Collecting the Information

How and Why it began

Stage 1

Early followers of Jesus met to talk and pray about Jesus. They may have listened to first-hand witnesses and memorised the stories!

Stage 2

The groups got larger and became 'churches', which grew in number. As eyewitnesses died, it became necessary to write down everything about Jesus. The Gospels of Matthew, Mark, Luke and John were begun.

Stage 3

Apostles and Christian community leaders wrote letters to Christian communities that were far away. The letters were about Jesus, faith, worship and the future.

Acts of the Apostles: 'The accounts of the beginnings of Christianity.'

- By A.D. 200, the Church was officially using the four Gospels as the authority on Jesus' life, death and resurrection. These, together with the Acts of the Apostles, were used for teaching.
- The letters of **St Paul** to Christian communities were accepted as being of equal importance.
- **Revelation** was used and read widely by the third century. The Letter to the Hebrews was accepted at this time also.
- Peter 2 / John 2 and 3 / James and Jude were later accepted for the New Testament.
- In A.D. 363, at the Council of **Laodicea** (a small town in Turkey), in A.D. 397 at the Council of **Carthage** (in Tunisia, Northern Africa) and at the Council of **Trent** (Northern Italy) in 1545, the bishops began to put together and finalise the appropriate books in the New Testament.

They wanted to be sure that the books they included in the New Testament truly represented the witness and experience of the Apostles — the men who lived closest to Jesus.

1. What was Stage 1 in collecting the information?
2. Why did the early Christians begin to write down the stories of Jesus?
3. What was Stage 3 in collecting information for the New Testament?
4. What information was the Church using by A.D. 200?
5. Which books were later additions to the New Testament?
6. Name the three Councils that helped to finalise the books of the New Testament.
7. Where is Laodicea?
8. Where is Carthage?

To do

Draw a bookshelf. On it draw all the books of the New Testament.

Fill in the blanks:

The early followers of ________ met and ________ about Jesus. They ________ the stories. Later the ________ grew in number and eye ________ began to ________ off. It became necessary to ________ everything down. ________, ________, ________ and ________ are examples of this. The leaders in the ________ communities wrote ________ especially St ________. The letters were written to Christian ________ around the area. The ________ of the ________ recounts the beginnings of Christianity.

More Qs to do

A. Why was it important for the early Christians to write down the stories of Jesus?

B. Why were letters written to the spreading Christian communities?

C. Why were the 'Acts of the Apostles' important?

D. What did the bishops want to achieve at the Councils?

Find out what is in the book called 'Revelation'!

Let's Check a Reference in the Bible

We'll look up this reference:

Matthew, Chapter 2: Verses 1-6.

Number 2

Go to the chapter, which in this case is 2

(Usually the big number on the page!)

Number 1

Go to the book named. In this case it is 'Matthew' (Matt.)

(Remember to look in the New Testament for this book.)

Number 3

Find the verses, in this case 1-6

(Usually the smaller numbers down the edge. There is a number for each line.)

NB The numbers may also be on the line itself.

Now try these

Matthew 2:13
Q. What did the Angel say to Joseph?

Mark 1:1-3
Q. What did the prophet Isaiah write?

Luke 24:1-8
Q. What did the men in white say to the women?

Exodus 15:1-3
Q. What song did the Israelites sing?

When you have done all that, you've found Matthew 2:1-6

(Book) (Chapter) (Verses)

A Look at Judaism

Before we delve into the religion of Christianity, we will take a brief look at the background to Judaism, the prominent religion in Israel at the time of Jesus Christ. Later, in Volume 2, we will give Judaism our full attention!

TO KNOW

Covenant = agreement, sacred bond.

1900 B.C.

The **Old Testament** contains what we need to know about Judaism

Abraham is called by God to travel to Canaan (Israel) from his town in Mesopotamia (Iraq) (Genesis 12).

God makes a **Covenant** with **Abraham**.

'Worship God and the land will be yours and your descendants" (Genesis 17)

Abraham and the Hebrews settle in Canaan and worship one God.

Famine strikes **Canaan.** Abraham's grandson, **Jacob**, leads the people to **Egypt**.

Pharaoh and the Egyptians eventually make the Hebrews into slaves.

The Hebrews believe that God will free them.

Moses is chosen by God.

His mission is to free **'God's People'** (Exodus 3:1-20).

Moses demands from Pharaoh that he 'let the Hebrews go. Plagues are sent on the Egyptians (Exodus 7).

Let my People go!

The **Exodus**

Moses leads the Hebrews to safety. Pharaoh lets them go.

They cross the Red Sea.

Through Moses, God works to free the Hebrews.

The **Ten Commandments**

On their journey back to the Promised Land, God gives the people the Law to live by. It is called the Ten Commandments.

New Covenant

Keep these Laws!

Hebrews settle in Canaan, remove earlier settlements, and make Saul their King. All the tribes are united.

David becomes the next **King**.

Encourages the people to worship God continually.

Jerusalem

Under King David, Jerusalem is made the capital and the country becomes **'ISRAEL'**!

David dies 970 B.C.

Solomon, David's son, becomes King. Inherits a wealthy country with many trade routes with neighbours!

Solomon builds the great Temple in Jerusalem. The Ark of the Ten Commandments is kept there! He calls on the Hebrews to worship God.

Solomon dies in 930 B.C.
Israel splits in two – Israel to the North; **Judah** to the South (Jerusalem is the capital of Judah).

Jerusalem

Time of the **'Prophets'**.

Isaiah, Jeremiah, Amos, Elijah, Hosea ...

The prophets speak out against the wrongs that the people are committing. They call on the people to turn back to God and live by God's laws.

Assyrians attack Israel – 722 B.C.

Israelites taken and scattered throughout the Assyrian Empire.

Babylonians attack **Judah** – 586 B.C.

Babylonians take Jews into captivity in Babylon. Work as slaves there.

New thinking in Babylon

- Because they no longer have a temple, they meet in groups to pray and practise their religion. From this comes their day of rest, **'Sabbath'**, and meeting-house, **'synagogue'**.
- They begin to write down all that they believe about God and their relationship with God, also their history and laws. This becomes the **'TORAH'** and, later, **'Old Testament'**.
- **'Rabbis'** appear as teachers of Jewish law and students of the writings.

539 B.C.
Set free from Babylon by the Persians.

Realise that because of their turning away from God and the Covenants, all that disaster happened!

Further invasions by **Greeks** and **Romans**.

The Jews believed that God would send a new leader to overthrow the Romans. A great king like King David of old and from his household! Even today, the Jews still await the Messiah (in Greek, 'Christ').

They waited for **'The Messiah'**.

TO KNOW →

As well as the law and the development of their relationship with God, the Jews also developed rites and rituals around important moments in life and festivals over the year, e.g. circumcision (removal of the foreskin of the penis as a sign, in flesh, of the Covenant) and Bar Mitzvah (celebration of a thirteen-year-old boy's journey to an adult and a son of the law).

Q1. What book would you read to find out about Judaism?
Q2. With whom did God make the first Covenant?
Q3. What does 'Covenant' mean?
Q4. What was the Covenant to Abraham?
Q5. What was the name of the country that the Hebrews went to?
Q6. Why did Jacob, Abraham's grandson, go to Egypt?
Q7. What happened to the Hebrews in Egypt?
Q8. Who rescued them from Egypt?
Q9. What was the name of that event?
Q10. What did God give to the Hebrews on their way home?

The Hebrews settled in ______. Their first King was ______. Their second King was ______. David made ______ his capital city. He died in ______. His son, ______, became the next ______. He made a great ______ in Jerusalem. In the Temple was the ______ of the ______ ______. He died in ______ and the land split into ______ in the north and ______ in the south, Jerusalem was in ______.

Finish these sentences

Three prophets were ______.
They spoke out against ______.
They called on people to turn ______.
The Assyrians attacked ______ in ______.
The Babylonians attacked ______ in ______.
In Babylon, the Jews were ______.
Because they had no temple, the Jews ______.
They wrote down ______.
Rabbis were ______.
In 539 B.C. the Jews ______.
They were invaded by ______.
The Jews await ______.

More Qs

A What made the Jews realise that they had turned from God?

B Who told them about their wrong ways?

C What happened to the Jews in Babylon?

D What changes did they have to make to their religious practices?

E Why are they awaiting the Messiah?

CHRISTIANITY

The Followers of Jesus

- The religion of **Christianity** is based around the life, death and resurrection of a man called Jesus. He lived in what is today called Israel. In his time, it was known as **Palestine**.

TO KNOW

The name 'Palestine' comes from a group of people called Philistines who lived in the region.

- To help us to understand this religion and Jesus fully, we need to step back in time and look at these important things: **the place** he lived in, **the history** around him and **the people** who lived at this time. **These three together, we can call**

The Context

Words to know and remember:
Palestine.
Resurrection.
Tetrarch / Tetrarchy.
Herod.

... Looking at

The Place

where Jesus lived and grew up!

When we read about any famous person or thing, we always like to know what sort of place the person lived in or where the thing came from. It's the same here – we need to look at where Jesus lived and grew up and where the religion of Christianity sprang from.

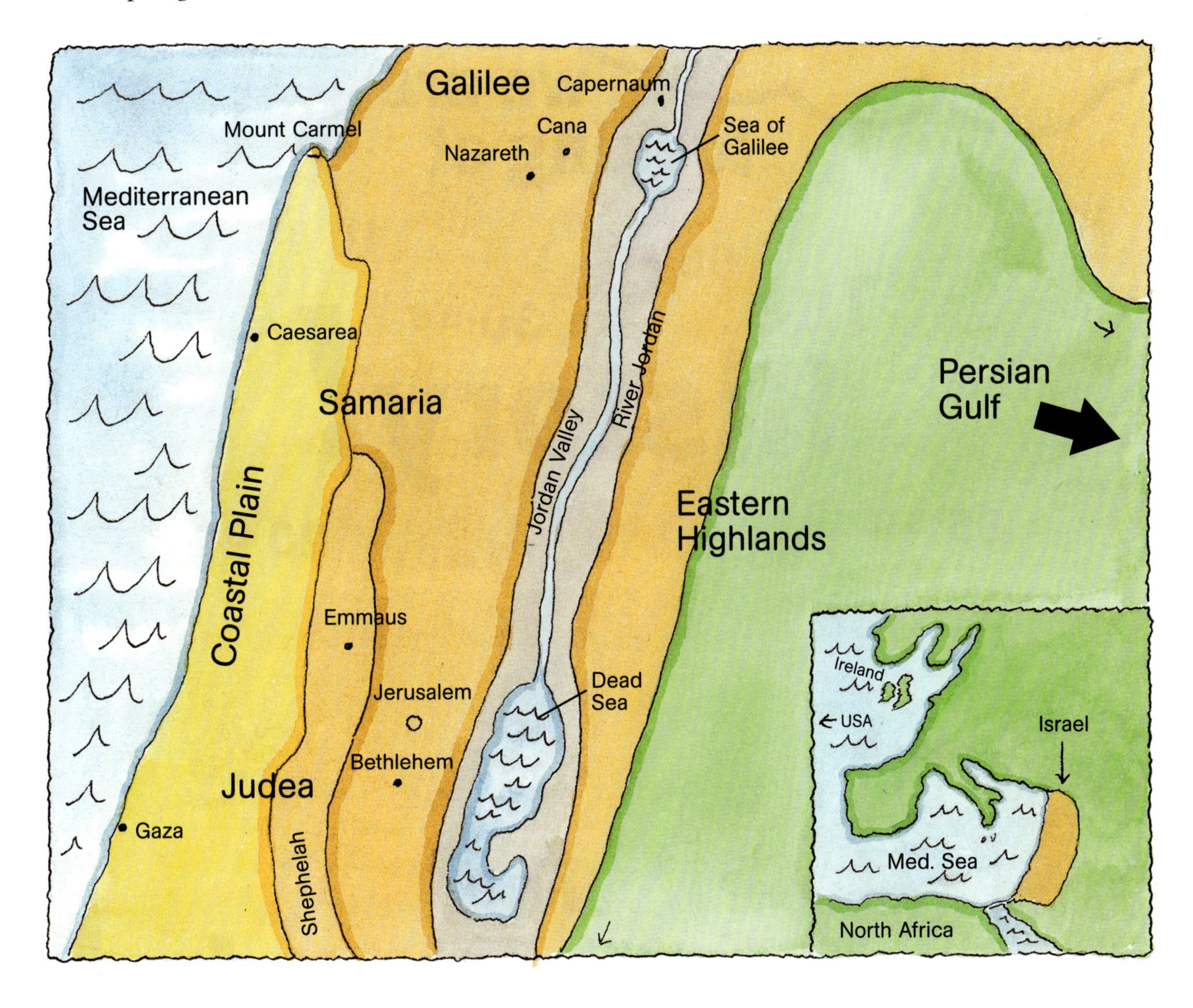

Palestine at the time of Jesus.

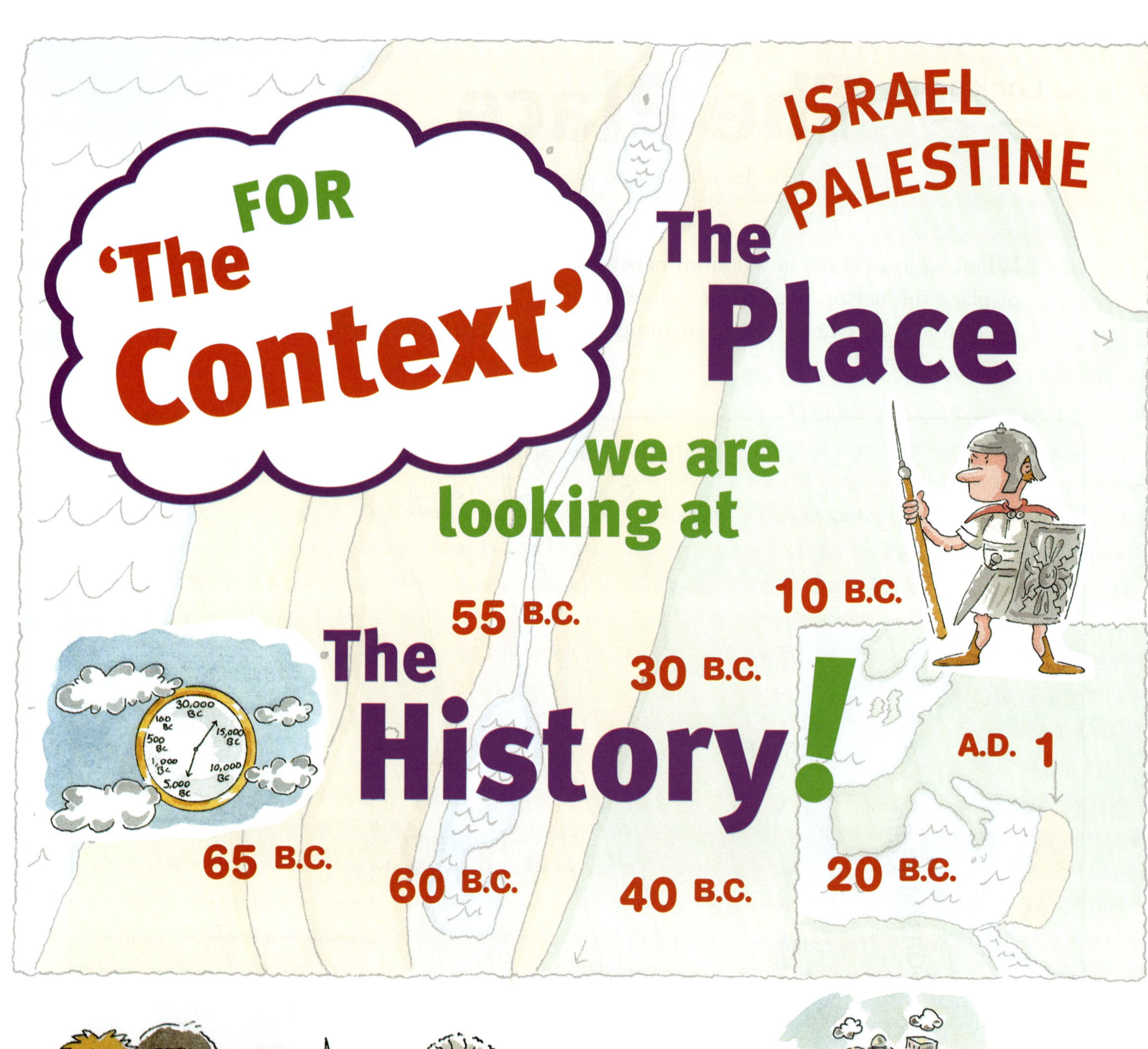

'The Context'
FOR
The Place
ISRAEL
PALESTINE
we are looking at
The History!
55 B.C.
10 B.C.
30 B.C.
A.D. 1
65 B.C.
60 B.C.
40 B.C.
20 B.C.

The People!

One-word answers to write in your copy.

1. The place where Jesus grew up.
2. What Palestine is called today.
3. The religion of the followers of Jesus.
4. One word that covers **THE PLACE**, **THE HISTORY** and **THE PEOPLE** that we are studying.

In your copy, write out the sentences that are TRUE and correct the FALSE ones:

A. The religion of the followers of Jesus is called Hinduism.

B. Christianity is based around the life, death and resurrection of Jesus.

C. Jesus grew up in the country that was called Palestine.

D. When we look at 'The Context', we mean the place, the people and the history.

E. The Mediterranean Sea is beside Palestine.

F. The river that flows through Palestine is the Liffey.

G. There are two lakes in Palestine – the Dead Sea and the Sea of Galilee.

The place Jesus grew up in was called **Palestine**. As we know from our brief look at Judaism, Palestine also had other names, like **Canaan, Israel and Judah**. Today it is called Israel again.

TO KNOW

The Name PALESTINE comes from a group of people called PHILISTINES who lived in the region.

The story behind Jesus takes place in a small area at the eastern end of the Mediterranean Sea. This land of Palestine lies between the sea and the huge Arabian deserts. In geographical terms, the land separating the sea and the desert is called the

'Fertile Crescent!'

This is the name that covers the well-watered, fertile land that stretches from Egypt through Palestine and up to the Persian Gulf (see previous map).

TO KNOW

Because of this and the overall geography of Palestine, it was a good place to invade and take over.

The overall size of Palestine was small compared to that of modern countries.

Length: 230km (150 miles)

Width: 80km (50 miles)
(north of Dead Sea to the coast)

Running through the land of Palestine is the

Jordan Valley!

This is where the River Jordan flows. The river itself rises (begins) near **Mount Hermon**, flows south through Lake Huleh and the Sea of Galilee to the Dead Sea. The Dead Sea is in an area called the **Ghor Plain**. The valley has steep sides and the river has cut into the floor and created a winding shape. The areas each side of the valley are the Eastern Highlands and the Central Highlands. Further west is the Coastal Plain.

... Here are some Qs

1. What other names did Palestine have?
2. How did the country get the name Palestine?
3. Where is Palestine situated?
4. In geographical terms, what is the land of Palestine special for?
5. Why was Palestine invaded?
6. How big is Palestine? What goes through the middle of Palestine, from top to bottom?

Now, fill in the blanks in your copy:

The story behind _______ takes place in a small area at the _______ end of the Mediterranean Sea. This land of _______ lies between the _______ and the _______ deserts. This area separating the sea and desert is called the _______ _______. The _______ _______ is fertile land from _______ to the _______ _______. The land has been _______ or _______ many times. Palestine itself is _______ long and _______ wide!

Let's have a look at some of those areas.

Travelling around this land you would come across a variety of plants and animals, e.g. lentils, wheat, cinnamon, roses, deer, camels, leopards and eagles, to name but a few.

... fancy a bit of artwork?

In your copy, draw a picture of the Coastal Plain, Central Highlands and Eastern Highlands, putting them all together to form one big map. (Remember to include rivers and cities mentioned.)

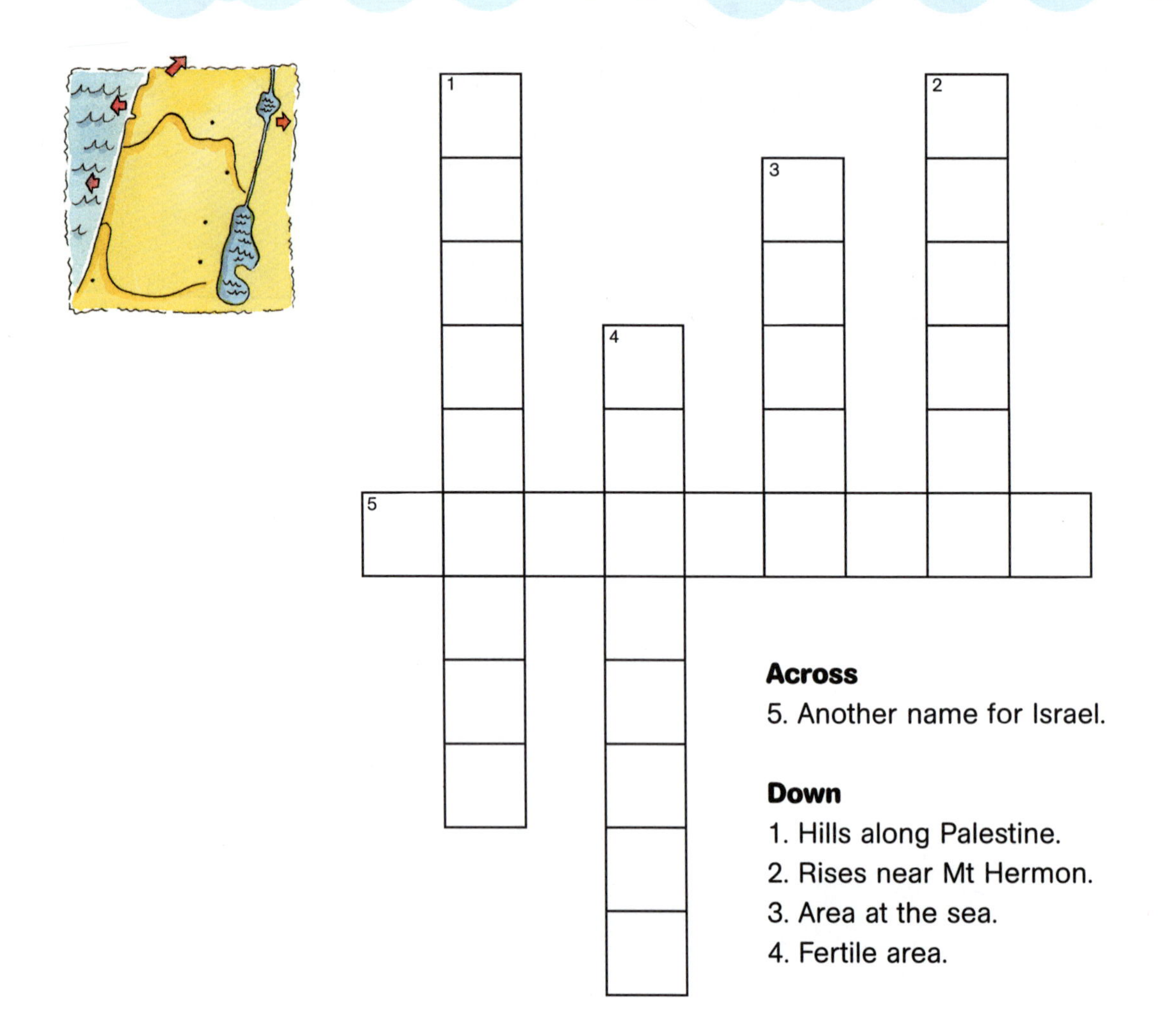

Across

5. Another name for Israel.

Down

1. Hills along Palestine.
2. Rises near Mt Hermon.
3. Area at the sea.
4. Fertile area.

Palestine – Land of Extremes

... that's the land. What's the weather like?

NB ➡ summers can be very hot and temperatures can be as high as 40°C. In winter, temperatures could go to 15°C.

As we continue to look at the **Context** of life in Palestine, it's time for the

History of Palestine

Just before Jesus was born ... **Roman Empire** spreads, and eventually reaches **Palestine**.

63 B.C. General Pompey and the Roman Empire take over Palestine.

Palestine becomes part of the **Province of Syria** (north of Palestine).

37 B.C. **Herod the Great** is appointed **'King of the Jews'**. (He creates new taxes.)

30 B.C. Augustus becomes new Roman Emperor. Rome continues to rule Palestine.

(Jesus is born.)

4 B.C. **Herod the Great** dies. **Palestine** is divided between his three sons.

When Herod the Great was the Roman ruler of Palestine, the **three political regions** of

Galilee, (to the north of Palestine)

Samaria (middle)

and Judea (southern Palestine)

were united, but when Herod died, the three were divided up and given to his sons.

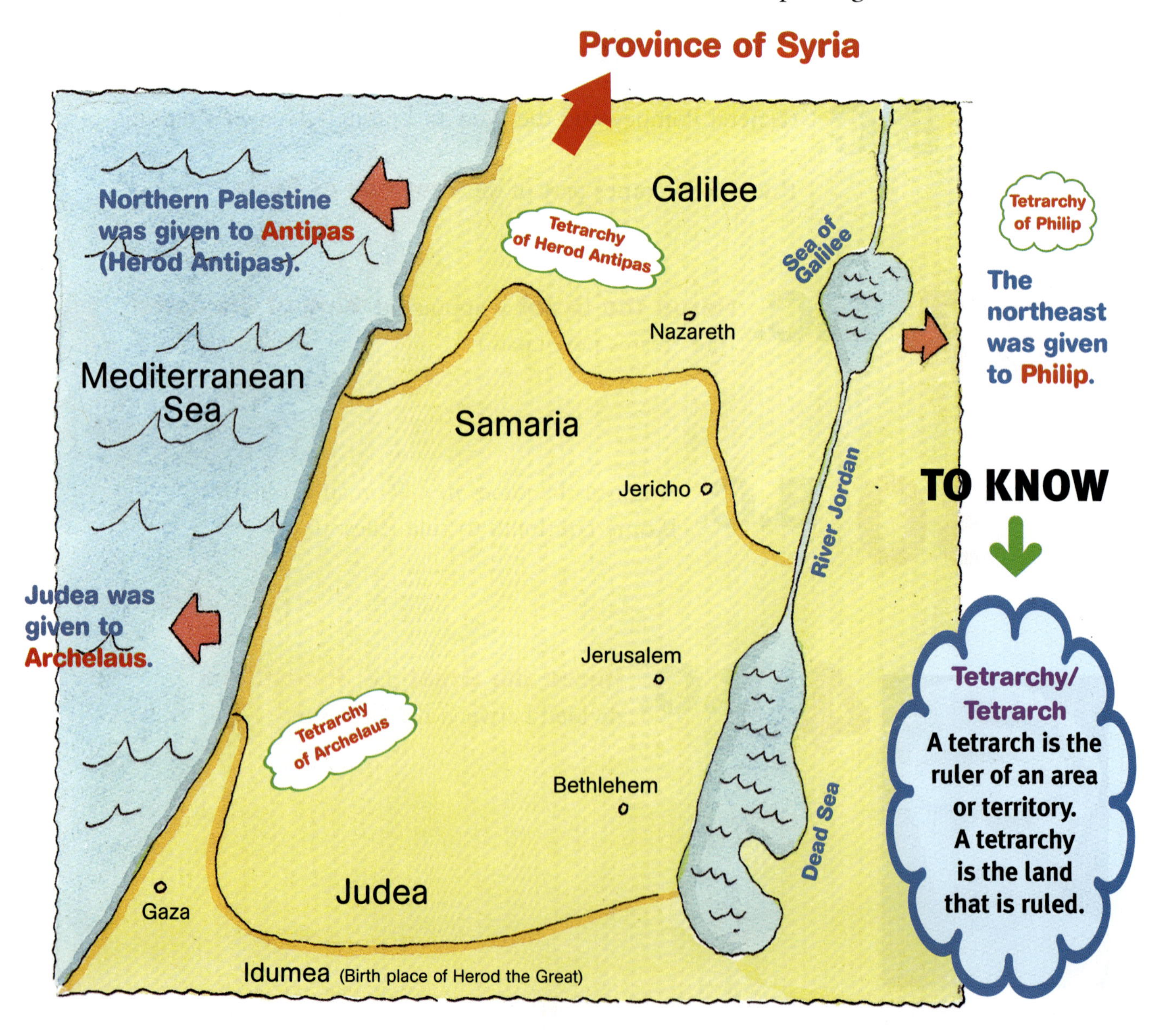

TO KNOW

Tetrarchy/ Tetrarch
A tetrarch is the ruler of an area or territory. A tetrarchy is the land that is ruled.

... let's ask ourselves ... 

A Find the words in this puzzle wheel:

GALILEEMSOUJUDEASTLPOMPEYMPTRORXEMPERORKALSTURAUGUSTUSTYCDEFHERODIJKOXYT

When you find them, write them in your copy and use each one in a sentence.

B Draw a timeline like this in your copy and fill in the important dates and events that we have read about.

70 B.C. — 2 B.C.

C Draw this map of Palestine in your copy. Complete it by marking in the following:

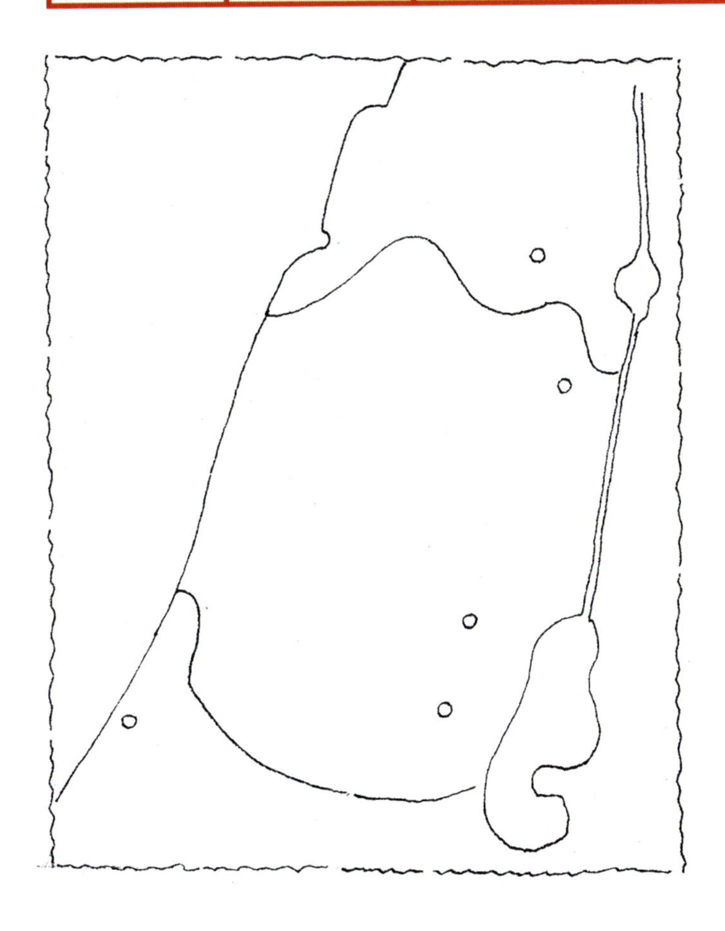

1. Seas.
2. Political regions.
3. Towns marked with dots.
4. River Jordan.
5. Tetrarchy of Herod Antipas.
6. Birthplace of Herod the Great.

Identify what happened on each of these dates ...

63 B.C. _ _ _ _ _ _ _ _ _ _
37 B.C. _ _ _ _ _ _ _ _ _ _
30 B.C. _ _ _ _ _ _ _ _ _ _
4 B.C. _ _ _ _ _ _ _ _ _ _

?

some Qs for you ...

1. Who was the Roman Emperor who took over Palestine in 63 B.C.?
2. Name the province that Palestine became part of.
3. Who became the King of the Jews in 37 B.C.?
4. When did Herod the Great die?
5. What happened to Palestine then?
6. Name the three political regions of Palestine.
7. What does 'Tetrarchy' mean?
8. Where was the town of Nazareth located?

Let's take a look at ...

Herod the Great:

- Born around 73 B.C. Half-Jewish.
- Younger son of Antipater, an **Idumaean** chieftain.

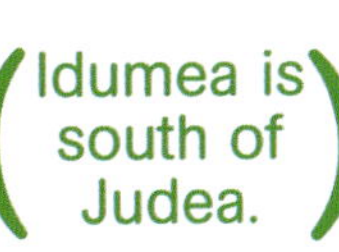

- Appointed as Governor of Galilee in 47 B.C. by Roman Emperor, Julius Caesar.

Julius Caesar, Roman Emperor.

- Made King of Judea in 37 B.C. by Marcus Antonius. Also ruled under Emperor Augustus.
- Loyal to the Roman Emperor, and efficient.
- Good with money. Made big cities in Judea.

(Began construction of new Temple in Jerusalem.)

- Said to be a cruel man.
- Died in 4 B.C..

Herod the Great.

Philip, son of Herod the Great

(Tetrarch of Iturea and Trachonitis):

- Became Tetrarch during A.D. 4 and ruled until A.D. 34.
- Given northeast of Palestine to rule.
- Founded the town of **Caesarea Philippi** at the foot of Mount Hermon.

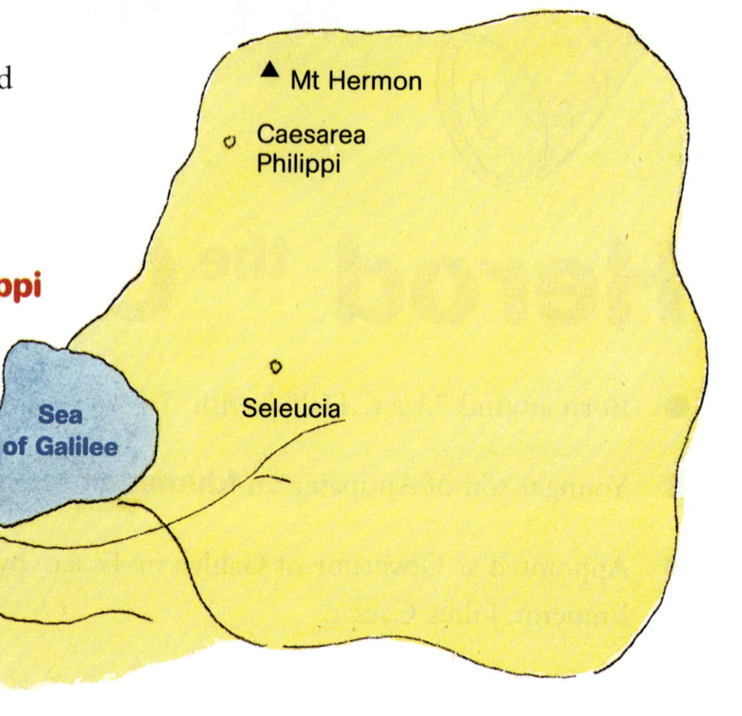

Herod Antipas, son of Herod the Great

(Tetrarch of Galilee and Perea):

- Became Tetrarch during A.D. 4. Ruled until A.D. 39.
- Given northern Palestine to rule – the area called Galilee and the small region called Perea. (Galilee included the town of Nazareth, where Jesus grew up.)
- Had a good relationship with Roman Emperor Tiberius.
- Built the town of Tiberias by Lake Galilee.
- Had John the Baptist beheaded, and was involved in the trial of Jesus.

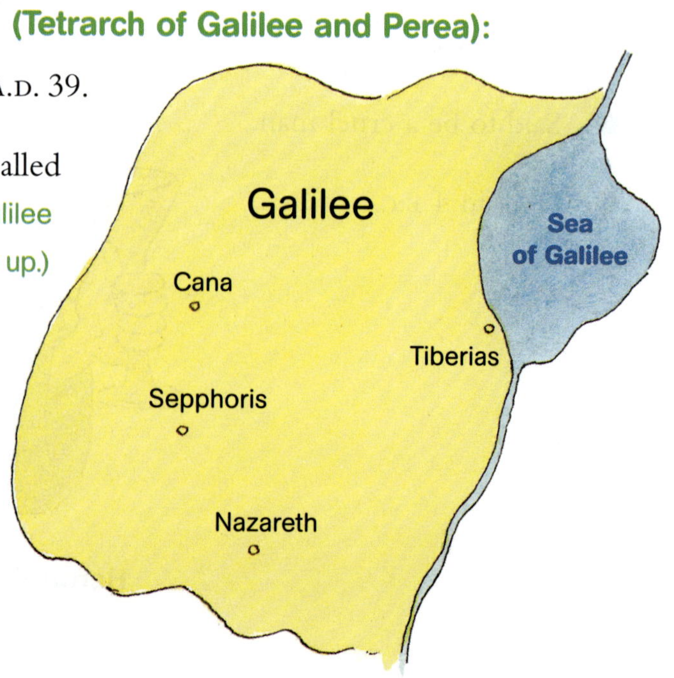

Archelaus, son of Herod the Great

(Ethnarch of Judea, including Samaria):

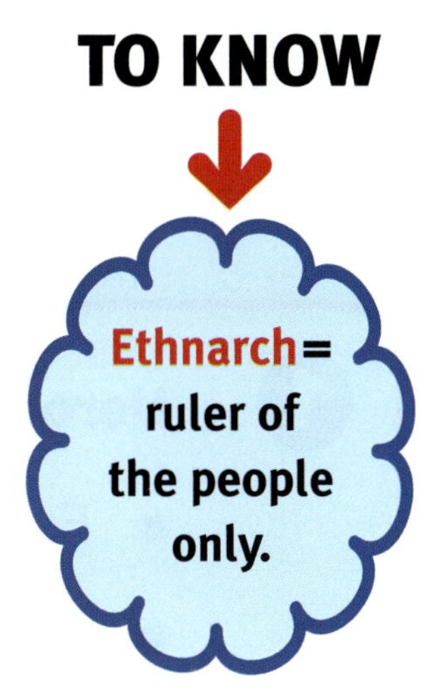

- Became **Ethnarch** in A.D. 4.
- Ruled for ten years.
- Not liked by the Jews of the territory.
- Removed by Rome.

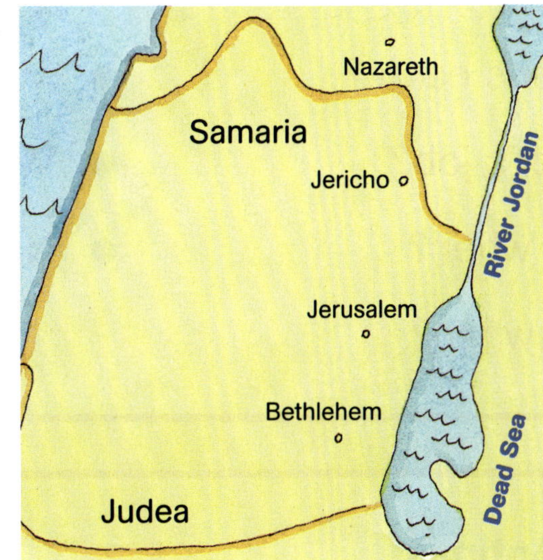

Well, around A.D. 6, Judea itself became a province of the Roman Empire, which meant that it had closer links with Rome and Roman rule. Because of this, Judea was given a new ruler called a **Procurator**. One of the best-known, and the one who concerns us the most, is:

Pontius Pilate

We will read more about him later.

Complete these two fact files:

1 **Herod the Great:**

- Father's name?
- Father's job?
- Born when?
- Died when?
- Made King in?
- Was King of?
- Name of Emperors?

2 **Herod Antipas:**

- Tetrarch of?
- Roman Emperor?
- Built which town?
- Name of father?
- Who did he have beheaded?
- Became Tetrarch in which year?

Answer these questions ...

A What does the word 'Tetrarch' mean?

B In what year did Philip become Tetrarch?

C What was the name of the town he built?

D In what year did Archelaus become Ethnarch?

E For how many years did he rule?

F What is the difference between the role of Archelaus as ruler and that of his brothers?

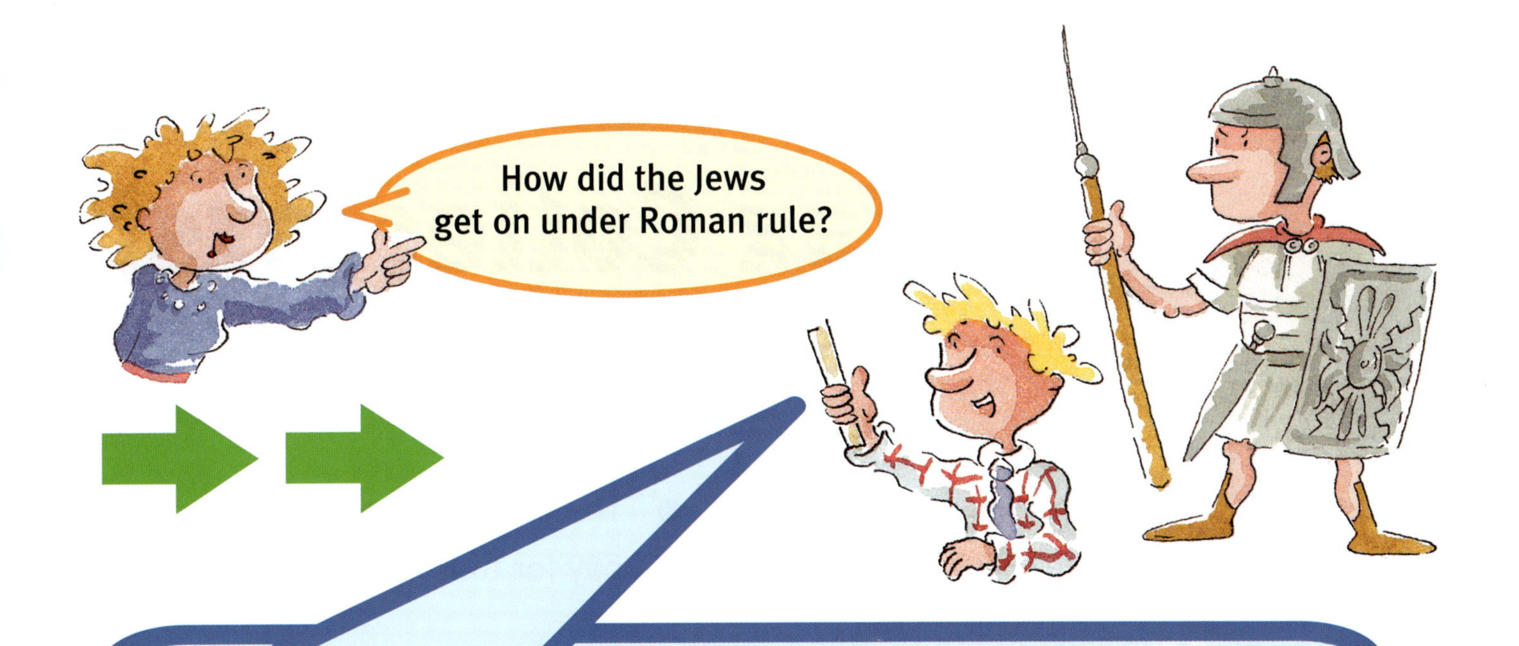

History tells us that the Jews were not altogether happy with Roman occupation.

Why? The Jews were convinced that they were God's chosen people **(Old Testament history)** and that they should be ruled by no one else except God. Because Rome wanted to rule the Jews, it therefore came into conflict with Jewish beliefs.

However, Rome gave the Jews a lot of **'self-rule'**. For example, each of the regions had its own 'council'. In **Judea**, this council was called the **'Sanhedrin'**. This council was allowed to make laws and decisions and hold trials, but it was never allowed to execute anybody.

... One of the biggest complaints the Jews had about the Romans was the appointing of

Tax Collectors!

Why was that a problem?

- The Romans needed taxes to pay for their growing Empire.

- So, every province of the Roman Empire had to pay taxes to Rome. This included Palestine.

- The right to collect taxes was sold to the Jew who paid the highest price. It was the job of this Jew to collect the taxes from the people and give them to the Roman authorities.

- Tax collectors were not popular because they worked for the Romans and were seen as traitors. They were also allowed to keep some of the money for themselves. They became, in some cases, social outcasts.

Matthew was a **tax collector** who became a follower of Jesus.

Jobs

Of course, tax collecting wasn't the only job you could do. There was also:

Fishing

Fishing was a family business. Sons followed their fathers into it. Some of Jesus' followers were **fishermen**. The Sea of Galilee was the big fishing lake.

TO KNOW

Many of the followers of Jesus were fishermen.

Carpentry

This was another popular job. Jesus' foster-father, Joseph, was a **carpenter**, as was Jesus himself when he was old enough.

Shepherding

To be a **shepherd** was a very responsible job. The sheep were valuable for their wool and milk. Jesus told many stories using shepherd imagery.

Farming

Farming is one of the oldest jobs. **Farmers** have an important job. It was probably one of the hardest jobs in the region because of the different types of soil and the climate in Palestine. Sometimes they hired helpers and had slaves. Farmers produced a range of products, from olives to flax.

Some other jobs were ...

Miner

Sandalmaker

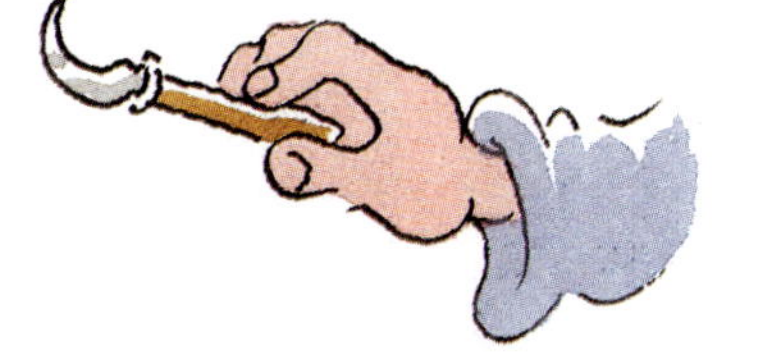

Doctor

Slave

Metalworker

Builder

Tailor

Hunter

Clothesmaker

Potter

Leatherworker

MONEY

Money, or **coinage**, seems to have come into existence around the seventh century B.C.!

In Jesus' time, there were three types of money in Palestine: Roman money, **Denari**; Greek money, **Drachma**; Jewish money, **Shekels**.

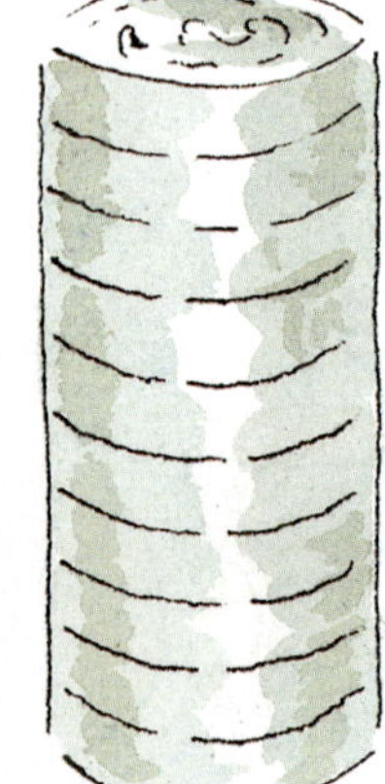

Answer the following questions ...

Q1. Why were tax collectors disliked?

Q2. How did tax collectors get the job?

Q3. Why did all provinces pay taxes?

Q4. Name five other jobs that people could do in Palestine.

Q5. Why was the job of shepherd so responsible?

Q6. What items did the carpenter make, do you think?

Q7. What natural conditions did farmers have to cope with, do you think?

Read these descriptions and name the job ...

A I work day and night.
I sell meat and wool.
I carry a staff.
Who am I?

B Good with money.
Not liked by people.
Bought the job.
Who am I?

C A family job.
Jesus' foster-father did it.
Common in Jesus' time.
Who am I?

D I don't like locusts.
I know the soil well.
I have flax.
Who am I?

... Let's try these ...

In your copy, unmuddle the following money and put them in sentences:

MDRHMCA

AEDNRI

KSEHEL

Q1. When did coinage come into existence?

Q2. Name the three types of coinage in use during Jesus' time.

Political and Religious Groups

When Jesus was growing up and when he was an adult, several groups of people were quite important in the land of Israel. These were:

The Sadducees!

The Pharisees!

The Essenes!

The Zealots!

The Sanhedrin!

All these groups were very prominent in Palestine during the time of Jesus and were involved in politics and religion.

... let's have a 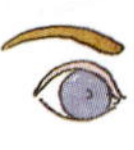  look!

SADDUCEES

- Mostly upper-class people.
- Many came from priestly families. (Priests had been around since the time of Moses. They became more important when the Temple was built. They acted as go-betweens for man with God.)
- Had a lot of political power.
- Had great commitment to the Temple and worship.
- Were religious conservatives.
- Co-operated with the Romans.
- Made up most of the Sanhedrin.
- Accepted the Torah only.
- Didn't accept Resurrection.

PHARISEES

- Name means 'Separate Ones'.
- Made up of laymen and students of the Old Testament.
- Members included 'scribes'.
- Rivals of the **Sadducees**.
- Accepted other scriptures as well as the Torah (e.g. Talmud).
- **Commitment** to the law rather than the Temple.
- Politically conservative – no compromise with the Romans.
- Respected by the common people.
- Believed in Resurrection.
- Waited for the Messiah to free them from Roman rule.

ZEALOTS

- Freedom-fighters.
- Wanted Jewish independence.
- Wanted to overthrow the Romans.
- Believed the **Messiah** would be a great soldier to free them.
- Believed in violent action.
- Jesus' Apostle, **Simon**, was a Zealot.

ESSENES

- Regarded Jewish leaders (political and religious) as weak.
- Withdrew from Jewish society.
- Observed strict religious traditions (law, Sabbath, etc.).
- Had small communities in out-of-the-way places.
- Believed that only **THEY** understood the Torah.
- Expected two Messiahs.

Over to you!

Who am I?

Guess to which of the four groups mentioned each of the following belongs:

- 'I am expecting two Messiahs!'
- 'I think that the political and religious leaders are weak!'
- 'Only my friends and I understand the Torah!'

I am an ____________________

- 'I am a rival to the Sadducees!'
- 'I am committed to the law!'
- 'The common people respect me!'
- 'I believe in Resurrection!'

I am a ____________________

- 'I am from the upper class!'
- 'I have a lot of political power!'
- 'I am committed to the Temple!'
- 'I am also a member of the Sanhedrin!'

I am a ____________________

Q

1. Name the four groups of people in Palestine in Jesus' time.
2. Give four details about the Sadducees.
3. How were they different from the Pharisees?
4. Did they believe in the Resurrection?
5. How did they get on with the Romans?
6. Where did most of the members of the Sadducees come from?

The Pharisees' name means ________ ________. They were mostly made up of ________ and ________ of the Old Testament. They were rivals to the ________. Their commitment was to the ________ rather than the ________. They were ________ by the common people, and believed in ________. They waited for the Messiah to ________ ________ from ________ ________.

More Qs

A. What religious traditions did the Essenes observe?

B. Where did they live and why, do you think?

C. What did the Zealots want?

D. What Messiah did they expect?

E. How would they get rid of the Romans?

The High Priest

The Sanhedrin – the Jewish Ruling Council

- Name means 'assembly' or 'senate'.
- Official governing body of the Jews.
- Recognised by the Romans.
- Seventy members plus a president.
- President was the **HIGH PRIEST**.
- Made up of priestly family members, scribes, elders (important Jewish laymen).
- Many Sadducees, few Pharisees.
- Had own police force (Temple Guard).
- Voted on laws, and controlled everything to do with religion.

- The High Priest was the head of all the Temple priests.
- He was a spiritual leader.
- He was anointed as the High Priest.
- He wore special clothes.
- He lived in a luxury palace.
- He had a lot of influence over religion and politics.
- He was Head of the Sanhedrin.

So, as well as the ordinary Jew on the street, these are the different types of people with whom Jesus would have come into contact during his life in Palestine.

Over to you!

True / False?

- The High Priest was Head of all Temple priests. **T / F**
- He was given a medal to become High Priest. **T / F**
- He lived in a small house. **T / F**
- He had no influence over politics. **T / F**
- He had a lot of influence over religion. **T / F**
- He wore plain clothes. **T / F**

1. What does the name Sanhedrin mean?
2. How many members in the Sanhedrin?
3. Who was part of the Sanhedrin?
4. Who was the president?
5. What did the Sanhedrin vote on?

SANHEDRINOUYMESSIAHXOUXZEALOTUROPHARISEETURSPIASIMONOUPSADDUCEEOUYTEMPLEARUPZHIGHPRIESTOUASTESSENESPTOUIAA

Find the words in the puzzle wheel and put them into a sentence in your copy.

- ____________________
- ____________________
- ____________________
- ____________________
- ____________________
- ____________________
- ____________________
- ____________________
- ____________________

So, for us to find out more about the person of Jesus and his life, death and resurrection, we need to look at the material that was written about him ...

Gospel is from old English, **'God-Spell'**, meaning 'Good Tidings'.

The New Testament

The New Testament (Christian Scriptures) is made up of **27 books** dealing with the life, death and resurrection of Jesus, his followers and the spread of his message.

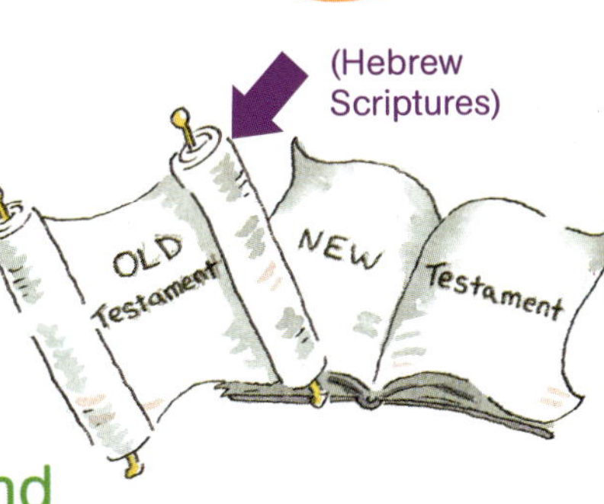

The New Testament goes hand in hand with the Old Testament. Christians believe that the person of Jesus fulfilled all the Old Testament prophecies about the Messiah. Jesus was the New Covenant between God and man.

As well as all these books, there are four that are especially important to finding out about Jesus' message, his life, death and resurrection. These are:

All that Christianity teaches about Jesus is taken from these four books (and other New Testament books).

TO KNOW

Collectively, Matthew, Mark, Luke and John are called the Evangelists, meaning proclaimers.

1. Where do we look to find out about Jesus' life?
2. How many books are in the New Testament?
3. Name six books from the New Testament.
4. Why does the New Testament go hand in hand with the Old Testament?
5. What does the word 'Gospel' mean?
6. What four books are especially important for reading about Jesus?
7. What name is used to describe the writers of the Gospels all together?
8. What does 'Evangelist' mean?

Match these up

Gospel	An Evangelist
Evangelist	New Testament goes hand in hand with
Matthew	Another name for New Testament
27	The Evangelists
Mark	A writer of a Gospel
Galatians	Written record of Jesus' life, death and resurrection
Proclaimers of Good News	A book from the New Testament
Good Tidings	Meaning of 'God-Spell'
Old Testament	The number of books in the New Testament
Christian Scriptures	Another Evangelist

... Now, it's important to keep in mind that the Gospels were not written while Jesus was walking and talking in Palestine. They appeared quite some time later, in stages. Have a look!

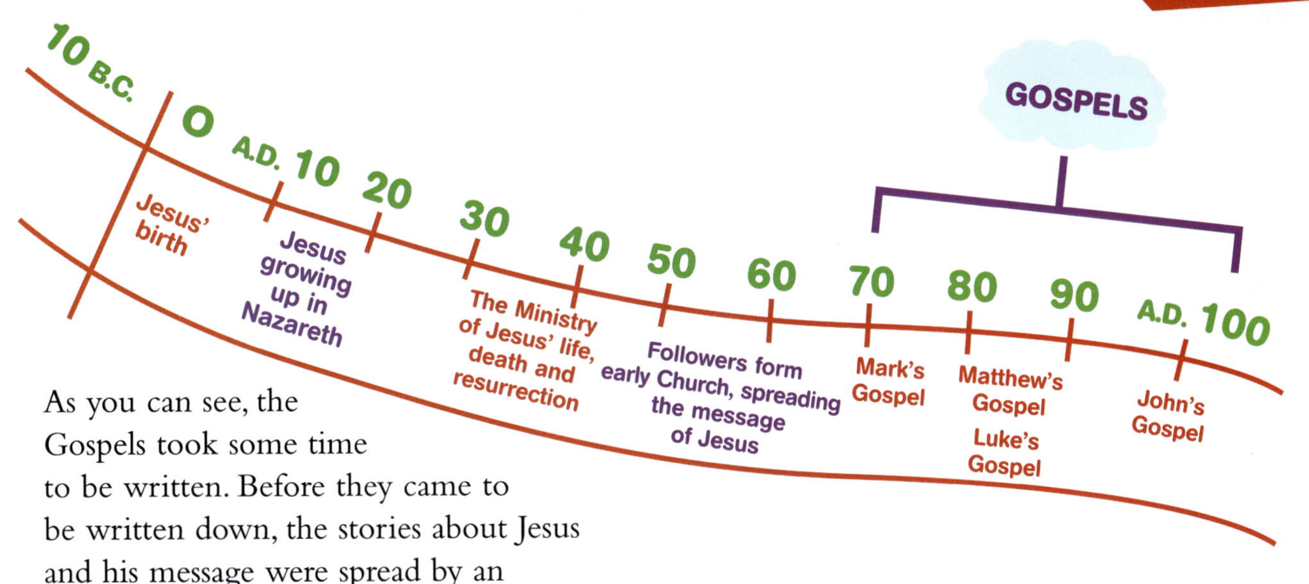

As you can see, the Gospels took some time to be written. Before they came to be written down, the stories about Jesus and his message were spread by an

Oral Tradition

(people recalling Jesus' life, death and resurrection by word-of-mouth)!

What made them write it down?

Good question!

1. The witnesses to Jesus' life, death and resurrection were getting old and dying. Their words had to be preserved.
2. Jesus' Second Coming in Glory would not be as soon as hoped, so the Christian community would be around for some time.
3. For the future Church and future generations, the essentials about Jesus had to be preserved and recollected accurately.
4. There was a continual need to instruct and inspire the communities already created around the Mediterranean.

Each of the **Evangelists** gathered pieces from all the stories told about Jesus. Each writer then put these pieces together for his readers.
The Gospels are written for people with different needs in different locations.

Why were the Gospels written down?

Explain the Oral Tradition

Design a poster that has the timeline on it from around 10 B.C. up to A.D. 100, indicating Jesus' life and the development of the Gospels!

FIGURE THESE OUT

THE	DIT	TRA	AL	ION	OR

NGE	EVA	TE	LS	WRO	THE	TS	LIS	GO	SPE

The Gospels

Four Portraits of Jesus

TO KNOW

Scripture scholar: a person who studies and knows about the Old and New Testaments.

Theologian: a person who studies God and religion.

Scripture scholars and theologians tell us that the Gospels are not simply the work of four men sitting down and writing about their memories of Jesus. It is more likely that each Evangelist had quite a bit of information and material to work from!

The Evangelists would have used:

- The words of Jesus used in prayers and recollections.
- The stories about Jesus told in the communities.
- Ideas and insights from preachers about the meaning of Jesus' life, death and resurrection, and connections to the Old Testament.
- The Gospels of the other Evangelists.
- **'Q Source'** (German world *Quelle*, meaning source – early collections of Jesus' sayings and teachings.)

Synoptic means: seen together.

It's important to remember this:
Matthew, Mark and Luke's Gospels are called the **Synoptic Gospels** because the three authors had the same materials and stories, as well as each other, available to them while writing their Gospels. They can be fully understood only when looked at side by side.
John's is different and unique. Its language and structure are much more image-filled and symbolic.

Who were the Evangelists...?

TO KNOW

'Gentile': a person who was not a Jew.

Symbols of lion/ox/man(angel)/eagle inspired by Revelations 4:7. '4 Living Creatures that surround God's throne.' Also mentioned in Ezekiel 1:1-14.

From their study of the history of the New Testament, Scripture scholars can tell us about who exactly **the Evangelists** were. Let's have a look.

Mark

Scripture scholars believe that the author was a **John Mark** who lived in Jerusalem. He learned about Jesus from the **Apostle Peter**. In the New Testament book, **The Acts of the Apostles**, John Mark is mentioned as a companion of St Paul (12:25). This Gospel was written between A.D. 65 and A.D. 70.

Luke

This Evangelist is also said to be the author of 'The Acts of the Apostles'. Luke is believed to have been a non-Jew **(Gentile)**, and a well-educated doctor, who converted to Christianity. It is thought that this is the Luke mentioned by St Paul in his **Letter to the Colossians (4:14)**. He is mentioned three times in the New Testament as a companion of St Paul. He may have had Mark's Gospel available to him when writing his. Luke's Gospel was written in approximately A.D. 85.

Matthew

There is disagreement over the authorship of Matthew's Gospel. Many Scripture scholars believe it to have been written by **Matthew the Apostle** of Jesus. Other scholars say that the author uses too much of what Mark and Luke have written to have been an eyewitness to Jesus' life. This Gospel was written around A.D. 80–100.

John

This Gospel is written differently from the three **Synoptic Gospels**. Scholars and the Church believe the author to be the Apostle, John. It is believed that he wrote this after a long life of prayer and reflection on the person of Jesus. He is also thought to have written 'The Book of Revelation'.

... Let's do some work

1. What is a Theologian?
2. What is a Scripture scholar?
3. What information did the Evangelists have available to them?
4. What is the 'Q Source'?
5. Name the 'Synoptic Gospels'.
6. What does Synoptic mean?
7. How is John's Gospel different from the others?

Which Evangelist am I

- I wrote 'The Acts of the Apostles'.
- I am a Gentile.
- St Paul mentions me.

- I lived in Jerusalem.
- I listened to the Apostle, Peter.
- I am also a companion of St Paul.

- I prayed and reflected on Jesus' life.
- I wrote the Book of Revelation.
- Some scholars believe I am the Beloved Disciple.

- Many scholars believe that I wrote a Gospel.
- I was an Apostle.
- I wrote around A.D. 80–100.

To do

In your copy, draw each of symbols of the Evangelists. Explain why these symbols are used!

Read through St John's Gospel. Compare his writing to that of the Synoptic Gospels. What's different? What's similar? What does he not have? What does he highlight?

Gospels Info. File

TO KNOW

The Evangelists wrote about the meaning of Jesus' life, rather than a biography of Jesus. The Gospels are documents of faith, not an historical encyclopaedia.

St Mark ...

- Shows us the human Jesus, his suffering and emotions.
- Was written for non-Jewish readers (Gentiles), probably in Rome.
- Has Jesus' death as a central point.
- Explains that suffering is an essential part of Christian life.
- Shows Jesus as both human and Divine.
- Is the shortest of the four Gospels.

St Matthew ...

- Shows Jesus as the expected Messiah of the Jews.
- Is organised like the 'Pentateuch' (OT).
- Shows Jesus as the fulfilment of Old Testament promises.
- Presents Jesus as a teacher of Jewish law – a 'new Moses'.
- Has a focus on Christian community (Church) life.
- Is good for educating new Christians.
- Contains five discourses by Jesus.
- Is presented first in the New Testament.

St Luke ...

- Shows Jesus as the Saviour who is compassionate and merciful.
- Was written for Christians to help them to have a deeper understanding of Jesus.
- Makes connections between Christianity and Judaism.
- Highlights the Holy Spirit in Jesus' life.
- Says that Jesus' message is for all people and that God accepts all.

St John ...

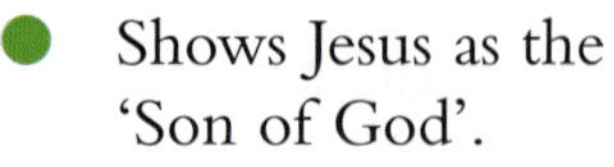

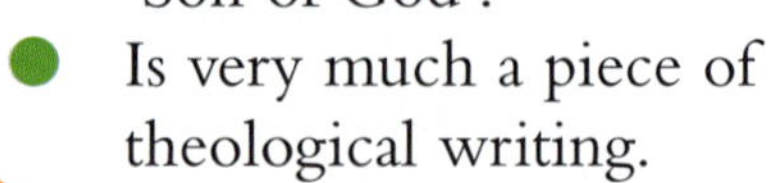

- Shows Jesus as the 'Son of God'.
- Is very much a piece of theological writing.
- Is prayerfully written.
- Presents Jesus as 'Bread of Life', 'Good Shepherd', 'Light of the World'.
- Gives more emphasis to Jesus' true identity to help believers understand.

1. Which Gospel was written for 'Gentiles'?
2. Which Gospel stresses Jesus' mercy and compassion?
3. Which Gospel is especially good for educating new Christians?
4. Which Gospel is a piece of theological writing?
5. Where would you look to find Jesus' five discourses?
6. Which Gospel has an emphasis on Jesus' emotions?
7. Are the Gospels biographies of Jesus? Why?

Put these sentences in the appropriate Evangelist box.

- Written for Gentiles.
- Connections between Christianity and Judaism.
- First in the New Testament.
- Helps to understand Jesus' true nature.
- Written prayerfully.
- Jesus presented as 'new Moses'.
- Organised like the Pentateuch.
- Shortest Gospel.
- Shows Jesus' love for all people.
- Piece of theology.
- Jesus' death is a very central point.
- Shows human nature of Jesus.
- Helps Christians to develop a better understanding of Jesus.
- Uses 'Good Shepherd' image.

St Mark

St Matthew

St Luke

St John

Now that we know a little about the Evangelists, when they wrote, why they wrote and who they wrote for, let's look at *what* they wrote!

The Life of Jesus

Piecing together Jesus' life involves reading what the Evangelists wrote about him and what the Apostles preached about him.

It's important to always keep in mind that these writings about Jesus are not history lessons or biographies. The writings tell us who Jesus was, what his mission was and the overall meaning of Jesus' life, death and resurrection.

How did it all begin?

Here's a picture that most people would be familiar with – the Birth of Jesus. Would you be surprised to learn that not all the **Evangelists** have written about Jesus' birth?

Narrative means: telling a story.

Only **St Matthew's and St Luke's** Gospels have the story, properly called:

'Infancy Narratives'.

Infancy Narratives

These narratives by St Matthew and St Luke, about the birth of Jesus, are answers to questions by the early Christian communities, telling them and us about the identity of Jesus.

TO KNOW

Emmanuel.
Magi.
Annunciation.
Magnificat.

St Matthew's Version

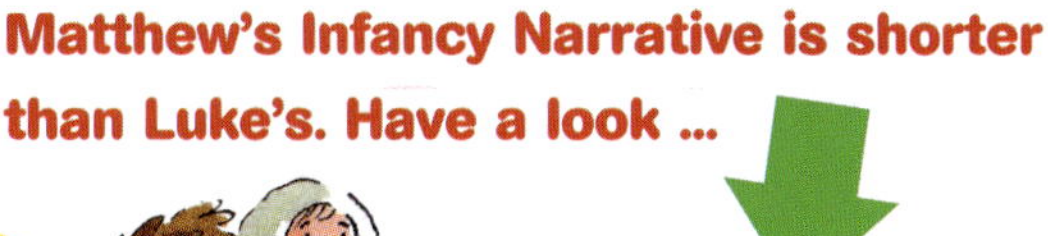

Matthew's Infancy Narrative is shorter than Luke's. Have a look ...

'Genealogy back to Abraham' (1:1-17).

Story of Mary and Joseph – **'Joseph, take Mary as your wife'** (1:18-25).

Jesus' birth and naming in Bethlehem **'a son ... called Emmanuel'** (1:18-25).

Three Kings visit

Magi (2:1-12).

Flight into Egypt.

Return to Nazareth (2:19-23).

St Luke's Version

In Luke's Gospel, before the story of Jesus' birth he tells us about the birth of John the Baptist (1:5-25).

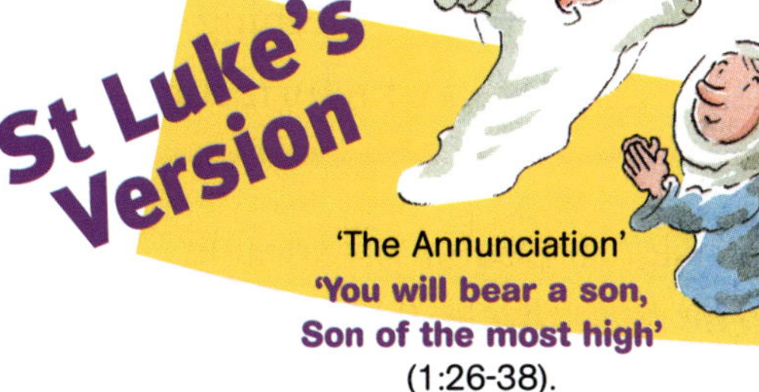

'The Annunciation' **'You will bear a son, Son of the most high'** (1:26-38).

Mary visits Elizabeth (her cousin) **'Blessed is the fruit of thy womb'** (1:39-45).

My soul proclaims the greatness of God

The Magnificat (Mary's prayer of thanks!) (1:46-55).

Birth of John the Baptist (1:57-80).

Mary and Joseph travel to Bethlehem for the census (2:1-5).

Jesus' birth, placed in manger. **'No room at the Inn'** (2:5-7).

Shepherds told of birth. They visit Jesus. **'in the city of David a Saviour is born'** (2:11).

Jesus presented in the Temple (2:21-38).

Put St Matthew's Infancy Narrative in the correct order:

1. ________
2. ________
3. ________
4. ________
5. ________
6. ________

- Flight to Egypt.
- The Three Kings arrive.
- Jesus' family tree.
- Story of Mary and Joseph.
- Birth of Jesus and naming.
- Return to Nazareth.

Put St Luke's Infancy Narrative in the correct order:

1. ________
2. ________
3. ________
4. ________
5. ________
6. ________
7. ________
8. ________

- Mary's prayer of thanks.
- Jesus presented in the Temple.
- Mary and Joseph travel to Bethlehem.
- Shepherds visit Jesus.
- Mary visits Elizabeth.
- Jesus' birth.
- Shepherds told of birth.
- The Annunciation.

Some artwork to do!

1. Read Luke 2:11. Draw a picture of that event.
2. Read Matthew 2:1-12. Draw a picture to go with a part of that narrative.
3. Read Luke 2:5-7. Draw a picture that represents this.

Fill in these blanks:

Piecing together Jesus' ________ involves reading what the ________ wrote about him and what the ________ preached about him.

It's important to keep in mind that the ________ about Jesus are not ________ ________ or ________. The writings are trying to say what ________ was, what his ________ was, and the overall meaning of Jesus' ________, ________ and resurrection.

Some Questions

A Why are the Gospels not biographies?

B How do we piece together Jesus' life?

C Which two Evangelists write about Jesus' birth?

D What is an Infancy Narrative?

E What are the main differences between the two Infancy Narratives?

F What is Mary's 'Song of Praise'?

G Where would you find information on John the Baptist?

TO DO Design a poster presenting ***The Magnificat*** (Luke 1:46-55).

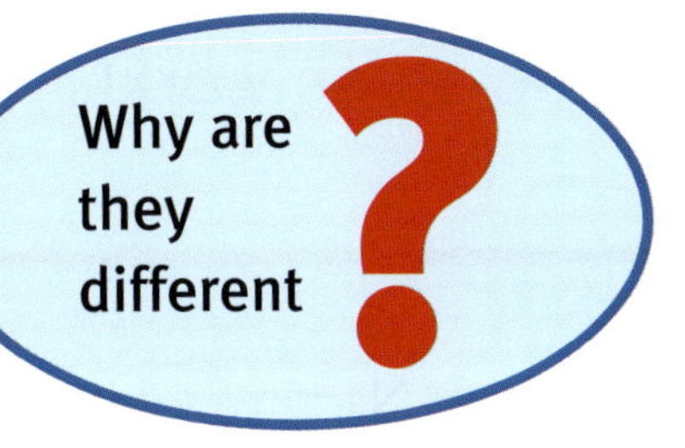

The Gospels explain Jesus' life, death and resurrection for different groups of people and make different points about Jesus' identity.

Let's see what points they are making!

St Matthew's Message

'New Moses'

St Matthew uses images like those associated with Moses from the Old Testament. Just like **Moses**, the Holy Family escaped Egypt and travelled to safety. Jesus fulfilled the law of Moses, leading the people to safety.

Jesus, the Messiah

In his writing, St Matthew wanted to show his **Jewish** readers that Jesus was the Messiah they had waited for. This is especially emphasised by the **Family Tree** all the way back to the prophet **Abraham**. He also includes that Jesus was born in **Bethlehem**, the town always associated with the **Great King David**.

Gentiles Accept Jesus

The **Magi** or Three Kings visit Jesus in St Matthew's version. Basically they symbolise people other than Jews – **Gentiles**. These Gentiles worship Jesus while not all Jews worship him.

St Luke's Message

Jesus' Message for All

St Luke wrote his Infancy Narrative for Gentiles, or non-Jews, so he doesn't have too many references to the Old Testament, though he does highlight Jesus as Messiah. St Luke focuses on the fact that the **Good News is for everyone** – all people who are poor, hungry, downtrodden, helpless, in slavery ... the shepherds represent the poor who would recognise Jesus. Later, in 3:23-38, there is a family tree that goes back to Adam. Luke is telling his readers that Jesus' message is for all humanity.

Let's do some work!

1. Why are the Infancy Narratives different?
2. Why do St Matthew and St Luke emphasise different aspects of the birth of Jesus?
3. Why does the Gospel of St Matthew have a family tree?
4. Why does St Matthew mention Bethlehem?
5. Who do the 'Magi' (Three Kings) represent? What do the shepherds represent?
6. What is St Matthew saying about Jesus and Moses?
7. Who is St Luke writing for?
8. What does St Luke focus on?
9. What's different about St Luke's family tree?
10. According to St Luke, who is Jesus' message for?

Finish these sentences (in your copy):

St Matthew was showing that Jesus was the _______.
His family tree goes back to _______.
According to St Matthew, Jesus was born in _______.
This town is associated with _______.
The Magi symbolise _______.
St Luke is writing for _______.
The Good News is for _______.
The shepherds symbolise _______.
The family tree in St Luke's Gospel goes back to _______.
This means that Jesus' message is _______.

Bible Wordsearch

```
N I S N N E E S K U V S B S T
U A H C U S Y G E R E V A H S
M O I N R N E C A V A R E E I
J A E G O I R L I S A M K P L
A I T P O U P T I M S G U H E
E D T T O L A T A T R E L E G
R I A S H R O I U E N I M R N
C K Q M R E C E E R R E P D A
T L G A H A W K H B E R G S V
E C N E I D U A E T A A H Y E
G P O R T R A I T A D L E B C
G O S P E L S O P V E O B Q Q
N S A B R A H A M H R H R A Q
Y C N A F N I R U S S C E B E
M A G I F S E S O M A S W Y P
```

ABRAHAM
AUDIENCE
GOSPELS
INFANCY
MAGI
MESSAGE
PORTRAIT
SCHOLAR
SYNOPTIC

ADAM
EVANGELIST
GREEK
JOHN
MARK
MOSES
QSOURCE
SCRIPTURE
THEOLOGIAN

ARAMAIC
GENTILES
HEBREW
LUKE
MATTHEW
NARRATIVES
READERS
SHEPHERDS

When was Jesus born?

Scripture scholars and theologians believe that Jesus was born in either **5 B.C.** or **6 B.C.**. From reading the Gospels, we know that Jesus was born during the reign of **King Herod** (Matthew 2:16). Herod died in the year 4 B.C., so **Jesus was born** before that date.

Choosing 25 December

Why?

When the Roman Empire took on **Christianity** as its official religion, the Romans named **25 December** as the feast of **Jesus' birth**. This replaced the older feast day to the Roman sun-god, Mithris. Jesus was seen as the new **'light of the world'**.

Jesus Growing Up

TO KNOW

The Gospels **(Matthew, Mark, Luke, John)** actually have very little to say about Jesus growing up as a young boy. Indeed, there seems to be a big jump from his birth right up to when he began to preach and teach the Good News as an adult.

Why? Overall the Evangelists wanted to tell us the meaning of the stories, miracles, life, death and resurrection of Jesus.

St Luke is the only **Evangelist** to mention Jesus growing up:

> 'When they had done everything the Law of the Lord required, they went back to Galilee to their own town of Nazareth and as the child Jesus grew to maturity, he was filled with wisdom and God's favour.'
>
> **(Luke 2:39-40)**

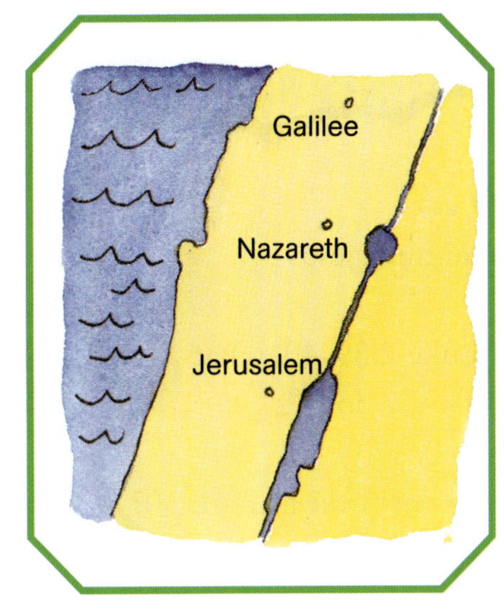

Luke also mentions, in 2:41-50, that, as a young boy, Jesus was in the Temple listening and speaking to the teachers and the Rabbis. Mary and Joseph thought that he was lost. When they found him, Jesus said, 'Did you not know that I must be in my Father's house?' This indicates the relationship between God, the Father and God, the Son.

The Gospels tell us that Jesus grew up in Nazareth, Galilee. Galilee lies to the north of Israel, spreading out beside the Sea of Galilee.

Nazareth, Jesus' hometown, was quite near some important trade routes along which foreigners, Romans and Greeks, passed. It was a small Jewish village. Around it were many non-Jewish villages. It was 90 km (56 miles) from the capital, Jerusalem.

Complete this cloze test

The _______ say very little about Jesus _______ up. There is a big _______ between Jesus' birth and his _______ as an adult. Overall the _______ wanted to tell us more about the _______ of Jesus' life. _______ is the only Evangelist to mention Jesus growing _______. 'When they had done _______ the _______ of the _______ required, they went back to _______ to their own town of _______. And as the child grew up to _______ he was filled with _______ and God's _______ was with him.'

So, from reading the _______ we know that as a _______ and young adult, Jesus grew up in _______ in the area of Galilee.

Some Qs to do ...

Q1. Which Gospel mentions Jesus growing up?

Q2. According to St Luke 2:39-40, what did Jesus and his family do?

Q3. Where did Jesus grow up?

Q4. What does St Luke mention in 2:41-50?

Q5. Draw a map of Israel and pinpoint where Nazareth is.

More Qs

A. Why do Evangelists hardly mention Jesus growing up?

B. What information do we have about Jesus growing up?

C. What does this information tell us about Jesus, Mary and Joseph?

D. What experiences would Jesus have had growing up in Nazareth, do you think?

E. What did Jesus mean when he said:

'Did you not know that I must be in my Father's House?'

COPY AND COLOUR

Growing up in NAZARETH

As we said, we know very little about Jesus growing up. But we can say a bit about what life would have been like growing up in Nazareth, Galilee, in Jesus' time thanks to the work of historians, archaeologists and scientists.

What was his house like?

Have a look

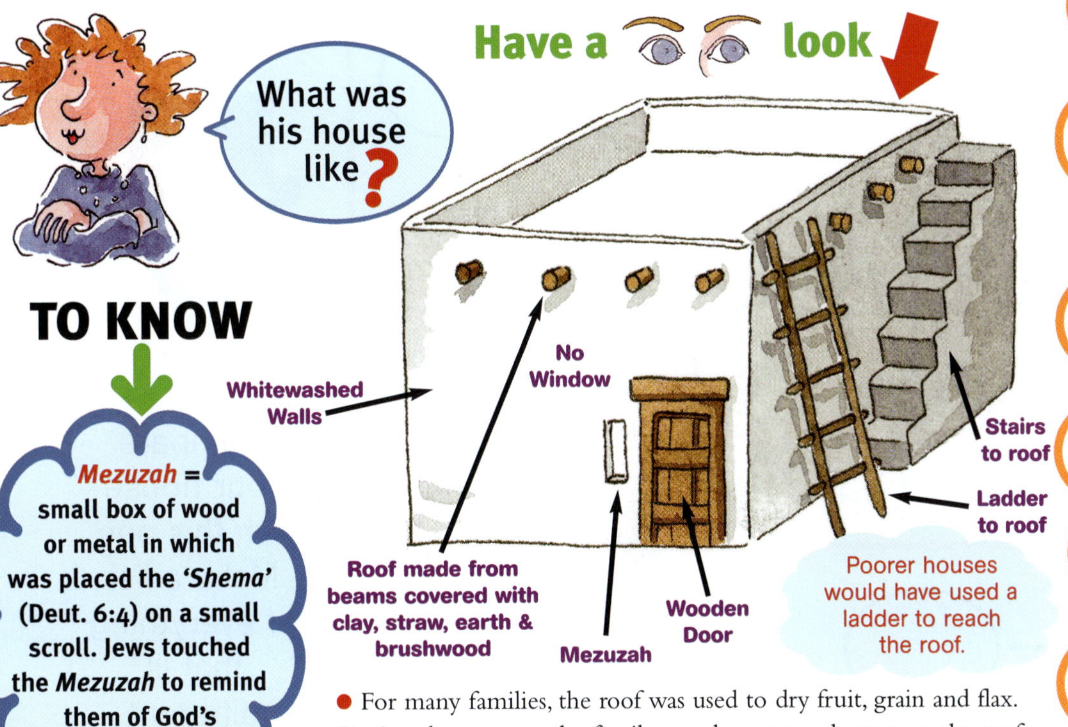

TO KNOW

Mezuzah = small box of wood or metal in which was placed the *'Shema'* (Deut. 6:4) on a small scroll. Jews touched the *Mezuzah* to remind them of God's Covenant.

- For many families, the roof was used to dry fruit, grain and flax. During the summer the family may have sat and eaten on the roof.
- A lot of insects during summer
- Smoky during winter
- No bathing facilities

Have a look inside

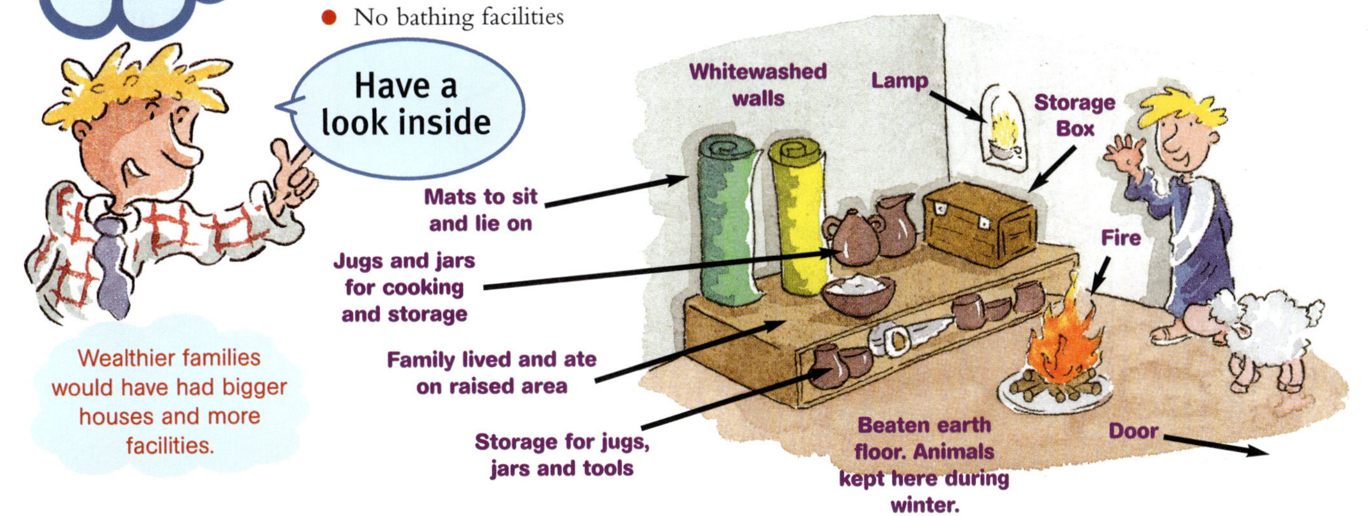

Wealthier families would have had bigger houses and more facilities.

Artwork to do!

In your copy, draw these boxes, then draw and complete the picture.

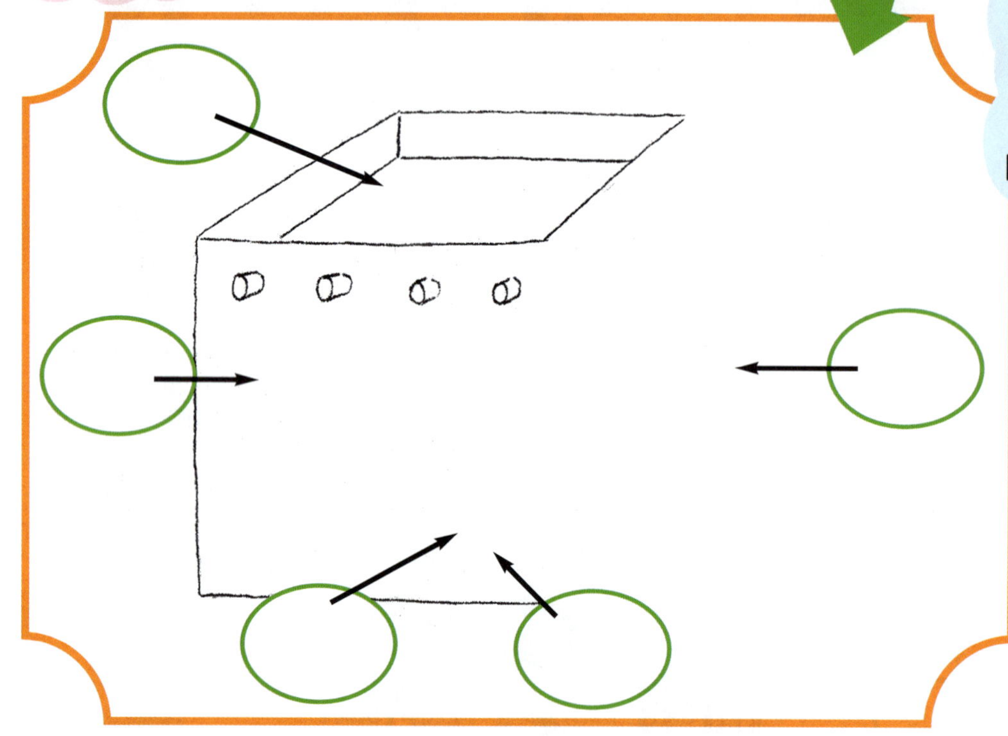

Research

Find a picture of a '*Mezuzah*' and draw it. Write out Deuteronomy 6:4.

Label each item

To do

Compare your house with this one. Make a list of everything that is different between your home and these houses.

This house is probably the type of house that Jesus would have lived in growing up in Nazareth.

NB a synagogue was the place of worship and prayer and also of learning and wisdom.

During his childhood, probably from the age of eight to thirteen years, Jesus would have gone to school. The **school** was usually a room attached to the synagogue.

Most of his study would have been from the Scriptures, and about the history of the Jewish people and their relationship with **Yahweh** (God).

Jesus would have known of, learned and spoken four languages:

HEBREW, GREEK, ARAMAIC and LATIN!

TO KNOW

Aramaic = the local language of people living in Palestine.
Hebrew = the traditional language of the Jews from ancient times.
Greek = the language used by traders and was left over from Greek occupation.
Latin = the language of the Romans.

In school, the teacher was called **'Rabbi'** **(Hebrew for 'My Master')**. The Rabbi was a person with great Old Testament knowledge. He was also a spiritual leader.

TRY THESE

True / False?

- Jesus was in school until he was eighteen. **T / F**
- The school was a room beside the synagogue. **T / F**
- He studied the history of the Egyptians. **T / F**
- He read from the Koran. **T / F**
- He spoke three languages. **T / F**
- Hebrew was a new language for the Jews. **T / F**
- Greek was the language of the Romans. **T / F**
- The teacher was called Rabbi. **T / F**
- Rabbi means 'my master'. **T / F**

1. At what age might Jesus have started school?
2. Where was the school?
3. What is a synagogue?
4. What did Jesus study in school?
5. What did he read from?
6. What languages was Jesus familiar with?
7. What was Aramaic?
8. What was Hebrew?
9. What was a Rabbi?

Try your best to copy out some Greek.

...When he wasn't in school, Jesus would have spent some hours every day helping his foster-father, Joseph.

Joseph was a carpenter!

A Family of Faith

We can say from our reading of the **New Testament** that Jesus, Mary and Joseph would have been **devout Jews**. The family would have been the source and beginnings of Jesus' deep faith.

The Passover meal remembers the Exodus of Israel from Egypt: lamb, herbs, unleavened bread, wine.

The Jewish family was seen as a small **religious community** in its own right. As a family, Jesus, Mary and Joseph would have celebrated all the Jewish feasts and festivals, remembered the Sabbath and attended synagogue, and have made a special effort to celebrate the **Passover** and to have **the Passover meal**.

'May the Lord bless you and take care of you;

May the Lord be kind and gracious to you;

May the Lord look on you with favour and give you peace' (Num. 6:24-26). **(Rabbi's blessing on *Bar Mitzvah* boy.)**

When Jesus was **thirteen**, he would have celebrated his *Bar Mitzvah*.

Bar Mitzvah is Hebrew for:

'Son of the Law'

that means, becoming an adult Jew!

For his *Bar Mitzvah*, Jesus would have worn the following:

Jesus and his family would have gone to the **synagogue** and joined other adult men. The **Rabbi** would have asked Jesus about the Old Testament, especially **the Torah**, and then he would have been allowed to read from **the Holy Scriptures** in Hebrew.

The next very important moment in Jesus' life was his **Baptism** – let's have a look!

In your copy, draw Jesus as a boy at his *Bar Mitzvah*.

On your drawing place his:

- *kippah;*
- *tallith;*
- *tefillin;*

Q

1. What does *Bar Mitzvah* mean?
2. At what age does it happen?
3. Where does it happen?
4. How does it happen?
5. What did Jesus wear for his *Bar Mitzvah*?
6. What Blessing did the Rabbi say?

Complete these sentences:

- Jesus' foster-father was ________.
- Joseph worked as a ________.
- Nazareth was a small ________.
- Jesus' family was a family of ________.
- Jesus, Mary and Joseph were ________.
- Jesus' family was a small ________.
- As a family they would have celebrated ________.
- The Passover meal remembers ________.

More Qs

A. Why is *Bar Mitzvah* important?
B. What does the Rabbi's Blessing mean?
C. Explain 'Son of the Law'.
D. Why is it a family celebration?
E. What influence did the family have on Jesus?
F. What did Jesus, Mary and Joseph do as devout Jews?
G. Why was the Passover meal important?

The Baptism of Jesus and His Public Life Begins

TO KNOW

Public = something done so that other people see and know.
Baptism = pouring of water over someone, or dipping them in water. A sign of new life and entering God's family.
Prophet = a religious person who spoke out against wrongdoing in society and warned of the consequences.

The Baptism of Jesus marks the beginning of his public life. From this moment, Jesus would preach and work miracles among the people of Palestine.

The person who baptised Jesus was

John the Baptist

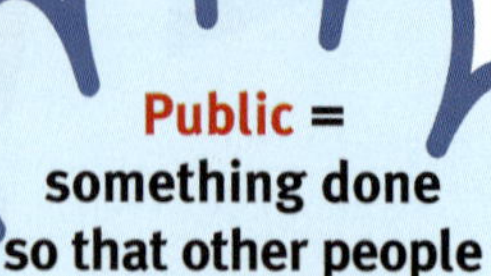

Who was John the Baptist?

Let's have a look

All the Evangelists say that he wore rough clothing, lived in the desert and believed that the Messiah was coming to redeem and save Palestine.

Fact File on John the Baptist:

- wandering prophet;
- announced the coming of the 'Messiah';
- called on people to repent of all they had done wrong;
- offered Baptism as a sign of a change of heart and that people were ready for a new age of the Messiah;
- son of Elizabeth (cousin of Mary) and Zechariah;
- read about him in Luke (3:21-22), Mark (1:9-11), Matthew (3:13-17), John (1:29-34).

This Messiah, he said, was among them. He also said that he himself was unfit to undo the sandals of the Messiah.

Quick Fact File:

John the ____________________

Job: ____________________

Called the: ____________________

Proclamation: ____________________

Offered: ____________________

Asked People: ____________________

Son of: ____________________

Read about him in: ____________________

____

Explain:

Baptism ____________________

Prophet ____________________

Q1. When did Jesus start his public life?

Q2. What does 'his public life' mean?

Q3. Who baptised Jesus?

Q4. What did John the Baptist want people to do?

Q5. What did he offer people?

Q6. What did he announce?

Q7. Where did he live?

Q8. What did he say about the Messiah?

Q9. What does Messiah mean?

More Qs

A Explain why John was baptising people.

B Read what the Gospels say about John ...
- what did he wear?
- what did he eat?
- how many people listened to him?

C Why was he unfit to undo the sandals of the Messiah?

The Moment of Baptism

'You are my son in whom I am well pleased!'

Jesus' baptism took place in the River Jordan. At that moment, a dove, symbolising God's spirit, came to Jesus and a voice was heard saying, 'You are my son in whom I am well pleased.' All the symbols of baptism show the relationship between God, the Father and his son, Jesus.

For Jesus, the moment of Baptism was:

- knowing that God loved him and that he was God's son;
- the beginning of his Ministry, when he was called by God;
- a time to proclaim the new kingdom.

Through his Baptism he was:

- seen as a suffering servant;
- acknowledged as the Son of God – unique relationship;
- given the power of the Spirit;
- called to reveal God's love and power.

Think about some of the images mentioned in the Baptism account!

Draw the **River Jordan**

Draw the **Dove**

What did the voice say?

The Dove means ________,

representing ________.

Q

1. Where was Jesus baptised?
2. Who performed the baptism?
3. What did the voice from Heaven say?
4. What did the dove represent?
5. What was John the Baptist asking people to do?

List some of the things that Jesus realised at the Baptism moment

1. ____________________
2. ____________________
3. ____________________
4. ____________________
5. ____________________

More to do!

A. From the baptism moment, what did Jesus realise about his relationship with God, the Father?

B. How important was it for Jesus to be baptised?

C. Explain, using Matthew 3:15, why Jesus was baptised.

Time to Think and Pray

We Pray …

For ourselves, that we will truly know our special and sacred, relationship with God. **Amen.**

That we will hear the spirit and feel its power to help create God's Kingdom. **Amen.**

That we will hear and recognise God in the people and the world around us. **Amen.**

That we will be proclaimers of Jesus' message and witnesses to Gospel values. **Amen.**

That we will live our baptism vocation to love one another as Jesus did. **Amen.**

'Lead me,
O Lord, lead me
this day and
everyday in all
I do and say,
in all I live
and pray …
Lead me,
O Lord, lead me.'

'Today I bring myself to the water. I join my fellow people and present myself to the Baptiser. This is what I must do. All righteousness must be done. These people are mine, my flock, and I will lead them – they are mine. Give me strength, O Spirit. Let me hear my Father. O God, prepare me for my mission. Baptise me!'

Read from Scriptures:
Mark 1:9-11
Matthew 3:13-17

Jesus is Tempted

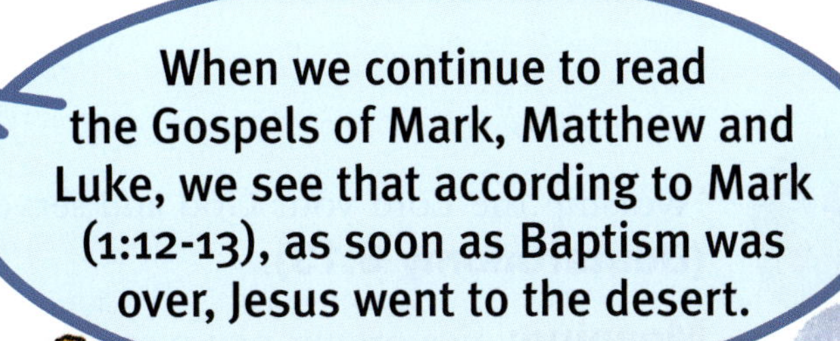

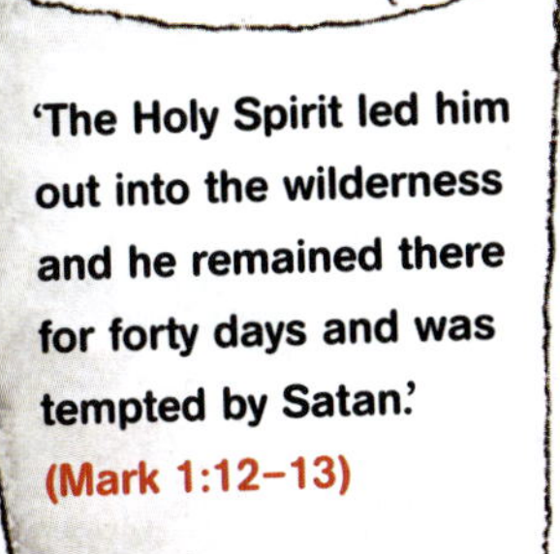

Now take a look at Matthew 4:1-11 and Luke 4:1-13. They tell us a bit more about this temptation story.

What do they tell us?

Have a look!

The accounts from the Gospels say that Satan tempted Jesus in three ways.

1. Satan suggested that Jesus turn stones into bread. By doing this, Jesus would have been using his power for himself.

2. Satan promised that if Jesus worshipped Satan, he would gain power and wealth from him.

3. Satan suggested that Jesus throw himself from the highest point of the Temple and have God catch him.

… to these three temptations Jesus had three responses!

'Man does not live on bread alone, but on every word that comes from the Mouth of God' **(Deuteronomy 8:3)**.

Meaning: although bread is really important for a person to survive, that person also needs God's help and words to exist!

2.

'Worship the Lord your God and serve only him' **(Deuteronomy 6:13)**.

Meaning: give proper praise and worship only to God. Jesus rejected the power and wealth because God's Kingdom would come through peace and love.

'Do not put the Lord your God to the test' **(Deuteronomy 6:16)**.

Meaning: Jesus realised that this was a very silly way to reveal God's love and power. Jesus would reveal God in different ways.

Why did all this happen?

Jesus spent forty days in the desert and didn't give in to temptation. In the Old Testament, the Jews also spent forty days in the desert. However, they did give in to temptation. Jesus was preparing himself for his mission to bring God's Kingdom of love and peace.

1. When did Jesus go to the desert?
2. How long did Jesus remain in the desert?
3. What happened to Jesus while in the desert?
4. Who, according to the Gospels, tempted Jesus?
5. How many ways was Jesus tempted in the desert?
6. Name the ways.
7. According to Jesus' response, 'Man does not live on _______ alone' (fill in the missing word).
8. In your copy, write out the meaning of Jesus' first response.

Fill in the blanks:

1. Worship the _______ your God and _______ only him.

2. Do _______ put the Lord _______ God to the _______.

3. Man does _______ live on bread _______ but on _______ that comes from the _______ of God.

For your copy!

1. Why, do you think, does man not live on bread alone?
2. What kind of things would tempt you in everyday life?
3. Why, do you think, did Satan want to tempt Jesus?
4. In what way did Jesus show his intelligence to Satan?
5. Jesus knew that he had a big task ahead of him and so prepared himself for it. In what way would you prepare for a task (for example, football game, exam)?
6. Do you agree that when preparing for a task you must be fit mentally as well as physically? Explain why.
7. Read the passage (Exodus 34:28) and see what the comparison with Moses is.

It begins ...

TO KNOW

Rabbi: Hebrew for 'My Master' – a teacher, especially of spirituality and Jewish law.
Disciple: Means pupil, usually of a religious teacher.

After his Baptism and Temptation, Jesus began his public ministry. This involved going around from place to place, preaching, teaching and working miracles. In Jesus' time, this wasn't uncommon – Rabbis did this, although most would have worked in synagogues and temples with not too much wandering. They would also have had some people follow them around – their pupils or disciples!

However, Jesus was very unique in what he had to say and do. He was different from the other Rabbis!

How?

- Jesus made reference to the Scriptures of the Old Testament, but fulfilled them and deepened them with his own interpretation.
- He preached with an authority that other Rabbis didn't have, by adding, 'But I say to you ...' **(Matthew 5:21-48)**.
- In his words and actions, Jesus was proclaiming the Coming of the Kingdom of God (through peace and love).
- This Coming of the Kingdom was connected to him – he personally would establish and embody it!
- He criticised the legalistic view of the Jewish laws (and so came into conflict with the authorities).
- He announced that he had come 'to complete the law and the Prophets' **(Matthew 5:17)**.
- He used dramatic 'Parables' and 'Miracles'.

For your copy!

1. List the qualities that a good Rabbi should have.
2. What does the word 'disciple' mean to you? Would you, as a student, be a kind of disciple? Give reasons why you would say yes and reasons to say no.

Put these words into sentences:

List four ways in which Jesus was different from other Rabbis.

Jesus' Disciples

TO KNOW

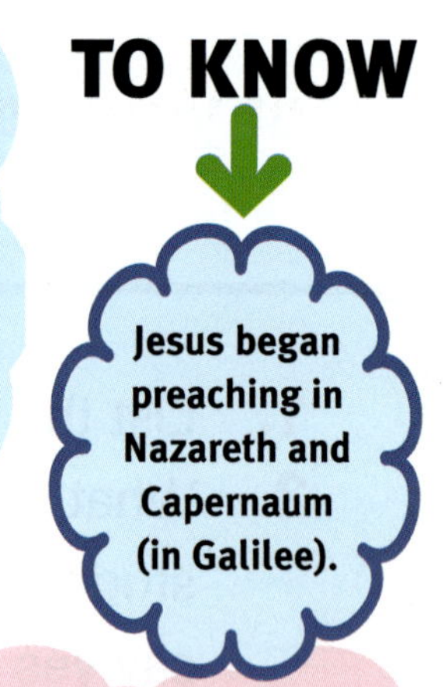

So, a Rabbi would have had a number of students with him. These students, or 'Disciples', would have learned all that the Rabbi taught, and then become Rabbis themselves and left their teacher.

The relationship between Jesus and his disciples was different because:

A They didn't choose him. Jesus 'called' his disciples.
(Mark 1:16-20 / Luke 5:1-11)

B They would never fully learn all that Jesus had to offer because there was always something new.
(Matthew 23:8-10)

C The disciples of Jesus did not only 'watch and learn' – they were called to share in the proclaiming of the Kingdom of God.
(Luke 9:1-6)

Calling a Disciple

For typical examples of Jesus calling disciples, take a look at:

Matthew 4:18-22: Jesus calls the disciples, and they drop everything and follow him!

Luke 5:1-11: Jesus preaches. The disciples explain their work. Jesus calls them, and they follow.

John 1:35-50: They meet Jesus and follow him. He calls them and they join him.

The Twelve Apostles

Jesus called these twelve men to be central to his mission on Earth.

Others may also have been his disciples.

Peter

James (Son of Zebedee)

John (James' brother)

Andrew

The word **'Apostle'** comes from Greek, meaning **'to send forth'**. Jesus called these men to go and spread the Good News of the Kingdom of God.

Philip

These twelve men were called the Apostles, and you can read their names in **Matthew 10:2-4, Mark 3:16-19, Luke 6:13-16**. Frequently, the Apostles are just called **'The twelve'**.

Bartholomew

Matthew

- The Apostles travelled with Jesus from place to place and were instructed in the truth that Jesus shared. Later, they continued Jesus' work, preaching, healing and forgiving.

Thomas

James (Son of Alphaeus)

Thaddeus

- According to Jewish history, there were twelve tribes that settled in the land of Israel, each having descended from one of the sons of Jacob, all of them starting a new life in the Promised Land.

They came from many backgrounds, and included **fishermen, a tax collector, a zealot** and **tradesmen**. Jesus saw in them great potential. Even though they didn't always understand him, or became afraid, they were strong when they needed to be!

Simon (the Zealot)

Judas Iscariot

- Now there were twelve Apostles, representing the new foundations for a new faith community, a New Israel. This new community would be **Christianity**.

1. Where did Jesus begin his preaching?
2. Where did the disciples gain all their knowledge?
3. What did disciples usually become after they had finished all their training from their Rabbi?
4. What was different about the way in which people became disciples of Jesus from the way in which people became disciples of other Rabbis?
5. Would Jesus' disciples become Rabbis themselves? Why?
6. The disciples of Jesus did more than 'watch and learn'. What else did they do?

Look up the chapters about Jesus calling disciples listed on the previous pages. Choose one and draw a cartoon strip.

Unscramble these words and say something about each one:

honj eetrp drawne
hppiil olowemhtarb
mesja tthewna masoht
mesja ddaeusth monsi dasjuriotisca

More to do!

1. Draw a map in your copy and mark on it where Jesus started his preaching.
2. Imagine you were a disciple. Describe how Jesus called you.
3. List the different backgrounds from which the Apostles came.
4. How, in your opinion, would Jesus call people today to be his disciples?
5. Why were twelve Apostles picked?

Disciple Wordsearch

L P N K T C Z R S S L M Y J Q I C L
R T A E Z X Y T L D U E O T Y B Z Z
Q A Z N Z D U E J A O H A F M B Z B
J V A Q Z D P T N A N Z P R U A B H
U F R N E S W R Q Q M K R D S R J M
D V E N O E E Y J N X E I O G I C W
A A T G L P G D O G Y X S Y H P S N
S S H V A T N D I S C I P L E S R W
J D E C C W I K H B D R Q O C A L R
S M F N H N H F U Z Q O R M E V B E
O U J M H H C O I A M D R L F I F K
I F E Z F T A L G S P A I B B R M P
J D F D K K E L N V H U T P E T E R
Z Z M U D G R O I N S E L T S O P A
X R J A E A P W L X O C R K H E H N
I X X U P A H B L A Z Z Z M A E A C
K I N G D O M T A K U T X E E D W Y
A Y S E B I R T C M G H A D X N R S

APOSTLE
CALLING
CAPERNAUM
DISCIPLES
FISHERMEN
FOLLOW
GOD
GOSPELS
ISRAEL
JAMES
JOHN
JUDAS
KINGDOM
LEARN
MATTHEW
NAZARETH
PETER
PREACHING
RABBI
STUDENTS
THADDEUS
TRIBES
TWELVE

TO KNOW

Parables = stories that have a special meaning. **Miracles** = actions brought about by God – by Divine intervention.

Proclaiming the Kingdom of God

What the Kingdom wasn't

- Jesus had a vision – a vision of the future, like the prophets of the Old Testament. Jesus' vision was the Kingdom of God.

- **His stories**, **the parables**, showed people his understanding of the Kingdom.

Many Jewish people at that time were totally fed-up with Roman rule. They were waiting patiently for their **Messiah** – the one sent by God to save them from the occupation. With this in mind, many expected that the Messiah would set up a new Jewish State, a new Jewish Kingdom. **Jesus had a different idea**.

- **His actions** – **the miracles** – were expressions that God was bringing about the Kingdom through Jesus. In teaching about the Kingdom of God, Jesus was certainly not trying to begin a new political reign over his people.
- He opposed any use of violence.
- He didn't have in mind a new nation – a geographical state.
- His Kingdom would have no boundaries and no borders.
- It wasn't just a plan for social reform either!

Over to You

1. What is a parable?
2. What is a miracle?
3. What was Jesus' vision of the future?
4. What two things helped to show Jesus' vision of the future?

To do

PARABLEMIRACLEVISIONFUTUREPROPHETINAUGURATINGMESSIAHOCCUPATIONPOLITICALGEOGRAPHICALBORDERSREIGN

Pick out the words in the circle. Make your own sentence with each of them in your copy.

A. What was Jesus' vision of the Kingdom?

B. What were the people of Israel expecting from the Messiah? Why?

C. In your own words, describe what type of Kingdom Jesus wanted to create.

What did JESUS mean?

TO KNOW → *Metanoia* = change of Heart.

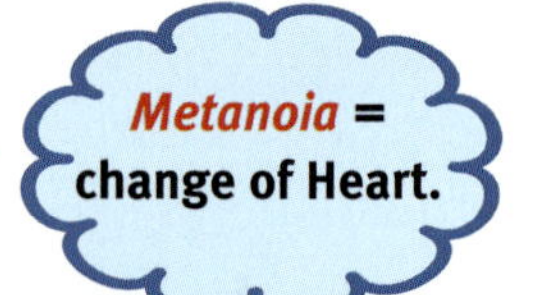

Jesus never gave us an exact image or phrase to describe the Kingdom. Instead, he used actions, stories and words to show us God's Kingdom. Put all these together and we have a good idea of the Kingdom of God brought about by Jesus!

To help us to understand better what Jesus meant by the Kingdom of God, we need to recognise the relationship that Jesus had with God the Father ...

Jesus spoke about God using the word

ABBA.

This was Aramaic for 'Daddy' (or Dada) **(Mark 14:36)**. It represented the affection and love between Jesus and his Father.

This love kept Jesus going and he gave this love to all he met. When people accept this love, they have a change of heart – '*metanoia*'. The Kingdom of God takes root in their hearts.

From this we can say that Jesus saw the Kingdom as the Rule of God's love over the very hearts of people, and then as a new social order and community based on people's unconditional love for one another – a time characterised by

PEACE, JOY, FREEDOM and LOVE.

... so we can say:

1. The Kingdom is a place where love, justice and peace reign!
2. People understand and accept with an openness and change of heart and act accordingly.
3. The Kingdom is in the here-and-now as a new society established by the coming of Jesus, his words and actions.

'The Words of the Kingdom'

To help us achieve a better understanding of the Kingdom, let's look at the words that both point to the Kingdom and show us its existence.

The Beatitudes

(Latin *Beati*, meaning 'Blessed')

The 'Our Father'

1. Why is it hard to explain the Kingdom?
2. How do we piece together what Jesus meant?
3. What helps us to understand what Jesus meant?
4. What does *Abba* mean?
5. Where can we read about that phrase?
6. How did Jesus see God, the Father?
7. What is needed for the Kingdom to take root in a person?
8. What did Jesus see the Kingdom as?

Read Mark 1:15: What is Jesus saying about himself and the Kingdom? Why does he say this

More to do!

- **A.** How has the Kingdom come?
- **B.** What are the characteristics of the Kingdom of God?
- **C.** How do love, justice and peace reign?
- **D.** What part do Christians play in this Reign of the Kingdom?
- **E.** How do people have an openness and change of heart to the Kingdom?
- **F.** How is the Kingdom in the here-and-now?
- **G.** What makes the Kingdom a reality in our lives?

The BEATITUDES

When we read St Matthew's Gospel, we come across the

Sermon on the Mount!

Part of the Sermon on the Mount in the **'Beatitudes'**. **(Matthew 5:3-12)**

This is an important part of the sermon that Jesus gave about the Kingdom.

'The Beatitudes are qualities or blessings of those who are members of the Kingdom of God!'

St Luke's Gospel has a shorter version, called 'The Sermon of the Plain' (Luke 6:20-23), and is a little different. Look it up to see and compare.

TO KNOW → **'Righteous' = good, just, upright, moral.**

1. **Poor in Spirit:** people who realise that they are weak, that they need God's strength and love in their lives.

2. **The Gentle:** people who show care and gentleness to everyone around them, creating God's Kingdom of peace and love. They are strong in showing God's Goodness.

3. **Mournful:** these are the people who have sinned and are sorry. They want God's love.

4. **Those who Hunger and Thirst for Righteousness:** these people long for God's Kingdom and do everything they can to bring it about.

5. **Merciful:** those who are merciful show God's love to others. They are forgiving and compassionate.

6. **Pure of Heart:** their hearts are pure, always focused on God and doing God's work.

7. **Peacemakers:** they bring God's peace to their situations and communities.

8. **Persecuted in the Cause of Righteousness:** they stand up against torture and mockery for God's Kingdom.

In your copy, list the **eight Beatitudes** and the rewards for each one.

Beatitude	Reward
1. ________	________
2. ________	________
3. ________	________
4. ________	________
5. ________	________
6. ________	________
7. ________	________
8. ________	________

Explain:
- Those who are 'Poor in Spirit'.
- Those who are 'Pure of Heart'.
- Those 'Persecuted in the Cause of Righteousness'.

Q

1. Where can we find the 'Sermon on the Mount'?
2. What is contained in the Sermon?
3. What are the Beatitudes? How many are there?
4. What does 'Beatitude' mean?
5. What will happen to those who are Merciful?

What do the Beatitudes tell us about the Kingdom of God?

RESEARCH
JOURNAL IDEA

Think of the world around you. Can you name a person, or people, or an organisation that might identify with each Beatitude? Make a list and detail your findings. Can you identify yourself with any of those?

... The Beatitudes of Jesus, contained in the Gospels of St Matthew and St Luke, give us four lessons to learn and to live by ...

The Kingdom is in the here-and-now!

The Beatitudes not only point to the future but also show us that the Kingdom exists in the here-and-now, brought about by Jesus.

The Kingdom will come!

The Beatitudes indicate to us that the future Kingdom will come. This is when God's reign over everyone's hearts is complete.

To be part of the Kingdom is to love!

The Beatitudes show us a life of loving service to others. Christians are called to hunger and thirst for righteousness, to be merciful and just, to suffer persecution for others and to care for the poor!

Beatitudes create the 'Reign of God'!

If believers live the Beatitudes, it is because they know and have faith that God's reign of love will triumph over evil in the world. Jesus is the role model as one who lived the Beatitudes totally.

IN YOUR COPY

True / False?

- The completion of the Kingdom is far away. **T / F**
- The future Kingdom is when God's reign over people's hearts is complete. **T / F**
- The Kingdom is in the here-and-now. **T / F**
- The Kingdom is here, brought about by Jesus. **T / F**
- To be part of the Kingdom is to hate. **T / F**
- We are not to live a life of Beatitude attitudes. **T / F**
- Christians are called to ignore Righteousness. **T / F**
- If Christians live the Beatitudes, God's Kingdom will come. **T / F**

1. What do the Beatitudes point to?
2. What is the future Kingdom about?
3. What do the Beatitudes demand of people?
4. What are Christians called to do?
5. Who is the role model for Christians, and why?

Design a poster saying:

What the Beatitudes are!

How we can live them!

What the world will be like when people do!

The 'Our Father'

The **'Our Father'** is also called the **'Lord's Prayer'** (because Our Lord, Jesus, gave it to us!)

'Our Father who art in Heaven, Hallowed be thy name. Thy Kingdom come, thy will be done on Earth as it is in Heaven. Give us this day our daily bread and forgive us our trespasses, as we forgive those who trespass against us, and lead us not into temptation, but deliver us from Evil, Amen.'

The prayer can be read in the Gospels of **St Matthew (6:9-13)** and **St Luke (11:2-4)**. It is the only complete prayer attributed to Jesus himself.

Praying like pagans.

Praying like followers of Jesus.

St Matthew tells us that Jesus is instructing his listeners how not to pray like pagans! St Luke's version has Jesus responding to a question from the disciples on how to pray like him!

'Kingdom of God Images'!

Contained in the 'Our Father', e.g.

'Hallowed be Thy Name' – shows the power and importance of God's name. All people are to put God's name above all others!

'Thy Kingdom Come' – asks for God's love to come into people's hearts and be shown in the world. Through Jesus' words, actions, life, death and resurrection, it becomes a reality on Earth!

'Give Us This Day' – calls on God to sustain us physically but also spiritually.

'Daily Bread' – calls on God to take care of our needs, as well as being present to us in the Eucharist, the Bread of Life.

'Forgiveness' – God forgives us and accepts us back. In God's Kingdom we must show the same forgiveness.

In your own words, explain each **Kingdom Image:**

'Hallowed Be Thy Name' • **'Thy Kingdom Come'**
'Give us This Day' • **'Daily Bread'** • **'Forgiveness'**

Q

1. What is the other name for the 'Our Father'?
2. Why is it called that?
3. Where can we read it in the Gospels?
4. What is the difference between the two accounts?
5. What is the full prayer about?

A What is unique about the 'Our Father'?

B What image does it present of God, the Father?

C What evil do you think we need to be delivered from?

D What temptations might we come across?

E What are 'trespasses'?

Draw a picture that goes with and explains **'The Lord's Prayer'**

‘Through our living of the Beatitudes and praying the ‘Our Father’, the Kingdom of God will come and is present in the here-and-now!’

TO DO IN YOUR COPY

Parables and Miracles

Now that we have looked at the meaning of the Kingdom of God in the Beatitudes and the 'Our Father', our next investigation takes us to the **parables** and the **miracles** of Jesus.

The **parables** are the stories of Jesus, showing the Kingdom of God at work in everyday situations!

The **miracles** are the actions of Jesus, letting us see that the Kingdom of God has arrived!

As you will see ...

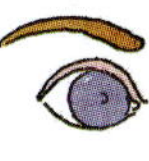
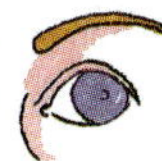

Parable Themes

- Stories of the way the Kingdom of God will be.
- Advice on how we can enter the Kingdom.
- Lessons on how we should treat others in the Kingdom of God.
- Sayings on what will happen when the Kingdom arrives.

Miracle Images

- Glimpses of the Kingdom of God.
- Signs of God's love for all.
- Responses to people's faith.
- Proofs of God's power, through Jesus, over the world and over evil.

Jesus, the 'Preacher'

Think for a few moments about something that has happened to you over the past few days. If it's a good story, you'll probably want to tell someone. If it's funny, you'll want to make people laugh. If it's important, you'll want to share it with your friends and people at home, and you'll want them to listen.

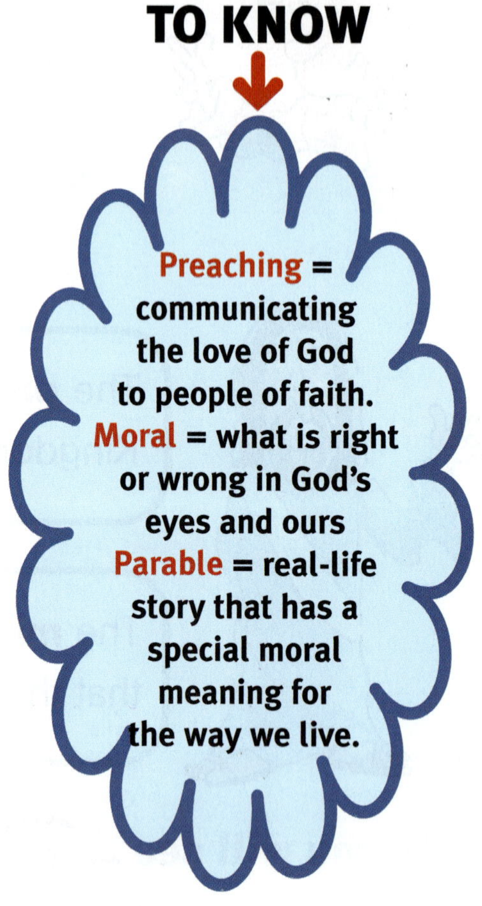

When he walked the roads of Palestine 2,000 years ago, Jesus loved to be listened to. That is one reason why he told so many stories. When he was telling the stories, he was **preaching**. The stories he told have a special name – they are called **parables**. Contained in them are examples of how to live in God's Kingdom!

The parables Jesus told had a **'moral'** meaning. Being moral means: knowing and doing what is right for the Kingdom of God. During his three years **preaching** in Palestine, Jesus told many **parables**.

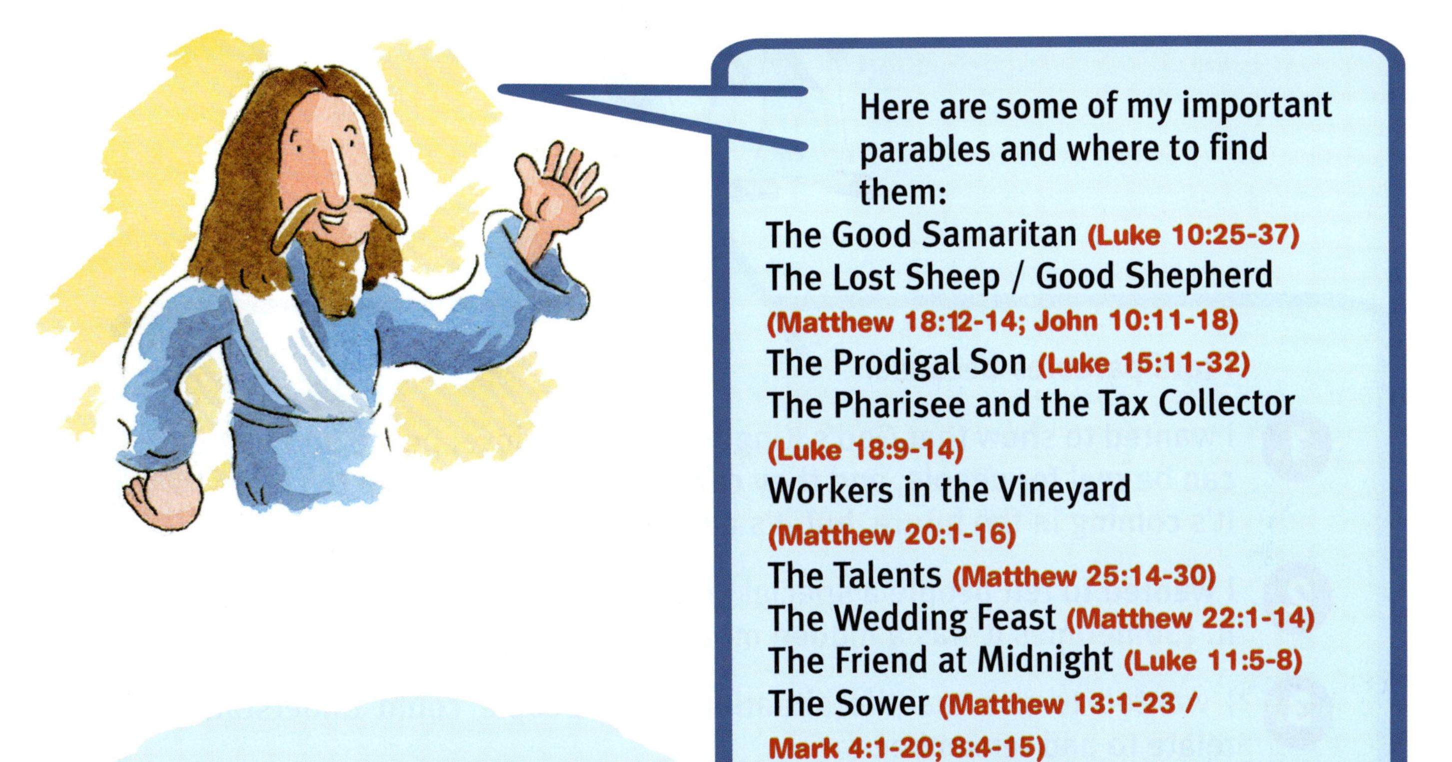

Now a quick cloze test:

Jesus went around Palestine p_______. Preaching means c_______ God's love to people.

J_______ liked to tell s_______ because he liked to be l_______ to. The stories Jesus told were called p_______. During his t_______ years p_______ he told many p_______. Three important ones are the G_______ S_______, the P_______ S_______ and the P_______ and the T_______ C_______.

Here are some other reasons why Jesus told **parables**:

I told parables because:

1. I wanted to show that God's Kingdom of truth, love, peace and justice can be real for people, and they can be part of it and help to create it. It's coming in the future, but it's also here, embodied in me.
2. I wanted to tell people a special story that had a **'moral'** message in it. (Sometimes it was a hidden meaning!)
3. I wanted to use real-life situations that people could understand, relate to and remember.
4. I wanted to show **'God's love'** / **'God's values'** at work through ordinary people and ordinary situations.

Time to find:

PREACHER
PARABLE
MORAL
LISTEN
STORIES
PALESTINE
KINGDOM
LOVE
TALENT

Jesus Wordsearch

B	E	F	G	N	E	T	S	I	L	M	P
S	T	O	R	I	E	S	J	L	A	A	U
Q	R	E	H	C	A	E	R	P	R	V	T
K	I	N	G	D	O	M	T	A	O	S	A
T	A	F	W	H	O	S	B	L	M	P	L
C	U	Y	X	K	R	L	V	O	R	U	E
D	G	V	M	P	E	W	T	V	L	O	N
P	A	L	E	S	T	I	N	E	S	E	T

From Jesus' life and the **Beatitudes** we know that in God's Kingdom there is no fighting, jealousy, envy, or killing. God's Justice means that everybody is equal in God's eyes, no matter what. And God's Love is a love that demands nothing back **(unconditional love)** and is given to everybody to accept and to return, and to give to the people we know around us, to the world and nature.

Let's ask ourselves:

Q1. What does God's Justice mean?

Q2. What is a parable?

Q3. Name three famous parables.

Q4. How can we create peace in our own area?

Q5. Where do we see injustice happening?

Q6. How can people be more 'loving to each other'?

Jesus' Parables

He preached his parables in
- Palestine
- Galilee
- Jerusalem
- Jericho

A story with a special moral meaning!

COPY AND COLOUR

They are stories about God's Kingdom

'The Good Samaritan'

'The Sower'

Here are three of Jesus' most famous parables and what they mean for us today:

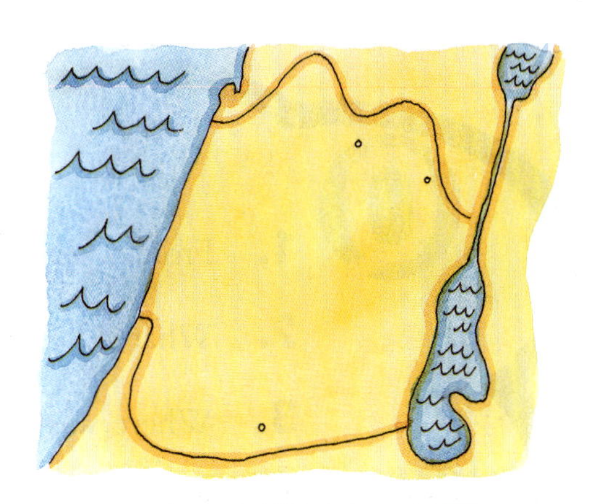

'The Good Samaritan'

(Taken from Luke 10:25-37)

TO KNOW

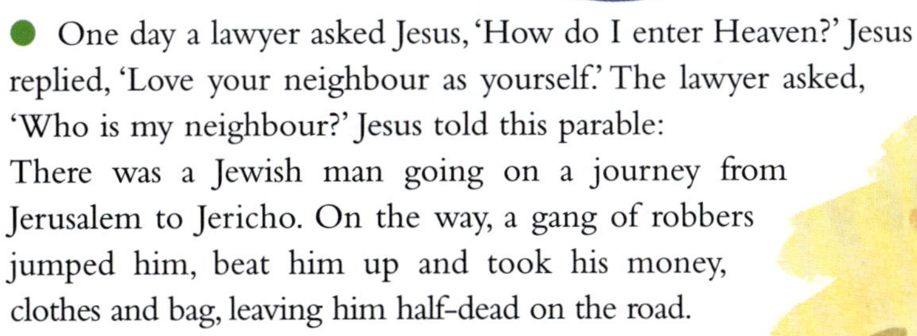

- One day a lawyer asked Jesus, 'How do I enter Heaven?' Jesus replied, 'Love your neighbour as yourself.' The lawyer asked, 'Who is my neighbour?' Jesus told this parable: There was a Jewish man going on a journey from Jerusalem to Jericho. On the way, a gang of robbers jumped him, beat him up and took his money, clothes and bag, leaving him half-dead on the road.
- About an hour later a Jewish priest from the Temple was walking along the road and saw the injured man. But he walked by, doing nothing to help him. A Levite walked along the road and saw the victim. But he also continued walking on, and did nothing.
- A little bit later a man from Samaria (a Samaritan) was walking along the same road. He saw the man and immediately felt sorry for him and wanted to help him. He cleaned his wounds and bandaged them. Then he put the man on his donkey and they made their way to the nearest guesthouse, where he took care of the injured Jew. The next day the Samaritan had to go, but he gave two silver pieces to the landlady and told her that whatever extra she spent looking after the man, he would repay when he returned.
- Jesus finished his parable and asked this question: 'Which of the three men was a neighbour to the beaten man?' The lawyer replied, 'The one who felt sorry for him and helped him.' Jesus said, 'Correct. Go then and in your life do what the Samaritan did.'

To Remember

Priests and Levites:
Levites – servants of God and the Temple. **Priests** – teachers of the law and givers of sacrifices. Seen as the holiest people and closest to God.

Q

1. From which Gospel is 'The Good Samaritan' taken?
2. What is a Samaritan?
3. Where was the Jewish man travelling to?
4. Which three people passed the injured man?
5. What did the Good Samaritan do?
6. What did Jesus say to the lawyer at the end of the parable?
7. What is a priest and what is a Levite?
8. Retell this parable using people and a situation for today.
9. Who would be the Good Samaritan today, and who would pass by?

Meaning for us today:

Jesus' listeners would have been really surprised at this story because it was the person most unlikely to help who helped. The moral meaning is that we must look at ourselves and see who we can be a **'neighbour'** to. Because people are Christians, they are called to be **'neighbours'** to all people in need, in trouble, or in bad situations – no matter who they are. The Samaritan reached out to a person who would normally fight with him: the Jewish man. This parable is a story calling us to be charitable and to take unconditional risks for others. It also shows us that sometimes people who we think are close to God may not be capable of love as shown by the Samaritan. Showing this love is helping to create **'The Kingdom of God'**.

Further Activities

1. Find the words in this word circle:

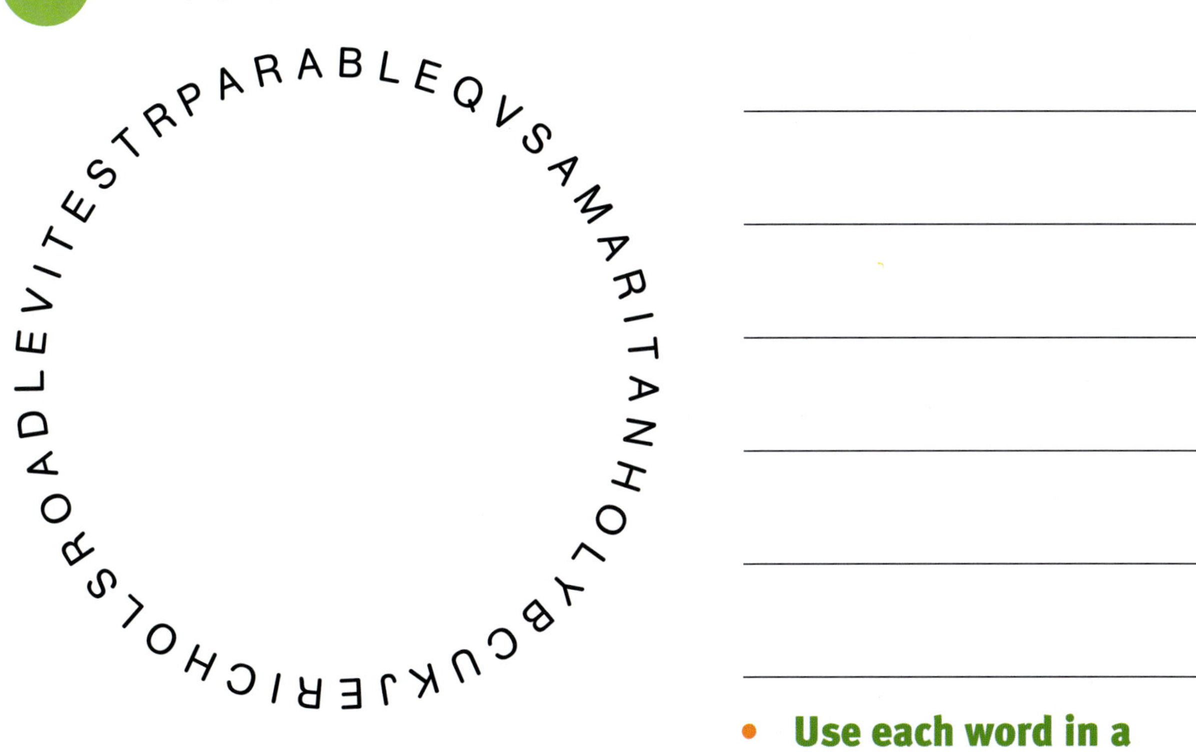

- **Use each word in a sentence in your copy.**

2. Put these sentences in the correct order:

- Later a priest and a Levite came along.
- Jesus asked, 'Which one was a neighbour to the man?'
- They passed him by.
- Jesus began the Good Samaritan parable.
- A Samaritan came and helped the injured man.
- A lawyer asked Jesus a question: 'Who is my neighbour?'
- He took him to a guesthouse and paid for his treatment and future needs.
- A man was walking from Jerusalem to Jericho and was mugged and badly beaten.
- The lawyer answered, 'The Good Samaritan.'

'The Prodigal Son'

(Taken from Luke 15:11-32)

TO KNOW

Prodigal means: spends a lot of money wastefully.

TO KNOW

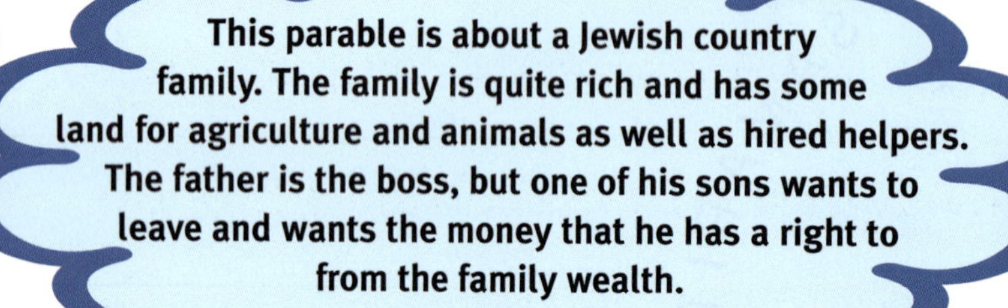

This parable is about a Jewish country family. The family is quite rich and has some land for agriculture and animals as well as hired helpers. The father is the boss, but one of his sons wants to leave and wants the money that he has a right to from the family wealth.

- Jesus said: There was a man who had two sons. One day the youngest asked his father if he could have his share of the land and estate in cash because he wanted to go away and do something different with his life. So his father gave him what he asked and the son left with his money and belongings. He went off to a distant land. While there, he wasted all his money shopping and spent it on gambling. With no money, he had to work. At the same time, a famine happened in the land. He eventually got a job on a pig farm, but he was so hungry now that he would have gladly eaten the scraps the pigs were getting.

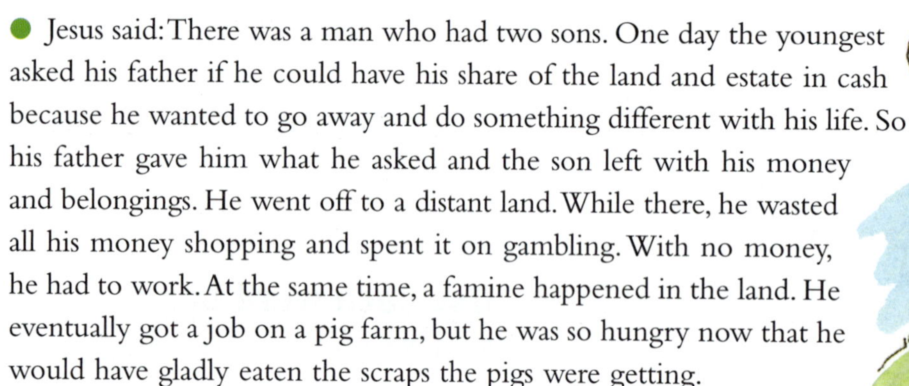

- Finally, he came to his senses and thought to himself: 'How many of my father's hired helpers have loads to eat, and here I am starving and with nothing. I've really made a big mistake.' He decided that he would go back to his father and say that he was very wrong and that he had treated his father and God with disrespect and had sinned. So he got up and started for home.
- Even when he was still a long way off, his father saw him and was delighted and deeply moved – so much so that he ran to meet him and threw his arms around him with great joy. His son said, 'Father, I have been disrespectful to you and to God. I have sinned and made a mess of things. I actually don't deserve to be called your son!' But the father turned to his hired helpers and said, 'Quick – get the best and most expensive clothes we have and put them on him and put a gold ring on his finger. Get the fatted calf and cook it. We will celebrate and have a party because this son of mine was dead and has come back to life. He was lost and is now found.'

Meaning for us today:

This **parable** has a very important message in it. First, we must look at the father – who is he? Basically, Jesus was saying that this is God the Father. The youngest son represents all of us – **humankind**. We think that we want freedom, and that God takes this away. In their search for liberation **(freedom)**, humans go away from God. While away, they lose everything and end up in slavery. Suddenly, they realise that life is so much better with the love, guidance and protection of God the Father. So, they turn back to God, expecting to be punished, but the Christian God is a loving God and accepts humankind back, with no judgment at all. Humankind was lost and is found, was dead and is now alive. Without God, we end up in slavery – slavery to money, famine, war, greed and all things that make us selfish, greedy, unloving and hating. Accept this love and the Kingdom is present.

1. From which Gospel and verses is this parable taken?
2. What did the youngest son want to do?
3. What happened to the youngest son when he went away?
4. How did the father react when the son returned? What happened?

Use your artistic skills!

Turn 'The Prodigal Son' parable into a cartoon strip, using the twelve boxes below.

1.	2.	3.	4.
5.	6.	7.	8.
9.	10.	11.	12.

A. What does the parable tell us about God the Father?
B. Who do you think is represented by the son?
C. Who might the brother be?
D. Tell this parable using modern-day people and images. Write your version in your copy!

Our last parable is the parable of:

'The Sower'

(Taken from Matthew 13:3-8; 18-23)

TO KNOW

Many of Jesus' listeners, as well as being fishermen, were men and women who farmed and worked on the land around Palestine, and earned a living from this. This parable is one to which they would have related very well.

Sow = to plant seeds for crops.

A farmer who worked on the land went out to his field one day to **sow** some seeds so that he could grow crops to eat and to sell. But as the seeds fell:

A. Some landed on the path and the birds flew down and ate them.

B. Some landed on rocks and rocky ground, but there was little soil, and they grew too fast, so the sun dried them up and they died.

C. Some landed on the thistles and thorn bushes. The seeds were choked and couldn't grow.

D. Some landed on very good soil, took deep root and grew an excellent crop.

Jesus continued to explain what this parable meant for his listeners and for us today.

The seeds that the sower is sowing are God's message revealed in Jesus Christ. The ground represents the listeners – it **represents** us.

A. So, the **PATH** represents the person who hears the message of Jesus, but doesn't take it to heart and is easily distracted from it.

B. The **ROCKY GROUND** is those who receive the message with great joy and enthusiasm, but when living the message gets hard, they give up and go back to their earlier lifestyles.

C. The **THORN BUSHES** represent those who hear the Word but are too busy with life and money to do anything about it.

D. The **GOOD SOIL** represents those people who hear the message, listen to it, understand it and think about it. They take it to their hearts and live a life according to Gospel values and the example of Christ.

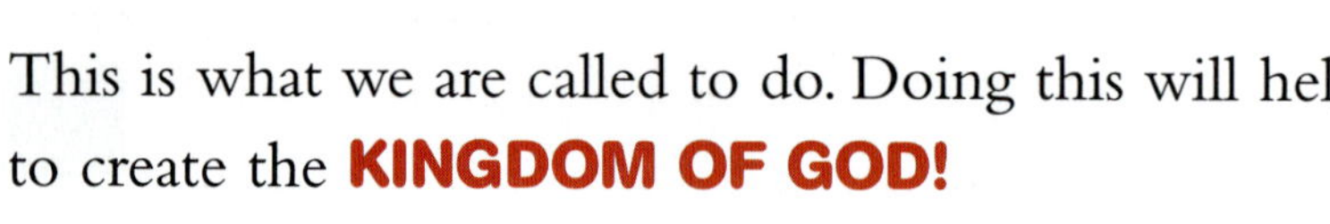

This is what we are called to do. Doing this will help to create the **KINGDOM OF GOD!**

Complete this CLOZE test:

The p_______ of the S_______ is taken from M_______ Gospel. It's about a s_______ who went out to s_______ his land. As he was sowing the s_______, some fell on the p_______. Other seeds fell on r_______ g_______. Other seeds fell on th_______ b_______, and some fell on good s_______. In this parable, the s_______ are God's m_______ and the g_______ is the l_______.

QUICK QUESTIONS

1. What does 'to sow' mean?
2. What type of ground did the seed fall on?
3. What did rocky ground represent?
4. What did the good soil represent?
5. What happened when the seed fell onto good soil?

Explain each of the parable images:

Path = _______________________________

Rocky Ground = _______________________________

Thorn Bushes = _______________________________

Good Soil = _______________________________

Q

1. Explain the overall meaning of this parable.
2. How does it relate to people today?
3. Who might fit into each image? Explain.
4. Where do you fit in?

FINAL THOUGHT

The parables were told to let us know how important it is to live our lives a certain way. This is the way Christ lived and wants us to live. The Gospel values contained in the parables will help us to create a society in which we can love and respect each other, our community and our world. It will create the **Kingdom of God!**

COPY AND COLOUR
The Parables Jesus told:
The Sower!
How We Accept God's Message
Rocky soil
Thorny soil
Birds eat it
Good soil
The Prodigal Son!
God accepts all people back
The Good Samaritan!
Showing God's Love
BAAH!
God will take care of everyone
The Lost Sheep!
The Lost Coin!
I've found it!

Time to Think and Pray

Opening Prayer:

We pray today that the message of Jesus, shown to us in his parables, will touch our hearts. We ask that we will understand the words of Jesus and live them in our daily lives for the good of ourselves and all people.

Gospel reading: Matthew 13:11-13

Prayers for the class group:

Let us pray for all people who hear God's word, that they may make it a reality for themselves and others.

Lord, hear our prayer

Let us pray that we may always be open to hearing God's word and to seeing it at work in the world and people around us.

Lord, hear our prayer

We pray that each one of us in our dealings with our family, friends and all the community may be the example of Christ's message.

Lord, hear our prayer

Music / Hymn Reflection: 'Servant Song'
'Thy word'
'Your words are spirit and life' (B. Farrell)

Let us pray: Lord, may we never fail to know that the way to live good and honest lives is through the message of the Gospels given to us by your Son, Jesus Christ. Amen.

To do in your copy!

'Jesus the Miracle-Doer'

TO KNOW

Messiah = Saviour, Chosen one, Christ.
Miracle = a marvellous event that is beyond nature – supernatural.
'Miracle' is made up of two words:
Mirari = to wonder
Miraculum = a marvel.

- Performing **miracles** was very much part of Jesus' work and **ministry!** Through them, he revealed the Kingdom of God.
- A miracle was a wondrous action that seemed unnatural.

Miracles are very important when looking at Jesus' life and message of the Kingdom. So let's investigate them!

– Why did Jesus perform miracles? There are several reasons

Miracles were ...

the Messiah!

- Signs to show that Jesus was the **Messiah** (as prophesied in the Old Testament).
- Signs of the **Kingdom of God** (glimpses of God's world).
- Signs of the **love of God for all people.**
- Signs of the **power of God over creation and the world.**

- Signs of the **future world that Jesus preaches** (the Kingdom of God).
- Signs that are **responding to the religious faith of his listeners and followers.**

TO KNOW

The **miracles** Jesus worked can be broken into four broad areas.

1. Raising to Life!

e.g. raising the widow's son ... Luke 7:11-17

2. Miracles of Nature!

e.g. calming the storm ... Matthew 8:23-27

3. Miracles of Healing!

e.g. healing the paralysed man ... Mark 2:1-12

4. Exorcism!

e.g. healing the demon-possessed man ... Mark 5:1-20

Raising to Life

Raising the widow's son ... (Luke 7:11-17)

Jesus went to a town called Naim. Many of his disciples went with him – a great number of people. As he reached the gate of the town, a dead man was being carried out. He was the only son of a widow. She was there together with a crowd of townspeople. On seeing her, Jesus had pity.

He said, 'Do not cry.' Then he came up and touched the stretcher, and the men who carried it stopped. Jesus then said, 'Young man, awake, I tell you.' And the dead man got up and began to speak, and Jesus returned him to his mother. All the crowd praised God and said, 'A great prophet has appeared among us; God has visited his people and the good news has spread.'

What does this Miracle tell us?

Let's See!

- Only Jesus has power over **Death!**
- It shows that Jesus is the giver of new life and will **rise** to eternal life himself with the Father forever!
- The woman is **suffering** – Jesus eases the suffering!
- Jesus understands the suffering that **people go through!** (The people see Jesus as a great prophet.)

1. What type of miracle is this?
2. What town did Jesus go to?
3. What happened when he reached the gate?
4. What did Jesus say to the woman?
5. What did he say to the dead man?
6. What did the crowd say?

Fill in the blanks:

No one but _______ has _______ over _______. It shows that _______ himself will _______ from the _______ through _______. The woman is _______. _______ eases the suffering. Jesus _______ the suffering that _______ go through.

More to do!

A. Why did the people think God had visited his people?

B. What future event does this miracle point to?

C. Jesus sees the woman's suffering. What does that tell us about Jesus?

D. Why was Jesus seen as a great prophet?

Looking closer at some miracles ...

Miracle of Nature

Calming the storm ... (adapted, Matthew 8:23-27)

Jesus got into a fishing boat one day, and his disciples followed him. Without warning, a heavy storm blew up. Jesus was asleep. The disciples woke him.

'Lord, save us! We are lost!' they said. Jesus answered, 'Why are you so afraid, you of little faith?' Then he stood up and ordered the wind and the sea; and it became completely calm. All the people were astonished. They said, 'What kind of man is he? Even the winds and the sea obey him.'

What does this Miracle tell us?

- The sea, in those days, could have represented badness, chaos and evil (eastern understanding).
- Jesus calming it could show his **Power** over **Evil!**
- Jesus sleeping in the back during the storm shows how confident he was of **God's help!**
- The disciples ask **questions**. They still don't fully **understand** who Jesus is!
- Calming the storm points to Jesus' true identity as the **Son of God!**

1. In this miracle story, why were the disciples afraid?
2. What did they say to Jesus?
3. What did Jesus say to them?
4. What did Jesus do?
5. What type of miracle is this?

To do

Draw a cartoon strip telling the story of this miracle!

Think!

Explain the meaning of this Miracle in your own words!

More Qs

1. What does the sea represent?
2. What power did Jesus show?
3. What does the fact that Jesus is asleep mean?
4. Overall, what does the miracle say about Jesus?

Miracle of Healing

Healing the paralysed man ... (Mark 2:1-12)

Jesus returned to Capernaum. As the news spread that he was there, many people came to see him – so many that there was no room outside the door. While Jesus was preaching the Word to them, some people brought a paralysed man to him. The men carrying him decided to open the roof above the room and lower him down to the ground on his mat. When Jesus saw the faith of the people, he said to the paralysed man, 'My son, your sins are forgiven!' He then said, 'Stand up, take your mat and go home!' The man stood up, took his mat and went home. All the crowds were astonished and praised God.

What does this Miracle tell us?

Well:

- It shows that Jesus is powerful in **word** and **deed!**
- It's made clear that he can **FORGIVE SINS!** (The authorities had a problem with this.)
- Jesus preached his **word** wherever he went, and had many **listeners!**
- The **FAITH** of the listeners is important to Jesus' words and deeds.
- This miracle points to Jesus' true identity as **Son of God!**

Let's Work!

To Do **Draw a cartoon strip detailing the events of the miracle!**

Think!

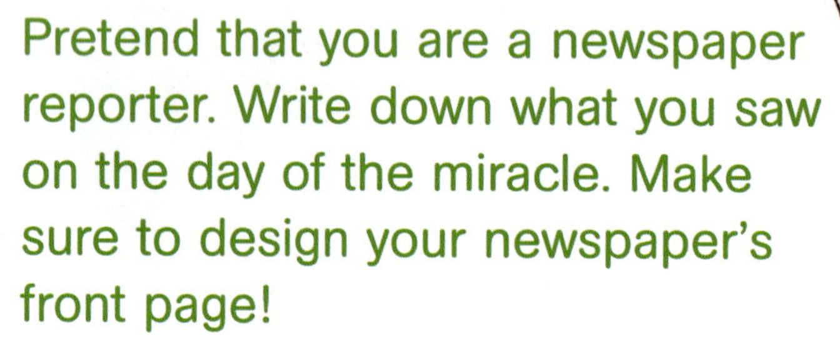

Pretend that you are a newspaper reporter. Write down what you saw on the day of the miracle. Make sure to design your newspaper's front page!

1. What happened while Jesus was preaching?
2. How did the people get the paralysed man to Jesus?
3. What was Jesus impressed by?
4. What did he say to the paralysed man?
5. What did the paralysed man do?

Explain in your own words what this miracle meant.

What does it tell us about the people's faith?

Exorcism

Healing the demon-possessed man ... (Mark 5:1-20)

Jesus and his disciples arrived at the other side of the lake called Gerasenes. As soon as he walked on the land, Jesus was confronted by a man possessed with evil spirits. This man had come down from the tombs on the mountain. He had often been tied up, but had broken free and nobody could control him. He was constantly screaming and beating himself with stones. He cried at Jesus' feet, 'What do you want with me, Jesus, Son of the most high God? Do not torment me!' Jesus commanded: 'Come out of the man, evil spirits. What is your name?'

The man replied, 'Legion is my name for we are many!' There were some pigs nearby and the spirits said to Jesus: 'Send us to the pigs!' So Jesus let them go, and into the pigs they went. When this happened, the pigs immediately ran and drowned themselves in the lake. People who had heard the news came to see the healed man. They were afraid and asked Jesus to go. Before he left, Jesus said to the man, 'Go home to your people and tell them how much the Lord has done for you and how he has had mercy on you.' So, the man went home and told his people, and they were astonished.

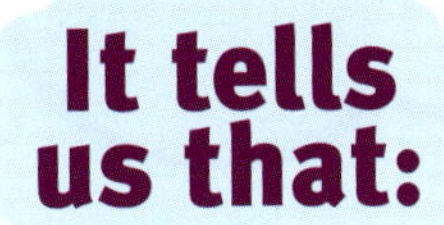

- This miracle points to Jesus' true identity as **Son of God.**
- He has power over **Evil** and **Satan!**
- The demon recognised Jesus' true identity!
- The **Kingdom of God** is very close (and yet also here)!
- Tombs were seen as places for demons.
- The pigs rush to the lake – again, the lake is seen here as a place of evil, according to tradition.

Some more to do

Imagine

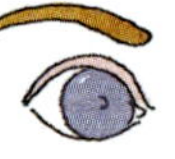
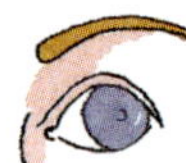

Imagine that you are a disciple of Jesus present at this miracle. Describe in your own words what you see!

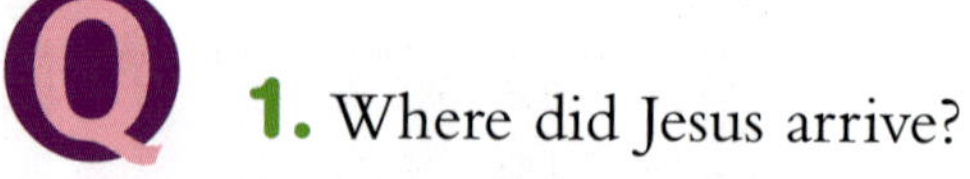

1. Where did Jesus arrive?
2. Who confronted Jesus?
3. Where did he come from?
4. What did he cry out?
5. What did Jesus command?
6. Where did Jesus send the spirits?
7. What happened to the pigs?
8. What did Jesus say to the cured man?

What does this miracle tell us about:

- Jesus?
- His power?
- The Demon?
- The Kingdom?

More Qs

A. Name the four types of miracle mentioned.

B. In what ways are they different?

C. What do they tell us about Jesus?

D. What would people think when they saw these miracles?

E. What do they tell us about the Kingdom of God?

RESEARCH

JOURNAL IDEA

Find out about some modern-day miracles. Where are they? When did they happen? Who was involved? Who are they attributed to? What do they say about God's Kingdom?

... In the Old Testament, miracles always meant something! God spoke and God acted:

'What he does is identical to what he says.'

At the Exodus **(Book of Genesis)**, **Moses worked wonders**

... not for effect, but to give a message.

The **Prophets** in the Old Testament used actions **to make a point!**

These actions showed God at work in the history of His people.

So, with Jesus the miracles are not just for effect, or to amaze people. **The Miracles:**

- are parables in action;
- are part of Jesus' message;
- are an extension of His words;
- show God's new society in action;
- present the challenge of the Kingdom of God;
- fulfil Old Testament prophecies.

To Do

Explain!

A. How are the Miracles 'Parables in Action'?

B. How do they show God's new society?

C. How do they fulfil Old Testament prophecies?

D. What is the challenge that the Miracles present?

Fill in the blanks:

In the _______ _______, miracles always meant something! God _______ and God _______. 'What he does is _______ to what he says.' At the _______ (Book of _______), Moses worked _______, not for _______ but to give a message. The _______ in the Old Testament used actions to _______ _______ _______! These actions showed _______ at work in the history of His _______. So, with Jesus the miracles are:

- ________________________________
- ________________________________
- ________________________________
- ________________________________
- ________________________________
- ________________________________

More Miracles

There are many more miracles. Here is a quick list from the Gospels:

Miracle	Matthew	Mark	Luke	John
Peter's mother-in-law healed	8:14-15	1:29-31	4:38-39	
Turning water to wine				2:1-11
Catching the fish			5:1-11	
Centurion's servant healed	8:5-13		7:1-10	
Calming the storm	8:22-37	4:35-41	8:22-25	
Exorcising a demon	8:22-34	5:1-20	8:26-39	
Healing paralysed man	9:1-8	2:1-12	5:17-26	
Jairus' daughter healed	9:18-26	5:21-43	8:40-56	
Widow's son raised	7:11-17			
Feeding the 5,000	14:13-21	6:30-44	9:10-17	6:1-14
Walking on water	14:22-23	6:45-52		
Feeding the 4,000	15:32-39	8:1-10		
Healing blind man				9:1-12
Epileptic boy healed	17:14-21	9:14-29	9:37-43	
Healing ten lepers			17:11-19	
Raising Lazarus				11:1-44
Bartimaeus healed	20:29-34	10:46-52	18:35-43	
Healing deaf man		7:31-37		
Man and withered hand	12:9-14	3:1-6	6:6-11	

To Do

Look up some miracles that interest you and try to figure out what they mean for us today!

Miracles Wordsearch

N J D G K M S B Q B Q C N S U
N M E J U D H L F 0 K A U F B
G L I M P S E S F A I T H O M
K S T R I M E M L R E G E L S
E J T G A R R I O L 0 0 A L I
A V N B U C S 0 C N R D L 0 C
Y S I T U T U A T A S R I W R
S R U L E O R L I S E W N E 0
K F T N M I D S U O M C G R X
J I E S M W I Q D M X 0 T S E
E R N M I N C I T Y L A R A P
S A G G G N M E S S I A H 0 H
U R E B D P I E F I L W E N T
S I R E W 0 P M N A T U R E A
A M L I F E M Q M D F T E K E
V Y V X X I F N I K V G S Y D

DEATH
DOUBTS
FOLLOWERS
GOD
KINGDOM
MESSIAH
MIRACULUM

NEW LIFE
RAISING
DEMONS
EVIL
FUTURE
HEALING
LIFE

MINISTRY
MIRARI
PARALYTIC
SIGNS
DOER
EXORCISM
GLIMPSES

FAITH
JESUS
LISTENERS
MIRACLE
NATURE
POWER
STORM

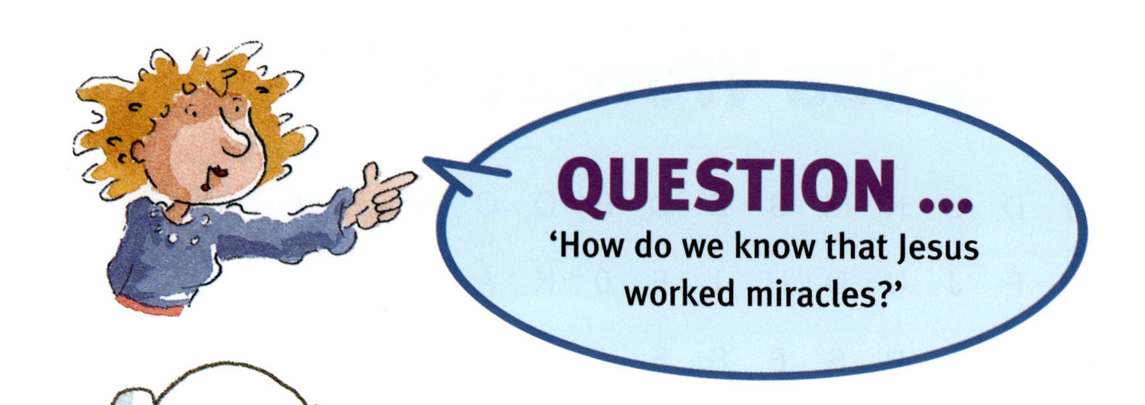

Looking into the **PAST** and at ancient history, we find **evidence** that supports the belief **that Jesus did perform miracles!**

The evidence can be found in ...

- **The Gospels!**
- **Jewish history!**
- **Early Christian preaching!**

We already know that the Gospels contain many **miracle** stories where people's lives were **changed** and **God's Kingdom** was revealed.

Let's look at

'Jewish history'

Flavius Josephus was an important Jewish historian who lived around A.D. 37–100. Josephus had great skill in **Greek** and **Hebrew** and could write and speak both languages. He was eventually appointed Governor of Galilee, because he was friendly with the Romans. He retired and lived in Rome. He wrote many books. One of the most important of these was ***Antiquities of the Jews***.

In this book, he writes:

About this time arose Jesus, a wise man, if indeed it be lawful to call him a man. For he was a **doer of wonderful deeds**, and a teacher of men who gladly receive the truth. He drew to himself many of the Jews and of the Gentiles. He was (called) the Christ; and when Pilate had condemned him to the cross, those who had loved him at first did not cease to do so, for he appeared to them again alive on the third day ...

Josephus tells us that Jesus did some extra-special things, was called 'Christ' and appeared to people after his crucifixion.

To do!

A. Why might some people not believe the miracle stories?

B. Name the three places where evidence of Jesus' miracles can be found.

1. Who was the writer from Jewish history?
2. What languages did he know?
3. What job did he have?
4. Where did he live when he retired?
5. Name one of the books he wrote.
6. What phrase did he write about Jesus?
7. How did he explain the last days of Jesus?

Finish these sentences:

The Gospels contain many _______.

_______ was an important Jewish historian.

Josephus lived around _______.

He spoke_______ and _______.

He wrote a book called _______.

He called Jesus _______.

He wrote that Jesus was condemned _______.

Jesus came back and _______.

Unmuddle these and put each into a sentence in your copy:

- EDEVINCE
- TPAS
- PSELGOS
- EWJHSI IORHTYS
- OEJSUPHS
- SWEJ fo eht NTQAIUTIESI
- ODWEFNRUL EDEDS

… in another Jewish history book called

the Talmud!

(A.D. 200–500)

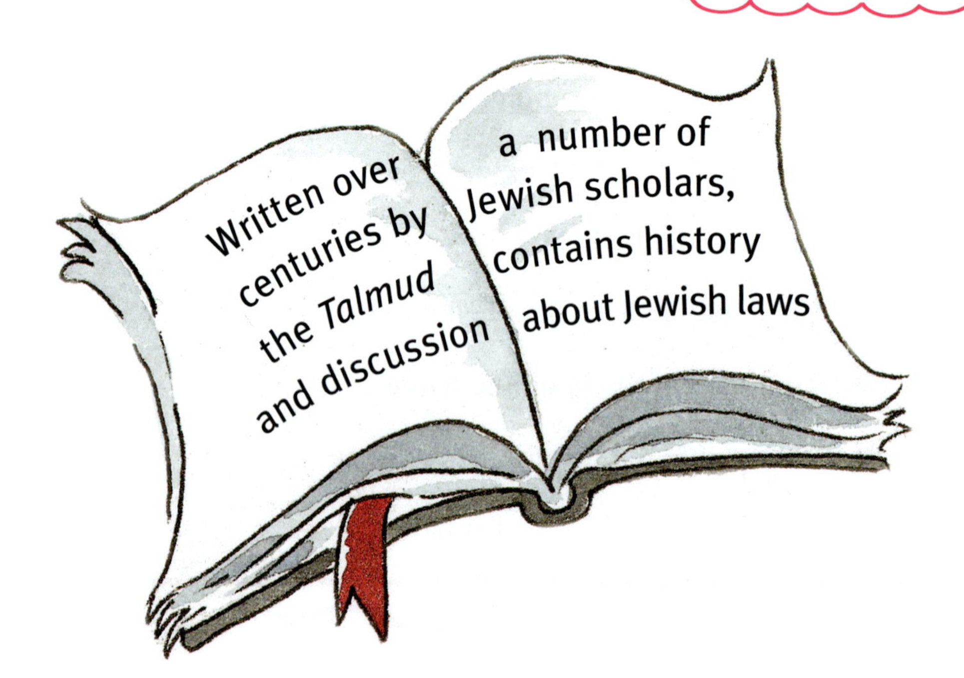

In this book it says that Jesus was executed because he practised **'sorcery'** and misled the people; they questioned whether his power came from God or the devil.

And one more ...

From Early Christian preaching

'The Kerygma'

Greek for 'Proclamation', or announcement.

This is the Apostles' and Early Christians' proclamation that:

'By His life, death and resurrection, Jesus has saved us from sin and death. Jesus is Salvation!'

In their writings, the Early Christians make many references to **Miracle-working**, e.g. Peter preaches about Jesus' mighty works and power over death.

NB: It's clear from the evidence that most people who knew anything at all about Jesus and his ministry believed that he had done remarkable deeds – and this belief was present whether or not they were Christians themselves!

1. What is the *Talmud*?
2. What does it say about Jesus?
3. What was the problem that people had with Jesus?
4. What does 'Kerygma' mean?
5. What is it?

More to do!

A. How important is the *Talmud* to historians?
B. From where did they think Jesus got his power to work miracles?
C. Why did the Apostles proclaim the Kerygma?
D. How did Jesus save us?
E. In what way did the Apostles spread the miracle message of Jesus?

Unscramble the tiles to reveal a message:

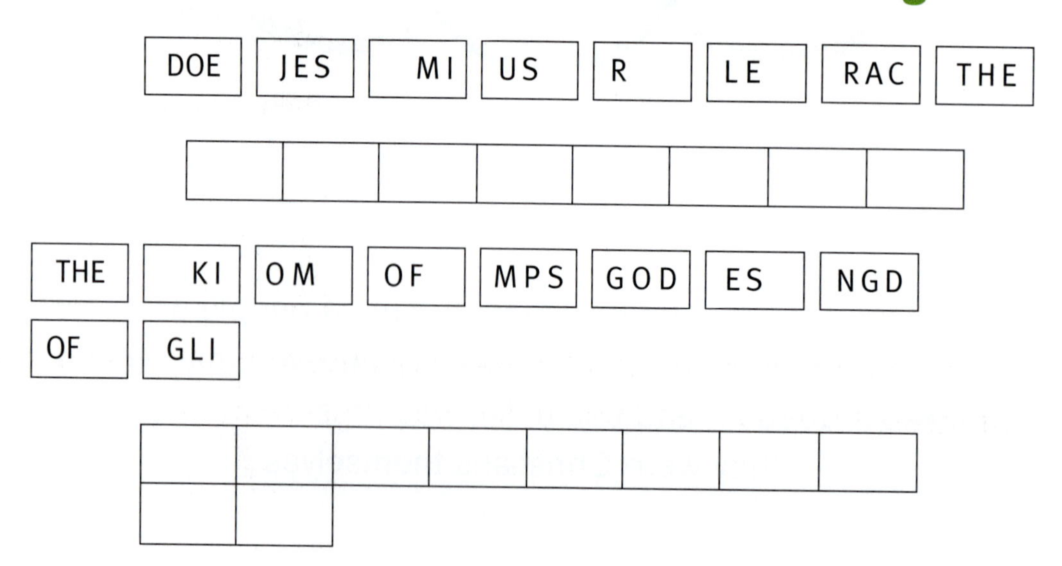

The Overall Meaning of Miracles

When we look at the **miracles**, we have to put them in the **CONTEXT** of all of Jesus' life, words and **ministry**. For many followers and believers, all of what Jesus said and did was against the **background of the Old Testament**. It says in the Old Testament that **'a Messiah, a Saviour would come to save Israel'!**

NB: All that was promised in the Old Testament was now happening – it was being fulfilled in Jesus!

NB: Through the miracles, the Kingdom of God was breaking through to the here-and-now, manifested and embodied by Jesus!

So, after looking at Jesus' words, Jesus' stories, Jesus' actions and keeping in mind his life, death and resurrection, we can try to piece together this chart showing the different aspects of the Kingdom of God.

Important points to remember!

John the Baptist called on people to repent because the Kingdom of God was close!

The Kingdom has arrived by and in Jesus. The Kingdom of God is offered to all who open their hearts to Jesus' message!

The Kingdom is created by relationship with God through prayer and through actions of love, peace, mercy, etc., which stem from that prayer!

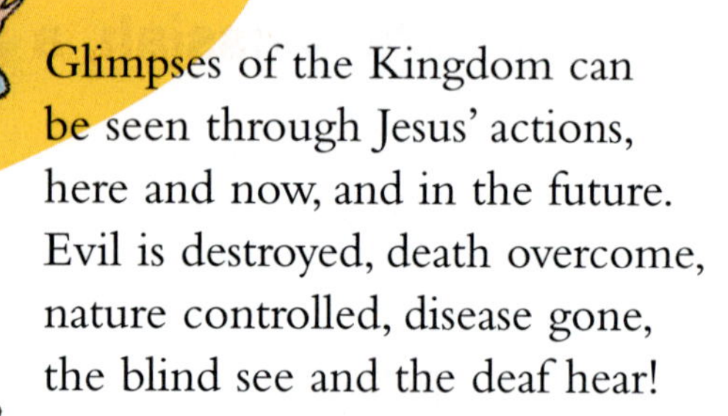

Glimpses of the Kingdom can be seen through Jesus' actions, here and now, and in the future. Evil is destroyed, death overcome, nature controlled, disease gone, the blind see and the deaf hear!

Jesus ate and drank with all people. This was called '**table-fellowship**', and indicated God's love for all people.

The Kingdom is still a mystery that will be revealed through Jesus at the end of time and through our prayers and good works!

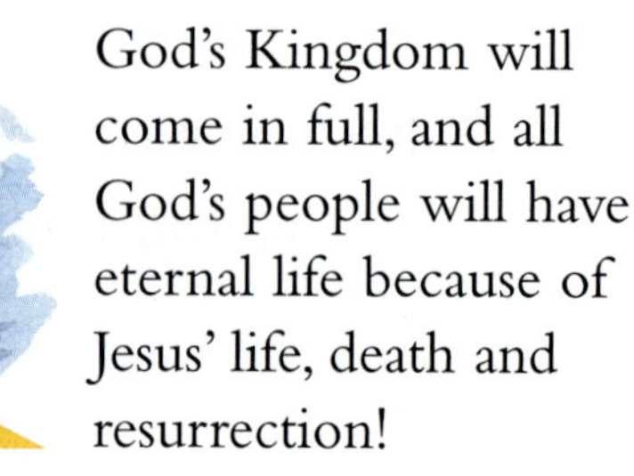

God's Kingdom will come in full, and all God's people will have eternal life because of Jesus' life, death and resurrection!

Followers of Jesus have a change of heart and live lives of love, peace, justice, caring, hope, compassion, humanity, purity of heart, and working for the Kingdom!

Try these

Q1. What does it say in the Old Testament about the Messiah?

Q2. How did Jesus fulfil this Prophecy?

Q3. How was the Kingdom breaking through?

Q4. From the Aspects chart, who is the Kingdom offered to?

Q5. What can we say about the Kingdom of God from Jesus' actions?

Q6. What was 'table-fellowship'?

Q7. What are followers of Jesus to have and do?

Q8. Why is the Kingdom a mystery?

Q9. Why will God's Kingdom come?

More to do!

A What kind of Kingdom of God is Jesus presenting?

B What role did John the Baptist have?

C How does the Kingdom come in and through Jesus?

D How do we create the Kingdom?

E According to the miracles, what sort of place is the Kingdom of God?

F Why is it all still a mystery?

RESEARCH JOURNAL IDEA

? Find examples of people and actions that are helping to create the Kingdom of God today! What are people doing? (Name some people who are helping.)

? Detail what Christians should be doing.

? What are you doing to help create God's Kingdom?

Time to Think and Pray!

Let us pray ...

I thank you God for letting us know what your Kingdom should be. Your son, Jesus, the doer of wonderful deeds, showed to us how the Kingdom of God should and will be. He also showed us how we play a part. Let me play my part, Lord!

(Read Mark 10:46-52 – 'The Curing of Bartimaeus')

We ask ...

- That we will have strength to work for God's Kingdom. **Amen!**
- That we will work tirelessly for the coming of God's Kingdom. **Amen!**
- That we will be inspired and joyous because of the glimpses that the miracles show us. **Amen!**
- That through our actions God's Kingdom will reign. **Amen!**
- Help me to believe that it will happen. **Amen!**

Reflection!

Bartimaeus was given his sight back, not only physically but spiritually. Bartimaeus, through that miracle, saw Jesus as the Son of God and the bringer of God's reign. Let me be Bartimaeus. Let me see Jesus the Son of God, as his coming Kingdom. Let me be healed from my blindness and given sight to see the Kingdom Come – that I am part of ... let it be. Amen!

TO KNOW

Crucifixion: Roman execution for non-Roman criminals.
Roman Army: occupiers of Palestine.
Religious Authorities: Sadducees, Pharisees, Sanhedrin.

The Last Days of Jesus

The last days of Jesus are those that are concerned with his **journey to the cross** – the crucifixion, death and resurrection of Jesus Christ as detailed in the Gospels of Matthew, Mark, Luke and John.

What Happened?

While Jesus travelled around Palestine, preaching, teaching and working miracles, he became famous and popular and had many followers. But he also had some **enemies**.

Jesus came into conflict with the religious and political leaders in Palestine.

The Romans were always very suspicious of a person who made a following for themselves. King Herod Antipas got rid of John the Baptist because he was afraid of political riots **(according to the writings of Josephus)**.

So they would have had a suspicious eye on Jesus because at one point he had a following of 5,000 who wanted him to be King **(John 6:15)**.

- Jesus' teaching was different from that of other Rabbis. He taught on his own **'authority'** (Mark 1:22).
- He did not hesitate to criticise the **Pharisees** and **Sadducees**, calling them **'blind leaders'** (Matthew 23:16-24) and saying that they were 'as rotten and worthless as a grave full of old bones' (Matthew 23:27).

Blasphemy:
- **irreverent comments and behaviour about religion and God;**
- **claiming authority from God;**
- **claiming to be divine.**

- Jesus had conflict with the Pharisees on a number of occasions while healing and preaching.

Read Luke 5:17-25 – 'Curing the paralysed man'

- At this healing miracle, some Pharisees were present.
- Jesus not only healed but also **forgave the man's sins.**
- The Pharisees considered this blasphemy.

- Jesus replied: **'The Son of Man has authority on Earth to Forgive Sins' (Luke 5:24).**
- They would have gone straight back to the religious authorities to report what they had heard.

Read Mark 3:20-30 – 'Exorcising the Evil Spirits'

- The religious authorities claim that Jesus gets his power to **exorcise** from the devil.
- Jesus replies, **'How can Satan drive out Satan? A Kingdom divided against itself cannot survive.'**

- Jesus goes on to say that anyone who blasphemes against the **SPIRIT** will not be forgiven, because the Pharisees were saying that there was an unclean spirit in Jesus.

Conflict also occurs when Jesus comments on:

- **Laws concerning FASTING and the SABBATH**

The Pharisees considered Jesus' views too easygoing and a wrong interpretation of the law.

(Read Mark 2:18-22; 23-27; 3:1-6)

Mark writes that Jesus claims that God is working through him in a direct way.

'The Kingdom of God has come near' (Mark 1:15).

This showed to the Pharisees that Jesus had an authority to interpret God's law!

The Pharisees were also critical of the way in which Jesus ate with sinners and tax collectors **(Mark 2:13-17).**

- For Jesus, this was 'table-fellowship'.
- Sinners were those who had broken the law of God.
- Jesus announced that these people had a place in God's Kingdom. Those who received Jesus would be received into God's Kingdom! **Jesus claimed that God was acting through him**.

OVER TO YOU

1. Why were the Romans suspicious of Jesus?
2. Who did Jesus come into conflict with?
3. What was the largest following Jesus had, according to Scripture?
4. Name two ways in which Jesus came into conflict with the religious authorities.

More to do!

A. Why did the Pharisees have a problem with Jesus after he healed the paralysed man?
B. What problems did the religious authorities have with the Exorcism miracle?
C. What two things were the Pharisees also critical of about Jesus, and why?
D. Why did Jesus eat and mix with sinners and tax collectors? What point was he making?
E. Sinners, according to religious law, were ________.
F. Who might Jesus mix with today?
G. Who might have a problem with Jesus' actions today?

Write a definition for each of these:

- Blasphemy
- Sadducees
- Conflict
- Exorcism
- Pharisees
- Sinners
- Crucifixion
- Sabbath
- Authority
- God's Kingdom

Jesus goes to Jerusalem

Sunday of Holy Week

WHY?

TO KNOW

'Passover': Jewish festival remembering freedom from Egypt. Special meal celebrated.
'Messiah': the Saviour of the Jewish people.
'Hosanna': means 'Save Now'.

- Jesus had to show and tell his message to the religious and political leaders **(The Pharisees / Sadducees / Sanhedrin)** centred in the capital – Jerusalem. It was his last step.
- He wanted to preach and work miracles in the Temple, the most holy site of Judaism.
- Jesus arrived at **Passover**. This was when the Jews remembered Moses leading them to freedom. According to Jewish tradition, this was the time when the Messiah would arrive to free them once more.

NB: Jesus explained that he had come to save people and to show God's love, not to bring about war.

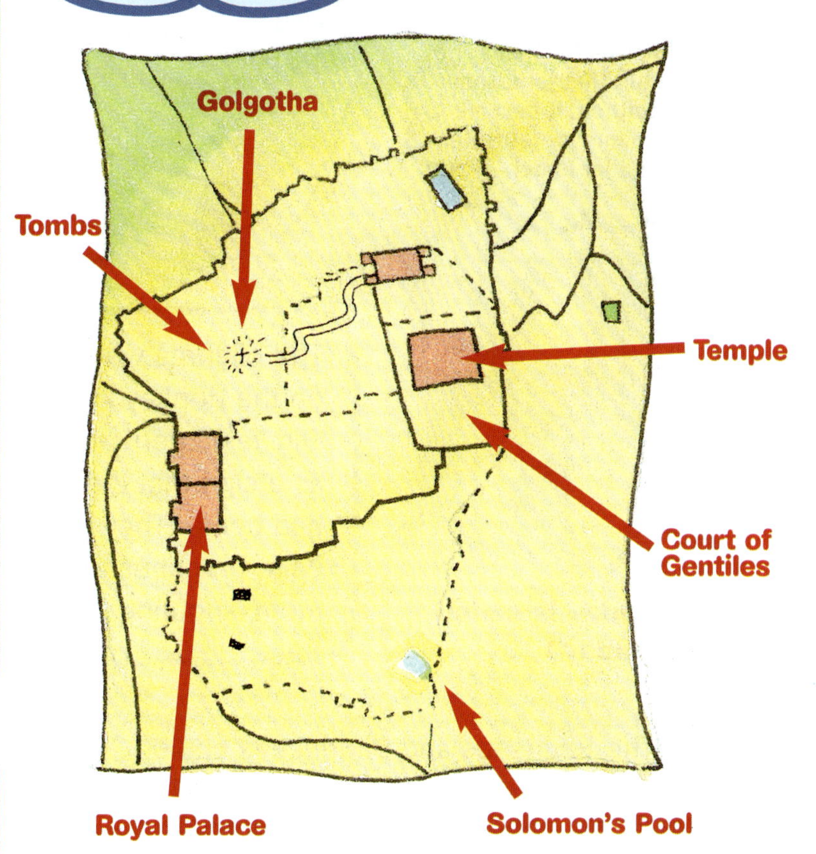

Jerusalem and the Temple

Palm Sunday

This way to Jerusalem and Passover festival

... So it was the time of Passover and many pilgrims were on their way to their capital city, Jerusalem, to celebrate the Passover. Jesus knew that he had to go as well.

But Jesus did not enter Jerusalem as a warrior, king or hero, as some expected. He entered as a person of service, peace and love.

'Rejoice heart and soul, Daughter of Zion. Shout for joy, Daughter of Jerusalem! Look, your King is approaching. He is victorious, humble and riding on a donkey ... he will proclaim peace to the nations' **(Zechariah 9:9-10)**

TO KNOW

Zion was the name of the hill that Jerusalem was built on. It became another name for Jerusalem and for Israel.

Jesus entered Jerusalem on a donkey, just as the Old Testament had said the Messiah would arrive! Jesus was to fulfil the Old Testament prophecies.

(That Sunday is called 'Palm Sunday')

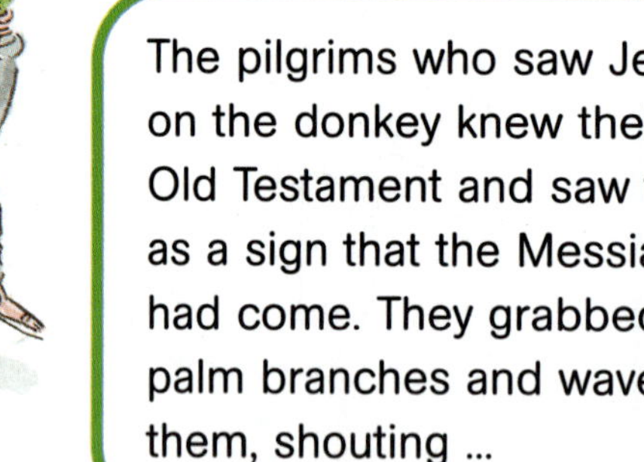

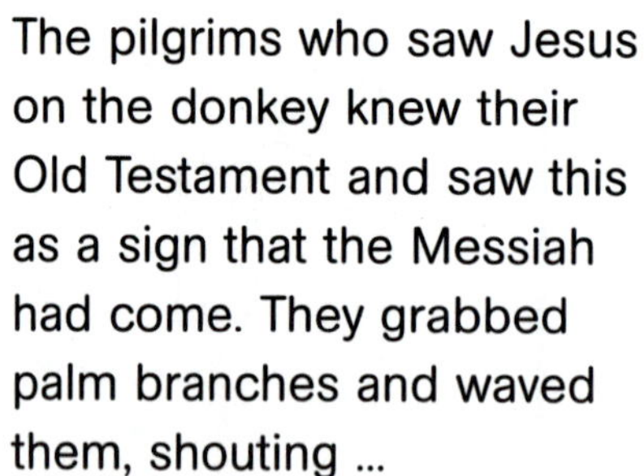

The pilgrims who saw Jesus on the donkey knew their Old Testament and saw this as a sign that the Messiah had come. They grabbed palm branches and waved them, shouting ...

'Hosanna ... to the Son of David ... Blessed is He who comes in the name of the Lord!'

NB: The Pharisees and Sadducees could have been very nervous about this and concerned this could upset their peace and comfort.

TO KNOW

The Messiah that was expected would come from the family line of the great King David of Jewish history.

To do!

1. What was the Passover?
2. Give two reasons why Jesus went to Jerusalem?
3. Who did Jesus want to preach his message to?
4. What was important about the Temple?
5. What was 'The Messiah'?
6. What type of Messiah did Jesus present?
7. Explain 'Hosanna'.
8. Why is 'Palm Sunday' so called?

Find each word and then write it in your copy in a sentence showing its meaning!

PEACEDONKEYPRSUZIONSTXPHOSANNAUSBAPASSOVERMUTMESSIAHOPZSADDUCEESCRUPHARISEESLOPA

Explain 'ZION'

Fill in the blanks:

It was the time of ______. Many pilgrims were on their way to ______ for the festival. They were going to ______ the fact that God, through ______, freed the people from ______ under the ______. Jesus and the ______ were on the way as well. Jesus entered ______ on a donkey. This action was to fulfil the ______ from the Old Testament about the ______ of the ______!

More to do!

A. What sort of Messiah were the people expecting?
B. Why was it important to arrive at the festival of Passover?
C. What was the significance of the fact that Jesus arrived on a donkey?
D. What did the people shout and why?
E. When they saw Jesus arriving on the donkey, what would have gone through the people's minds?
F. What sort of a Messiah did Jesus want to be and why?
G. How was Jesus the new Messiah?
H. How was this event going to be the new Passover?

RESEARCH
JOURNAL IDEA

Detail on a map all the important places that are mentioned in relation to the last days of Jesus in Jerusalem.

Jerusalem Crossword

Across

3. What Jesus sat on.
4. The city Jesus was going to.
5. The feast at that time.

Down

1. What the people shouted.
2. What the people thought Jesus was.
3. The people who were with Jesus.

HOLY WEEK

Holy Week: the week before Holy Saturday in the Christian calendar.

This is the name given to the week when we remember Jesus' last actions, from Palm Sunday to Good Friday.

SUNDAY (Palm Sunday)

Jesus arrives in Jerusalem, sitting on a donkey. The crowds wave palm branches and shout, **'Hosanna, the King of Kings!'**

MONDAY

Jesus goes to the Temple and turns over the traders' tables. The Pharisees and Sadducees see this and plot against Jesus.

TUESDAY

Jesus teaches in the Temple and is asked questions by the Pharisees and the Sadducees. They don't like his answers.

WEDNESDAY

The Apostle Judas Iscariot volunteers to betray Jesus and hand him over to the authorities.

THURSDAY

Jesus celebrates the Last Supper with the Apostles. He offers the bread and wine as his body and blood. Later, in the Garden of Gethsemane, Jesus is arrested by the Temple guards, with the help of Judas.

FRIDAY

Jesus is put on trial by Pontius Pilate. He is whipped and condemned to crucifixion. He dies on the cross.

The last days of Jesus are crucial to the Christian message!

Over to you!

In your copy, draw a chart like this one and fill in the proper information!

Day	Event	Drawing (to go with each event)
Palm Sunday	______	
Monday	______	
Tuesday	______	
Wednesday	______	
Thursday	______	
Friday	______	

1. Why is the Sunday before Easter called Palm Sunday?
2. What action did Jesus take on the Monday of Holy Week?
3. What event happened on the Wednesday of Holy Week?
4. What event happened on 'Good Friday'?
5. Why are the last days of Jesus given a lot of attention in the Gospels?

Trouble in the Temple

Monday of Holy Week

On the Monday of Holy Week, Jesus continued his mission and went to the Temple in Jerusalem, the holiest place for Jews.

TO KNOW

The Temple was in the control of the Temple priests, the Sanhedrin, and their Temple guards.

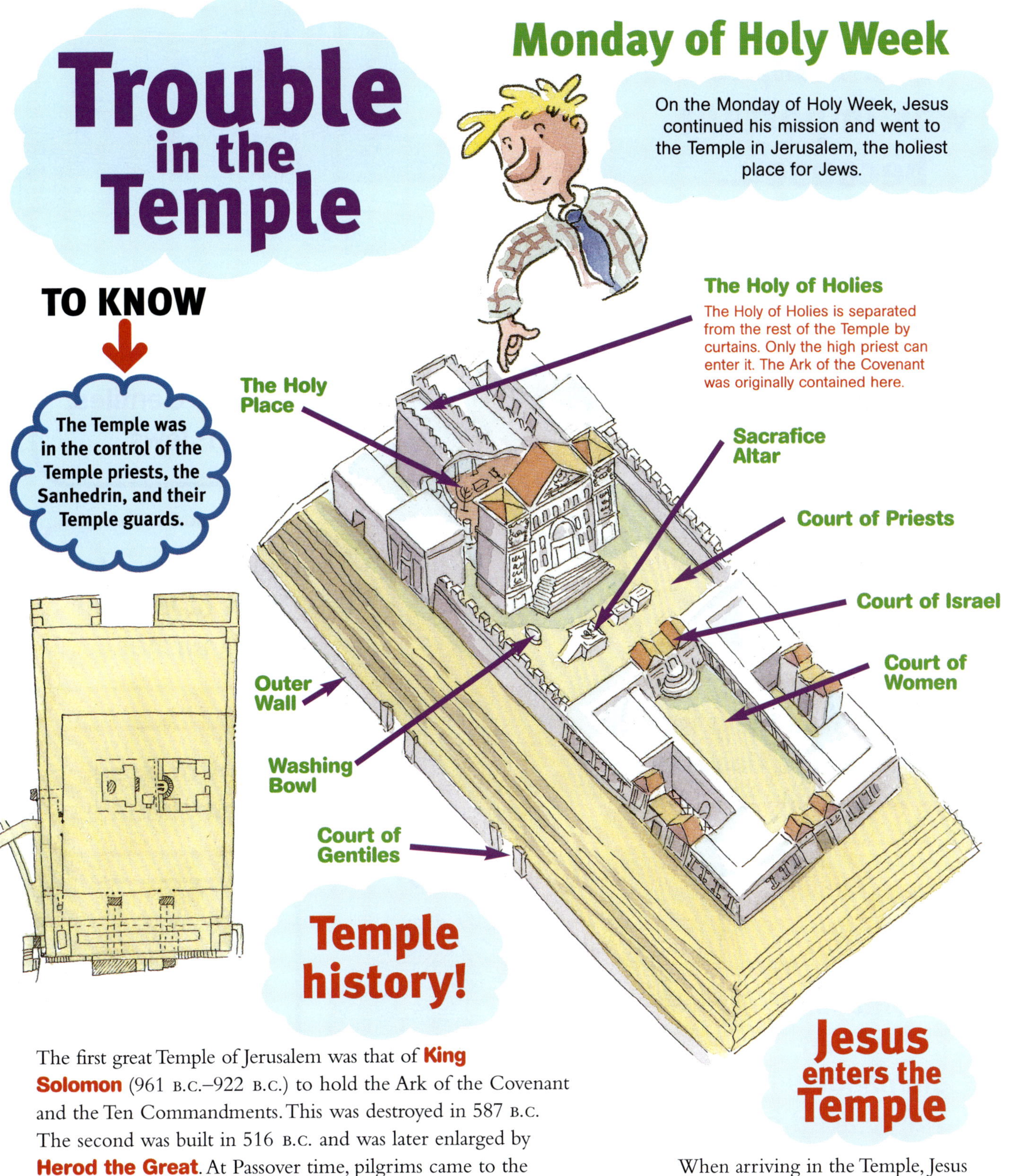

Temple history!

The first great Temple of Jerusalem was that of **King Solomon** (961 B.C.–922 B.C.) to hold the Ark of the Covenant and the Ten Commandments. This was destroyed in 587 B.C. The second was built in 516 B.C. and was later enlarged by **Herod the Great**. At Passover time, pilgrims came to the Temple to sacrifice an animal. Doves, cattle and sheep were sold. Pilgrims needed to change their money. The money exchanges cheated them. They also had to pay taxes to the Romans.

Jesus enters the Temple

When arriving in the Temple, Jesus saw money-changers and merchants selling animals in the area called the **'Court of the Gentiles'**.

The Temple was important because ...

In the Temple, God resided.

People focused their prayer and sacrifice on the Temple.

It was the 'marvel of the Universe'.

Outside was the Court of the Gentiles, for non-Jews.

The women went to the Court of Women and no further.

The Court of Israel was for Jewish males.

Originally, the Ark of the Covenant (box containing the Ten Commandments) was placed in the Holy of Holies.

Holy of Holies

The Holy of Holies was at the rear. Only the High Priest could enter.

- Jesus was very annoyed and called the place a 'den of robbers'. Then he knocked over the tables, scattered the money and shouted at the people about their selling and cheating!

- **The religious authorities, the Temple priests, allowed the selling and money-changing and this was a direct challenge to their authority.**

- At this, the **Pharisees and Sadducees** became annoyed with Jesus. However, over the next few days Jesus became very popular through his preaching in the Temple. **So they confronted him**. They wanted to trick and trap him.

The Sadducees did not believe in resurrection. Jesus meant that marriage was only for this life. All in Heaven live in a community of love, with no differences separating people. The Sadducees were disgusted by his answer and did not like Jesus' attitude. They asked no more questions.

The Pharisees asked Jesus ...
(Luke 20:20-26) (Mark 12:13-17)

Jesus knew that they were trying to trick him into answering that paying taxes to Rome was against Jewish law. If he had said this, he could have been arrested for outspoken opposition to Roman rule. But he knew better.

The Sadducees asked Jesus ...
(Luke 20:27-40) (Mark 12:18-27)

Fill in these blanks:

The first great Temple of _______ was that of _______ _______ (961 B.C. _______). This _______ was destroyed in _______ B.C. The second was built in 516 B.C. and was enlarged by _______ the _______. In A.D. 70 the _______ destroyed the Temple. The only remaining _______ of the _______ is the _______ _______ or ______ _______, a holy site for Jews and Jewish _______.

Q Explain in your own words why the traders and money-changers were in the Temple.

1. On what day did Jesus go to the Temple?
2. Why did Jesus get so annoyed?
3. What did Jesus call the place?
4. Why did the religious authorities consider this a challenge to them?
5. Why did the Pharisees and Sadducees confront Jesus?

More to do!

A. How did Jesus challenge the authority of the Temple priests?
B. What do you think was going through the minds of the religious authorities?
C. What was their reasoning behind confronting Jesus?
D. How did the Pharisees try to trick Jesus?
E. What words disgusted the Sadducees?
F. What do you think was going through Jesus' mind?

Think!

If you were part of the religious authorities, would you feel threatened, concerned, or afraid?

Why?

Write out your thoughts.

Read the Parable of the Wicked Tenants (Mark 12:1-15) (Luke 20:9-19). Jesus told this knowing that the religious leaders were listening!

Meaning ...

The vineyard is Israel, God's people. The tenants are the religious leaders; the father is God the Father, and the only son is Jesus. The servants are the prophets, come to help Israel and rejected on all occasions. The landlord will hand it all over to others: the Gentiles!

The Pharisees and Sadducees knew exactly what Jesus meant and that he was talking about them. Jesus was saying that they had neglected their responsibilities to the people and to God.

From that moment they wanted to stop Jesus ...

To do!

Tell the Parable of the Wicked Tenants using modern-day people and situations.

1. What grew in the vineyard?
2. How many servants did the owner send?
3. Why did he send them?
4. What happened to the servants?
5. Who was the last person sent by the owner?
6. What did the tenants do to the son?
7. At the end, what would the owner do?
8. Where can we read this parable?

Explain who the characters represent:

The vineyard owner: ____________________

His son: ____________________

The tenants: ____________________

The servants: ____________________

The vineyard is: ____________________

Q Why were the Pharisees and Sadducees angry with Jesus over this parable?

the Plan

The Saddducees and the Pharisees needed to stop Jesus, although he had not broken any laws. They knew that if they arrested him during the day and in public, there would be a riot. So it had to be quiet and at night-time (Matthew 26:3-5).

They were lucky because one person came to help them –

Judas Iscariot

Judas was one of the twelve Apostles. He had decided to betray Jesus to the High Priest. For this he would receive a reward of thirty pieces of silver **(Read Luke 22:4-6)**.

Why?

Different scholars believe different things:

- Judas was greedy and disloyal and would do anything for money (some scholars suggest that the name Iscariot is from **'Keriot'**, meaning 'man of falsehood').
- Handing him over would force Jesus to do something extraordinary as Messiah.
- It was preordained that Judas would do it as part of Jesus' overall plan.
- Nobody can know what Judas' true intentions were.
- After Jesus' arrest and crucifixion, Judas was so filled with remorse that he killed himself.

1. Why were the Sadducees and Pharisees so set on arresting Jesus?
2. Who stepped up to help them?
3. How much money was he to get?
4. What reasons are given as to why he did what he did?
5. What meaning is given for 'Iscariot'?

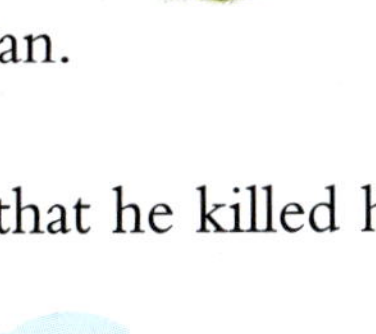

Think!

Imagine you are Judas Iscariot. Using one or more reasons, write an account of what you did, why and how you felt about it.

Thursday of Holy Week

TO KNOW

The Last Supper is the institution of the Eucharist. Bread and wine become Christ's body and blood.

The Last Supper

For the details of this 'last supper', look at the synoptic Gospels:

(Matthew 26:17-35)

(Mark 14:12-25)

(Luke 22:7-20).

At this meal, on Thursday evening before Passover, Jesus followed the usual custom. At the end of the meal, he said a prayer and blessing of thanksgiving. But then he did something different!

The three 'synoptic' Gospels detail that Jesus hosted a meal for his disciples. It took place on the Thursday evening in a room in a house offered to them by a friend in Jerusalem. This meal has come to be called **'The Last Supper'**.

Jesus took the bread, broke it, handed it to his disciples and said:

'This is my Body, given for you; do this in remembrance of me.'

After this, he took a cup of wine, blessed it and gave it to them ...

He said: 'Drink from this all of you, for this is my blood, the blood of the Covenant, poured out for the forgiveness of sins.'

Matthew, Mark and Luke say that this supper was a 'Passover Meal', but John makes no reference to that idea. He says that it took place before the Passover **(John 13:1)**.

What did Jesus mean by all this?

Good question! Let's try to answer it. First of all, we see how this meal was celebrated at

Last Supper is:
Memorial:
in memory of the event.
Sacrifice:
giving up Jesus' life for all humanity.

Passover time

In the Old Testament, the Hebrews, before leaving slavery in Egypt, ate a meal of lamb and bread. The blood of the lamb was put on their doors so that God would spare them from his wrath and save them from slavery.

At the **Last Supper**, Jesus said that his blood would be poured out for all people. This was a sign of the **New Covenant** between God and his people, brought about by Jesus' death on the cross. He is the **'Lamb to be sacrificed'**!

The Eucharist is both the memorial and the action of Jesus' sacrifice.

'Do this in remembrance of me'

Jesus knew that his time was coming to an end, so the meal was a message and symbol of this for his friends. Jesus made a connection between the meal and his upcoming crucifixion and death.

Jesus wanted the Last Supper to be celebrated always. The Last Supper is the model for the Catholic celebration of the Eucharist and explains the Catholic belief in the presence of Jesus in bread and wine.

The Apostles only truly understood what Jesus was doing after the Resurrection.

The Last Supper!

Bread was blessed and broken.

The bread became Jesus' body.

The wine, his blood.

The Institution of Eucharist!

Wine was poured and shared.

A Passover Meal

The Mass

The celebration of Mass or **'The Eucharist'** is based on the words and actions of Jesus at the Last Supper and was developed by the Early Christians.

More to do!

BLOODEUOPSUPPERXPUSDISCIPLESESRUBODYJEFUMEMORIALEATSACRIFICESTULAMBSFLEPASSOVER

When you find the words, use them and explain them.

Fill in the blanks:

At the meal on ________ evening before the ________, Jesus followed the usual custom. At the ________ of the meal he said a ________ of thanksgiving. Then he did something different. He took bread and ________ it, handed it to his disciples and said, 'This is my ________, given for you; do this in ________ of me.' So too he took a cup of ________, gave it to them and said, '________ from this all of you. This is my ________, the blood of the ________, poured out for the ________ of sins.'

1. Which Gospels contain accounts of the Last Supper?
2. When did the Last Supper take place?
3. Where did Jesus and the Apostles have it?
4. What did Jesus do at the meal that was different?
5. What did he proclaim about the bread?
6. What did he say about the wine?
7. What was the Passover about?
8. How was Jesus the 'New Covenant'?
9. Why is the Last Supper a meal of memorial and sacrifice?
10. What message was Jesus giving?

Read over the synoptic Gospel accounts. Pretend you are a servant at the Last Supper. Detail what happened, from your point of view.

RESEARCH
JOURNAL IDEA

Research how the Mass compares with the Last Supper. Also find about Early Christian community gatherings and how they developed and expanded on the Last Supper.

More to do!

- **A** Why is the meal called the 'Last Supper'?
- **B** Why were the disciples surprised at what Jesus did?
- **C** How was this event the 'new Passover'?
- **D** Why was it a 'New Covenant'?
- **E** What is the Eucharist?
- **F** Why is the Last Supper the 'institution of the Eucharist'?
- **G** What connection has Mass to the Last Supper?
- **H** Did the disciples know what Jesus meant? (Why? / Why not?)

The Final Hours of Jesus

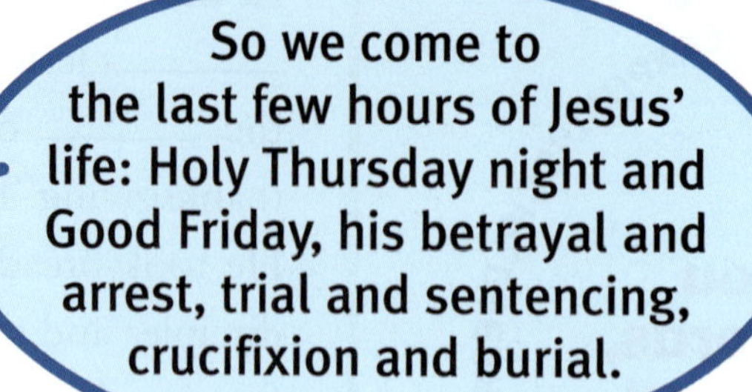

TO KNOW

- Gethsemane.
- Mount of Olives.
- High Priest Caiaphas.

On Holy Thursday evening, after the Last Supper, Jesus and the disciples went to the Garden of Gethsemane (across the Kedron Valley). Jesus wanted to pray for help during these last hours because he knew that the time was close **(Luke 22:39)**.

The disciples scattered, with the exception of Peter, who followed ...

After a while, the Temple guards arrived, with Judas leading them. They had come to arrest Jesus. Jesus knew that the time had come.

(Matthew 26:47-51)

Caiaphas was the High Priest at the time.

Jesus is Questioned

To Remember

It is at this point that we meet the High Priest. Go back and find out what his job was.

'By Annas'

Annas was a former high priest and father-in-law of **Caiaphas**. He questioned Jesus, and then sent him to Caiaphas.

While Jesus was being questioned, the Apostle Peter was outside. He denied knowledge of Jesus three times, just as Jesus had predicted. **(Luke 22:54-62)**

'By Caiaphas'

Jesus was brought to the **High Priest Caiaphas**. Caiaphas was not alone – he was the head of the Sanhedrin, the ruling **Jewish Council**. (Go back and read about the Sanhedrin.)

Let's Work!

True / False

- After the Last Supper, Jesus went to the Temple. T / F
- Jesus prayed in the Garden of Gethsemane. T / F
- Jesus asked for God's help and strength. T / F
- Judas led the Temple guards to Jesus. T / F
- Jesus and the disciples ran away. T / F
- All the disciples followed Jesus. T / F
- Jesus and the disciples became violent. T / F
- Jesus was brought to Caiaphas first. T / F
- Annas sent Jesus to the king. T / F
- Caiaphas was the High Priest. T / F

Unmuddle these ...

- NSMGTAEHEE
- LYOH SHUDYTRA
- RRTSEA
- CIIATRSO DJSAU
- AIPAHCAS
- SANAN
- HDSNIAERN

When you figure out each one, put it into a sentence in your copy!

More Qs

A. Why did Jesus not run away?
B. Why did Judas and the guards arrive at that time?
C. How might the disciples have felt, do you think?
D. Why was it that the disciples scattered?
E. Read Luke 22:54-62. What did Peter do that was such a let-down?
F. Why was Jesus brought to Caiaphas and the Sanhedrin?
G. What was the job of the High Priest? How much authority did he have?

Friday of Holy Week

Good Friday

... Before the Religious and Political Leaders ...

TO KNOW

- High Priest.
- Sanhedrin.
- Pontius Pilate.
- Herod Antipas.
- Blasphemy.

Caiaphas and the Sanhedrin.

They all met in the 'Court of Inquiry' (inner court of the Temple). This gathering was to decide what charge to bring against Jesus in a trial before the Romans.
(Only the Romans could execute people.)

The Sanhedrin wanted Jesus dead.

The members of the Sanhedrin had made up their minds that they wanted Jesus put to death. Because:

- Jesus challenged their authority.
- He questioned their loyalty to the people and to God.
- He exposed the Pharisees' hypocrisy.
- He was beginning to upset the status quo.
- As we will see, he claimed to be the Messiah.

Jesus, the Messiah?

After examination of Jesus by the Sanhedrin, Caiaphas finally asked the question: 'Are you the Messiah, the Son of the Blessed One?' **(Mark 14:61)**

Jesus replied,

'I am; and you will see the Son of Man seated at the right hand of the Mighty One and coming on the clouds of Heaven.' **(Mark 14:62)**

NB: For the Romans, claiming to be 'a king' was also blasphemous and treasonous.

TO KNOW

Blasphemy = words or actions that insult God. Also 'claiming' to be divine or to have divine authority.

By saying this, Jesus accepted the title Messiah, but added that he had a unique relationship with God – meaning that he was divine. This response was seen as **blasphemy**. The members of the Sanhedrin were enraged.
(Look at the same scene in Matthew 26:57-68; Luke 66:71)

Pontius Pilate, Roman Governor

With that, the Sanhedrin sent Jesus to the Roman Governor, Pontius Pilate, the only one with the authority to put Jesus to death. The Sanhedrin knew that blasphemy in this case was a religious offence, not a political one, so they added the following to the charges against Jesus **(Luke 23:2-5)**:

- encouraging the people to revolt against their Jewish leaders;
- opposing the payment of taxes to Emperor Caesar;
- claiming to be the Messiah or King. Overall: **'Treason'**.

On hearing and reading these accusations, Pontius Pilate considered Jesus to be **INNOCENT**. But the Sanhedrin protested and persisted. Pilate had an idea. Jesus was from Galilee so he would send Jesus to the ruler of Galilee – this was **HEROD ANTIPAS**. (He was the Jewish leader appointed by Rome over Galilee. We read about him a few pages back.)

Herod Antipas was delighted to see Jesus.

He had heard all about him and wanted Jesus to work a miracle **(Luke 23:8)**. Jesus did not, so a disappointed and angry Herod Antipas sent Jesus back to Pontius Pilate!

So, Jesus was sent back to Pontius Pilate, who still considered him to be innocent. But he did not want to annoy the Sanhedrin, so he questioned Jesus one last time.

TO KNOW

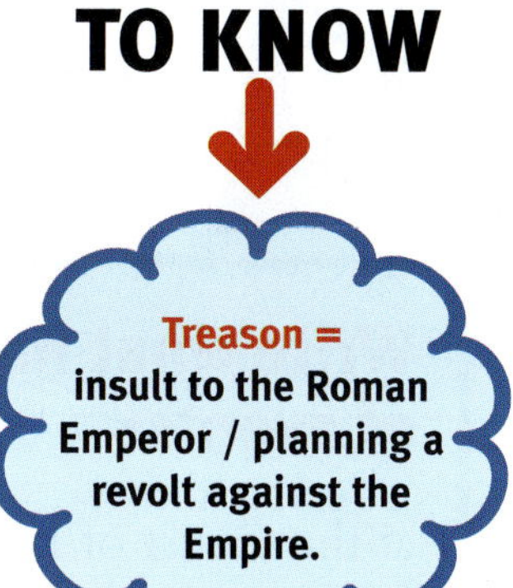

NB: Pontius Pilate was the Roman Governor (Procurator) of Judea. He was appointed by the Roman Emperor Caesar (Tiberius) to the area. He was not liked by the Jews.

(John 18:28-40)

TO KNOW

Claiming to be King of the Jews was a political offence against the Empire and Caesar.

Even with a response like that, however, Pilate could still find no charge against Jesus **(John 23:15-16)**, so he said that he would have Jesus whipped **('scourged')**.

Pilate had another idea. **(Mark 15:6-15) (Matthew 27:11-20) (Luke 23:14-25)**

It was the habit at Passover time that a prisoner be released by the Romans. Pilate gave the leaders and the gathered crowd outside the palace a choice – **'The Prisoner Barrabas'**, or Jesus.

The crowd called for Barrabas to be released.

The soldiers made fun of Jesus and put a crown of thorns on his head and a red cloak over his shoulders.

Mark's Gospel tells us that the Jewish leaders had put the people up to it, or indeed biased them **(Mark 15:11)**.

The crowds shouted for Jesus to be crucified!

According to **John 19:12**, Pilate was anxious to set Jesus free. But the Sanhedrin pushed for more action, and became very angry and increasingly persuasive!

John's Gospel adds that the crowd shouted to Pilate that if he set Jesus free, he was no friend of Caesar **(John 19:12)**. This frightened Pilate, who wanted to keep his job. So he gave in. Jesus was to be charged with treason and condemned to death. Pilate 'washed his hands' of the situation **(Matthew 27:24)**.

Complete this chart of events when Jesus was before the authorities ...

Write what happened and give details of events:

at the Court of Inquiry: ____________________

questioned by Caiaphas: ____________________

Jesus replies: ____________________

Sanhedrin response: ____________________

before Pilate: ____________________

over to Herod: ____________________

Q

1. Why was Jesus questioned by the Sanhedrin?
2. What did the Sanhedrin want overall?
3. Why did they want Jesus put to death?
4. What was Jesus' response to Caiaphas' question?
5. What charge did the Sanhedrin bring against Jesus?
6. What does blasphemy mean?
7. Why was Jesus sent to Pontius Pilate?
8. What extra charges were made against Jesus?
9. What did Pilate do and why?
10. What did Herod do and why?

More to do!

Read over the Gospel accounts and answer the following questions:

A. Why did Pontius Pilate initially find Jesus innocent?
B. What charges were brought against Jesus? Which charge was the political one?
C. Why was it important to have a political charge? What is treason?
D. Why did Pilate send Jesus to Herod? What was his thinking?
E. When Jesus was sent back, what happened?
F. Why was Jesus whipped? How did the soldiers mock Jesus?
G. What did Pilate really want to do with Jesus? How come he did not do what he wanted?
H. What plan did Pilate come up with? How did it go wrong?
I. What was the political charge brought against Jesus? Why did Pilate give in to the demands of the religious authorities and the crowd?
J. What was the symbolism of Pilate's washing his hands?

Match each statement with the person to whom it refers.

- Asked Jesus, 'Are you the Messiah?'
- Wanted Jesus to perform a miracle.
- Initially found Jesus innocent.
- Said, 'I am the Messiah.'
- Wanted Jesus dead.
- Accused Jesus of blasphemy.
- Sent Jesus to Herod.

- HEROD ANTIPAS
- SANHEDRIN
- CAIAPHAS
- JESUS
- PONTIUS PILATE

Last Days Wordsearch

T	T	P	S	B	B	H	R	S	C	G	L	C	H	D
E	L	S	P	U	S	L	E	D	U	M	A	S	O	E
M	S	J	E	I	I	L	A	A	N	I	E	U	L	G
P	E	U	S	I	P	T	R	S	A	B	M	S	Y	R
L	S	S	P	I	R	D	N	P	P	G	A	E	W	A
E	E	R	C	P	S	P	H	O	L	H	S	J	E	H
M	A	S	U	S	E	A	H	Q	P	K	E	C	E	C
F	I	J	U	O	S	R	M	G	L	V	H	M	K	F
D	F	S	A	N	H	E	D	R	I	N	T	N	Y	S
R	J	D	E	T	S	E	R	R	A	H	E	O	A	P
K	I	N	G	D	O	M	R	G	S	Y	G	N	E	R
E	T	A	L	I	P	R	U	O	B	D	N	A	F	A
N	S	W	L	N	L	S	H	E	D	A	K	G	T	Y
N	O	I	X	I	F	I	C	U	R	C	R	O	W	D
W	O	O	P	F	E	A	N	R	G	R	E	W	E	K

ANNAS
ARRESTED
BLASPHEMY
CAIAPHAS
CHARGED
CROWD
CRUCIFIXION
DISCIPLES
GETHSEMANE
GUARDS
HEROD
HIGH PRIEST
HOLY WEEK
HOURS
JESUS
KINGDOM
MESSIAH
PILATE
PONTIUS
PRAY
SANHEDRIN
SUPPER
TEMPLE

So, Jesus was charged with treason for **'calling himself a king'**, and was condemned to **crucifixion**. He began the journey to the cross.

The **Stations of the Cross** detail in a prayerful way fourteen aspects of Jesus' horrific journey to his crucifixion.

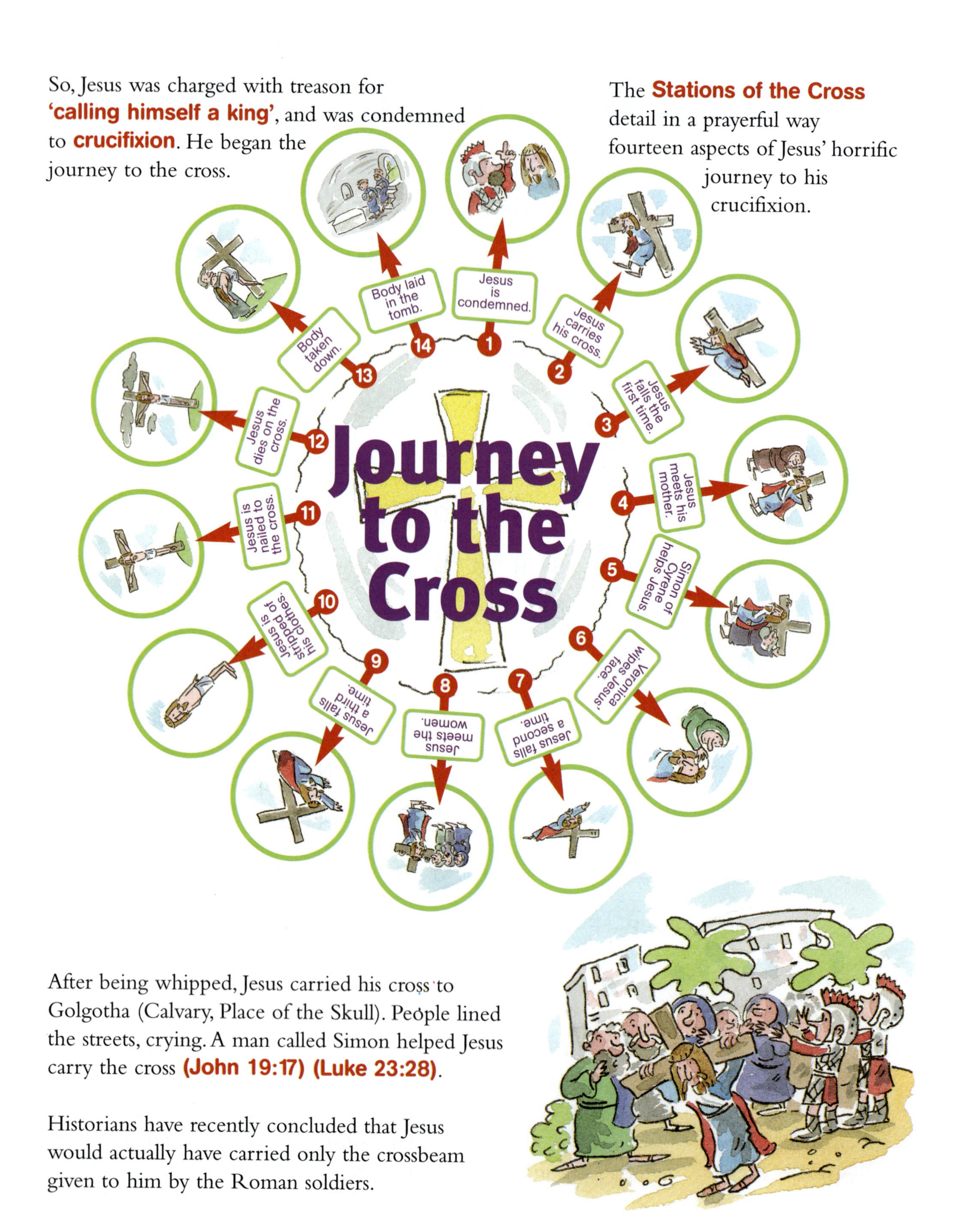

After being whipped, Jesus carried his cross to Golgotha (Calvary, Place of the Skull). People lined the streets, crying. A man called Simon helped Jesus carry the cross **(John 19:17) (Luke 23:28)**.

Historians have recently concluded that Jesus would actually have carried only the crossbeam given to him by the Roman soldiers.

In your copy, design your own Stations of the Cross. Draw a picture for each Station and beside it write the details of the Station. For example:

Station 3
Jesus falls the first time.

It might be an idea to make a set for your classroom or prayer room.

Imagine you are one of the Roman soldiers. Describe the scene as you lead Jesus to Calvary.

1. Why would Jesus have been exhausted?
2. What have historians recently told us about Jesus carrying the cross?
3. Where did the Romans lead Jesus?
4. What does Golgotha mean?
5. What is the 'Place of the Skull' in Latin?
6. What was Simon of Cyrene's role and why?

THE CRUCIFIXION

According to the Gospels, Mary, Jesus' mother, was there, together with the Apostle John (John 19:26-27) and Mary Magdalene.

When they reached Calvary, Jesus was nailed to the crossbeam (probably through the wrists). Then he and the crossbeam were nailed to a permanent pole on the hill.

Pilate ordered that this placard be put above Jesus on his cross. This really annoyed the Jewish authorities, but it was left there for all to see. It was written in Greek, Hebrew and Latin. He was crucified with a thief either side of him.

From the cross, Jesus heard a number of people mocking him from the ground: 'Save yourself, if you are the King'; 'He saved others; let him save himself' **(Luke 23:35)**. He also heard the thief beside him say, 'Are you not the Christ? Save yourself and us as well' **(Luke 23:39)**. Regarding the mockers and those who had crucified him, Jesus said, 'Father, forgive them for they know not what they do' **(Luke 23:34)**.

Q

1. Why was Jesus probably nailed through the wrists?
2. What did the placard say that Pilate had put up?
3. Why did it annoy the religious authorities?
4. What did Jesus say regarding those who mocked him?
5. What does this say about Jesus?

The Death of Jesus

The Evangelists write that around noon on Good Friday, a darkness covered the land and lasted until three o'clock that afternoon.

(Matthew 27:45; Mark 15:33; Luke 23:44)

Jesus cried out, and was given some vinegar on a sponge to keep him awake, then

he cried,

'My God, my God, why have you forsaken me?'

(Matthew 27:46; Mark 15:34)

Jesus was calling to God using **Psalm 22** from the Book of Psalms in the Old Testament.

NB: According to the Gospels, when Jesus died the curtain of the Holy of Holies in the Temple ripped. This is taken as meaning that Jesus, in dying for our sins, removed the barriers between God and his people.

St John's Gospel tells us that Jesus' last words were,

'It is accomplished'

and that 'bowing his head, he gave up his spirit' **(John 19:30)**. According to St Luke, Jesus said,

'Father, into your hands I commend my spirit'

and 'with this he breathed his last' **(Luke 23:46)**. These last words of Jesus show us his relationship with his heavenly Father.

1. How long did Jesus suffer on the cross before he died?
2. According to the Gospels, at what hour did he die?
3. What happened to the sky?
4. What was it that Jesus cried out?

More to do!

A. Why, do you think, did Jesus use the verse from **Psalm 22**?

B. If you were a bystander and heard that, what would you think?

C. How does **Psalm 22** end? (Look it up.)

D. What did Jesus mean by, 'It is accomplished'?

E. Read **Luke 23:45**. Why was the Temple curtain torn in two? What did that symbolise?

F. What does **Luke 23:46** tell us about Jesus' relationship with God the Father?

G. Have a look at **Luke 23:45**; **Matthew 22:51**; and **Mark 15:38**. What symbolism is used and what does each tell us about Jesus' death?

Jesus' Death – An Understanding

By reading the Gospel accounts of the death of Jesus and looking back on Jesus' life, preaching, teaching and miracles, we can make some important conclusions to help us in trying to understand and find meaning in the death of Jesus.

Jesus, the Suffering Servant

In the Old Testament, the prophet Isaiah speaks about a man who will suffer because of our sins. This man will rebuild the relationship between God and people **(Isaiah 42:1-4 and following)**.

Jesus, the Paschal Lamb

Just as the lamb's blood the Hebrews put on their doors saved them during the Passover, so too was Jesus' blood spilled to save us **(John 1:29)**.

Jesus, died for our Sins

Jesus died so that we would forever be able to have a relationship with God the Father through Jesus the Son.

Jesus, the New Covenant

Throughout the Old Testament, God made a Covenant with his people – with Abraham and with Moses. Through Jesus, God has created a new bond with his people.

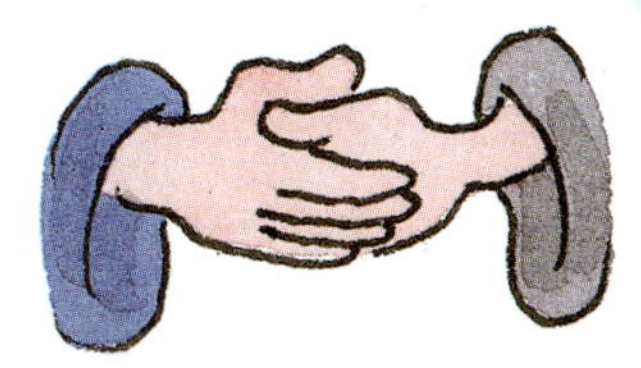

The Death of Jesus removed any barriers between God and us!

In your copy, explain in your own words each of the following:

- Jesus, the Paschal Lamb ____
- Jesus, the New Covenant ____
- Jesus, the Suffering Servant ____

Fill in these blanks:

The Prophet ________ in the ________ Testament speaks about God's 'Suffering ________'. This person would ________ greatly for our ________.

The Israelites, before gaining ________ at the Passover, ________ a lamb to eat and put its blood on their ________. So Jesus is the ________ lamb, whose blood is ________ out for ________.

Jesus' death was for our ________. The ________ between God and ________ is bridged.

Throughout the ________ ________ God made a ________ with his people through Abraham, ________ and finally ________. The death of ________ removed all ________ between God and ________.

Taken down from the cross

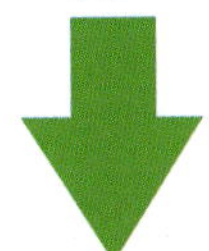

The burial had to be a rushed affair because the Sabbath was so close. The women who were present agreed that they would return to the tomb on Sunday morning, when the Sabbath was over, and complete the embalming of the body. Jesus was buried in a tomb that was nearby, close to the city gates **(John 19:42)**.

Jesus' Burial

As Good Friday evening was the beginning of the Jewish Sabbath, nobody was allowed to be left hanging on the cross.

... so they wrapped Jesus in a shroud and put him in a tomb cut into the stone ... (Luke 23:53)

To make sure that those who had been crucified were dead, the Romans used to break their legs. Jesus was already dead, so they pierced his side with a sword **(John 19:34)**. A Sanhedrin member and secret follower of Jesus, Joseph of Arimathea, helped them to take down the body and asked for permission to bury it.

A stone was rolled in front of the tomb entrance and the women, including Mary Magdalene, took note of where Jesus was buried.

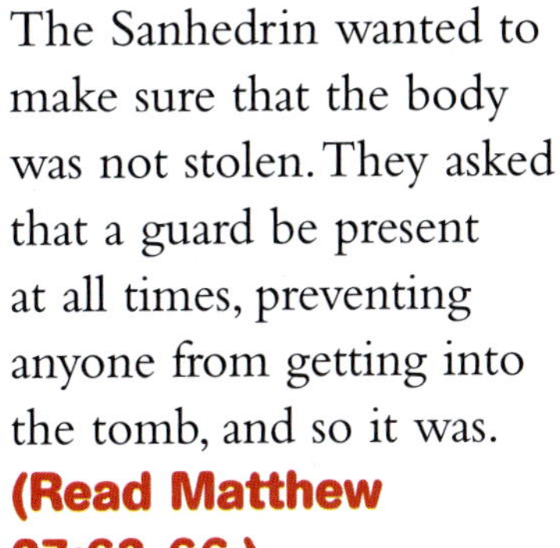

The Sanhedrin wanted to make sure that the body was not stolen. They asked that a guard be present at all times, preventing anyone from getting into the tomb, and so it was. **(Read Matthew 27:63-66.)**

1. Why did the bodies have to be taken down from the crosses?
2. What did the soldiers do to Jesus' body?
3. Who asked for permission to take and bury the body? What was his profession?
4. Why was the burial rushed?
5. Why was a guard stationed at the tomb?
6. Who made note of where Jesus was buried?

Death of Jesus Crossword

Across

1. Rolled in front of the tomb.
4. Sanhedrin member who took Jesus' body.
5. Placed there by the Romans.

Down

1. Reason to rush the burial.
2. Did instead of breaking Jesus' legs.
3. What Jesus was placed in.

More to do!

A. Read Deuteronomy 21:22-23. What is the law about capital punishment?

B. Read Exodus 12:46 / Psalm 34:20. How does this relate to Jesus?

C. Read Zechariah 12:10. How does this relate to Jesus' crucifixion?

D. Why, do you think, was Joseph of Arimathea a secret follower of Jesus?

E. The burial was not complete. Why not?

F. What was Pilate afraid of?

Easter Sunday

TO KNOW → Resurrection

The RESURRECTION

COPY AND COLOUR

What happened next is the core belief of Christianity. Jesus, whom the disciples and others had seen crucified, dying and being buried, rose from the dead and appeared to them.

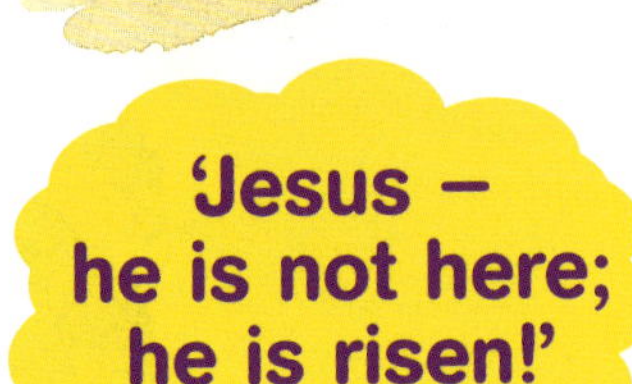

Mark's Gospel tells us that on Easter Sunday morning, Mary Magdalene, Mary the Mother of Salome and another woman went to finish embalming and anointing the body of Jesus. They were carrying spices to anoint the body according to Jewish tradition **(Mark 16:1)**. They went to the tomb and found it empty. John's Gospel says that a Messenger from God told them the Good News **(John 20:1)**. **(Read Matthew 28:2-6; Mark 16:5-6; Luke 24:1-8.)**

■ On hearing this amazing news, the women were shocked but overjoyed. They had to go and tell the disciples as quickly as they could. So they ran to where the disciples were hiding.

■ When the disciples heard the news, they couldn't believe it. They were still depressed and afraid because of all that had happened **(Mark 16:11)**. But Peter and John went to see for themselves. They discovered the tomb empty and the burial cloth on the ground.

'Jesus – he is not here; he is risen!'

COPY AND COLOUR

'Jesus had Risen from the Dead'

The Resurrection

'Jesus – he is not here; he is risen!'

Jesus, risen from the dead, rises to new life.

Breaks the chains of sin and death.

'Peace be with you.'

'Do not be afraid.'

'Go and make disciples of all the nations.'

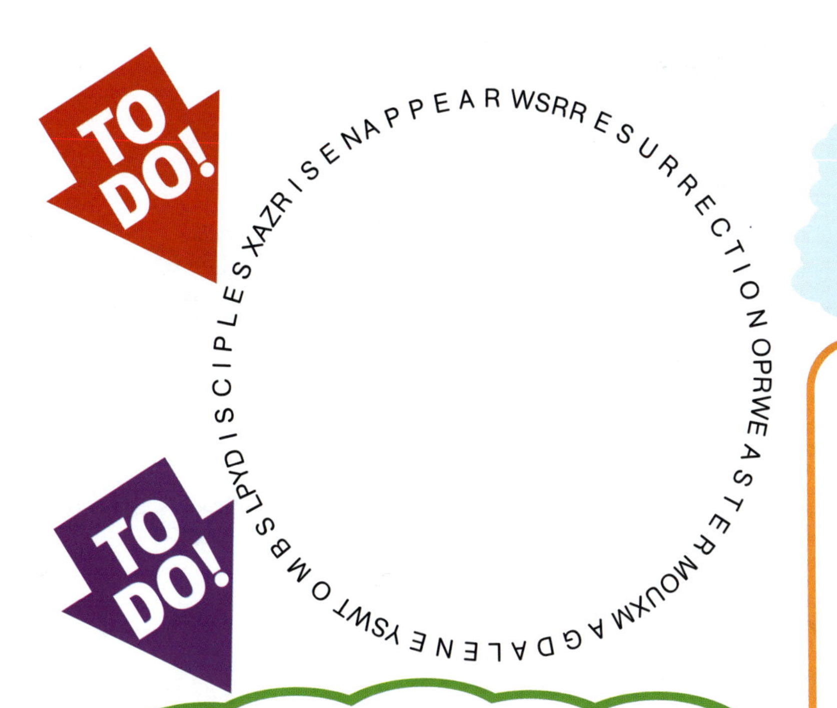

Find each of the words and use it in a sentence, describing its importance in the Resurrection events!

Imagine you are one of those people who went to the tomb. Retell the story from your point of view! (Read the Gospel accounts to help you.)

Fill in the blanks:

On Easter _______ morning, Mary _______, Mary the Mother of _______ and _______ women went to the _______. They wanted to _______ embalming the _______. They brought _______ with them. When they got to the _______, they found it _______. John's Gospel says that a _______ announced, 'Jesus – he is _______ _______; he is _______.' On hearing this _______, they ran to tell the _______.

Read the Resurrection accounts in the synoptic Gospels and John. **Mark 16:1-8 / Matthew 28:1-8 / Luke 24:1-8 / John 20:1-18.** Find out what is the same and what is different, comparing each of the accounts. Why might there be differences?

Try this!

In your copy, write an illustrated version of the Resurrection stories.

1. Who went to the tomb?
2. What did they go for?
3. What did they find when they got there?
4. What good news did they receive?
5. After hearing this news, where did they go?
6. Which Apostles went to the tomb?

More to do!

A. Why did the women need to anoint the body?
B. Name two ways that they knew Jesus had risen? (Read the accounts again.)
C. Why were the disciples in hiding?
D. Why was it that Peter and John went to the tomb?
E. How did this event clarify all that Jesus had said and done over the previous few days?
F. How did the disciples change?

Jesus Appears

■ Nobody actually saw the event of Jesus rising from the dead, but according to the Gospels, many people experienced him after the Resurrection.

■ The accounts of the Evangelists differ over certain details, but when we read them we see some common threads. These are:

- Jesus is transformed – different yet the same.
- Jesus appears unexpectedly.
- The people are initially depressed and downcast.
- They feel great peace and joy on learning that Jesus is risen and with them.
- Jesus greets them with a message of peace **(John 20:21)**.
- Jesus tells those to whom he appears to spread the Good News.

TO DO!

Read **Luke 24:13-35**, the 'Road to Emmaus' experience. Those mentioned meet Jesus and recognise him in the breaking of bread.

'Go, therefore, and make disciples of all the nations!'
(Matthew 28:19)

The Resurrection shows us ...

- **Jesus is the Messiah!**
  God resurrected his Son, Jesus, from the dead. The Messiah would have to suffer for our sins and die – Jesus fulfilled this Old Testament prophecy. He brought about the Kingdom of God for all people!
- **Good wins over Evil!**
  All believers will live with God. Sin will not reign. Death does not last. The Kingdom will come.
- **Death is not the end!**
  Life after death is promised to all believers. Jesus was the first to be born to new life with God.

The disciples were strengthened by their belief and faith, and ready to work for God's Kingdom!

True / False?

- Everybody saw Jesus rising from the tomb. **T / F**
- There are some common threads in the reports of the appearances of Jesus. **T / F**
- Jesus tells everybody that he is going to appear. **T / F**
- The people receive great peace and joy. **T / F**
- Jesus tells them to stay in the room. **T / F**
- Jesus greets them with the words, 'Peace be with you.' **T / F**
- In Luke, we read the story, 'The Road to Nazareth'. **T / F**
- Jesus says, 'Go, therefore, and make disciples of all the nations.' **T / F**

After reading 'The Road to Emmaus', what can we say about: The person of Jesus? • His listeners? • How Jesus was recognised?

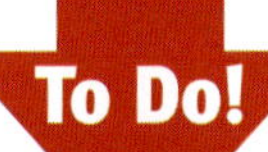

Draw a poster showing Jesus appearing to the disciples and announcing his message of peace and discipleship.

Think!

In your copy, explain the following: • **Jesus is the Messiah.** • **Good wins over Evil.** • **Death is not the end.**

How important is the resurrection to Christian belief? Explain.

Finish these sentences:

- Jesus appears to the people ________.
- The people are initially ________, but then ________.
- Jesus greets them with, '________'.
- Jesus also tells the disciples and listeners to '________'
- Jesus appears to two men in the ________.
- Jesus is the ________.
- Good ________.
- Death ________.

Resurrection Wordsearch

H	Y	A	E	Y	L	X	M	P	E	D	R	N	L	U
X	U	F	P	E	T	E	L	N	X	E	G	Q	Y	L
T	I	S	P	O	S	P	E	Z	S	T	O	T	O	Z
L	S	S	S	S	S	L	M	U	O	H	O	F	D	V
G	O	I	I	T	A	T	R	E	R	G	D	V	G	Y
G	O	A	L	D	O	R	L	I	O	I	M	Z	J	A
B	H	O	G	E	E	N	S	E	V	L	E	N	K	D
M	B	A	D	C	G	E	E	V	S	E	W	K	F	N
O	M	O	T	W	N	N	V	O	R	D	S	D	U	U
T	O	I	S	E	C	N	A	R	A	E	P	P	A	S
C	O	H	E	A	V	E	N	V	O	R	T	T	G	N
N	O	M	E	S	S	E	N	G	E	R	Y	S	U	E
L	F	B	C	K	R	Y	V	M	A	R	Y	F	A	I
C	S	U	S	E	J	G	N	Y	U	W	T	E	R	E
D	U	O	R	H	S	M	S	Z	N	L	Z	N	D	B

APOSTLES
APPEARANCES
DELIGHTED
EASTER
EMPTY
EVANGELIST

GOOD
GOOD NEWS
GOSPEL
GUARD
HEAVEN
JESUS

LIFE
MAGDALENE
MARY
MESSENGER
MESSIAH
RESURRECTION

RISEN
SHROUD
STONE
SUNDAY
TOMB

Time to Think and Pray!

Reflect ...

'Jesus has conquered Death. Eternal life is now given to all who open their hearts to Jesus, who are part of the family of God. I open my heart to eternal life!'

How could it be that the tomb was empty? 'It cannot be – where is Jesus?' The messenger said, "He is risen!" Oh yes, let it be! And it was. Jesus did not make us wait long. He told us not to be afraid and we are not – not now! Oh thank you, God – Jesus is the Messiah, the One. He has saved us, really saved us. We will live with God ...'

'Christ is our light, thanks be to God, risen in glory, thanks be to God!'

Let us pray ...

- Lord, we thank you for giving us eternal life. **Amen.**
- We rejoice in your resurrection. **Amen.**
- We look forward to eternal life. **Amen.**
- We know that we are now a resurrected people. **Amen.**
- Help us to see you in the world around us. **Amen.**
- Help us to see you in the people around us. **Amen.**
- Let us work for your Kingdom and wait to live in your presence. **Amen.**

'Rejoice, heavenly powers; sing, choirs of angels. Exult all creation around God's throne! Jesus Christ, Our King, is risen! Sound the trumpet of salvation. O Church of God, rejoice in glory; our risen Saviour is among us. Let us echo the mighty song of all God's people. Rejoice, Earth – you are radiant in the brightness of your King. Christ has conquered, glory fills you, darkness is banished forever ...
Let us praise God, the all-powerful Father, and his Son, Jesus, for Christ has freed and rescued us through his blood. His spirit is poured out for all.'

'*Exultet*' – the Easter hymn of praise (adapted).

Of course,
that's not the end!
In Volume 2, we will look at the
Ascension and Pentecost and
the spread of Christianity.